STANDS BEFORE HIS PEOPLE

May Enneagram work
deepen your understanding
of the Oshun and widen
your circle of care

Stephen Athauerger
29 July 2023

STANDS BEFORE HIS PEOPLE

― Enmegahbowh and the Ojibwe ―

VERNE PICKERING *and* **STEPHEN SCHAITBERGER**

Stands Before His People: Enmegahbowh and the Ojibwe © 2021
by Verne Pickering and Stephen Schaitberger

All rights reserved. No part of this book may be reproduced in any form whatsoever, by photography or xerography or by any other means, by broadcast or transmission, by translation into any kind of language, nor by recording electronically or otherwise, without permission in writing from the author, except by a reviewer, who may quote brief passages in critical articles or reviews.

Book design by Dan Pitts
Cover image, "Enmegahbowh," by permission of Minnesota Historical Society
Photographs on pages iii, 68, 69, 70, 71, 82, 115, 129, and 159 by permission of Minnesota Historical Society
Photographs on pages 78 and 133 by permission of Crow Wing Historical Society
Map illustrations by Lisa Kosmo
Managing Editor: Laurie Buss Herrmann

ISBN 13: 978-1-64343-930-3
Library of Congress Catalog Number: 2019905580
Printed in the United States of America
First Edition: 2021
25 24 23 22 21   5 4 3 2 1

Beaver's Pond Press
939 Seventh Street West
Saint Paul, MN 55102
(952) 829-8818
www.BeaversPondPress.com

To order, visit standsbefore.com. Reseller discounts available.

Contact the authors of *Stands Before His People* at standsbefore.com for school visits, speaking engagements, book club discussions, freelance writing projects, and interviews.

We dedicate this work to the Ojibwe people, with a hope for their well-being and improved relationships. Enmegahbowh and Charlotte accomplished much in improving the lives of the Ojibwe and improving their relationships to other Americans. May we all be strengthened by their examples.

CONTENTS

Preface by Stephen Schaitberger ix

Preface by Verne Pickering xi

Acknowledgments xiii

Introduction 3

Chapter 1: Enmegahbowh Raised as a Native and Educated by Armour and Evans, 1813 to 1834 7

Chapter 2: Methodist Missionaries in the Lake Superior Region 13

Chapter 3: The Ojibwe and the Americans until 1830 17

Chapter 4: The Treaty of 1837, the Pine Tree Treaty, Ceding Land in Wisconsin and Minnesota 25

Chapter 5: Enmegahbowh's Education as a Missionary and Service in Minnesota, 1837 to 1850 33

Chapter 6: Ceding the South Shore of Lake Superior, 1842, and Central Minnesota, 1847 47

Chapter 7: The Sandy Lake Tragedy, Late Fall 1850 51

Chapter 8: Ceding the North Shore of Lake Superior, 1854, and Mississippi Headwaters, 1855 61

Chapter 9: The Breck Mission to the Ojibwe, 1852 to 1858 65

Chapter 10: Henry Whipple Becomes Bishop of Minnesota, 1859 81

Chapter 11: The Hole in the Day Disturbance, 1862 93

Chapter 12: Treaties of 1863, 1864, 1866, and 1867 101

Chapter 13: Enmegahbowh and Hole in the Day Coexist, 1863 to 1869 109

Chapter 14: Enmegahbowh Removes to White Earth 119

Chapter 15: Joseph Gilfillan Comes to White Earth 131

Chapter 16: Strike! 145

Chapter 17: Red Lake Timberland Ceded, 1889, the Dawes and Nelson Acts 153

Chapter 18: Turtle Mountain Becomes a Reservation, 1888,
and the Ten Cent Treaty, 1892 161

Chapter 19: Whipple, Gilfillan, and Enmegahbowh, 1889 to 1903 163

Chapter 20: The Ojibwe at the Beginning of the Twentieth Century 173

Endnotes 177

Bibliography 189

Index 193

Photographs and Maps

George Copway 11

Anishinaabe Territory (map) 16

Fort Snelling 26

Land Ceded by the Ojibwe (map) 31

Peter Akers 33

Charlotte 38

Ojibwe Bands 1844 (map) 46

Fort Ripley 50

Flat Mouth 56

Buffalo 59

James Lloyd Breck 66

Ezekial Gear 67

Hole in the Day (the Younger) 68

Bad Boy 69

St. Columba Church 69

St. Columba Mission in 1855 69

Wautaub, Enmegahbowh, and Breck ... 70

George Bonga ... 71

E. Steele Peake ... 75

Crow Wing ... 78

Bishop Henry Whipple ... 82

Clement Beaulieu ... 95

Dole Encamped in Minnesota ... 97

Shabashkung, Mille Lacs Chief ... 113

Enmegahbowh in Priest's Robes ... 115

St. Columba Church ... 127

Consecration of St. Columba ... 128

Bishop Whipple Hospital ... 129

Front Street, Brainerd, Minnesota ... 133

Gilfillan ... 133

Ojibwe Deacons ... 134

Gilfillan in Traveling Furs ... 135

St. Columba Stone Church ... 141

George Johnson ... 148

Old Bug (with Other Ojibwe) ... 159

Cornelia Whipple ... 164

Whipple and Evangeline Whipple ... 164

Sybil Carter ... 165

Enmegahbowh in Old Age ... 168

Peter Marksman ... 169

PREFACE
by Stephen Schaitberger

The story of Enmegahbowh and the influence he had as the first Ojibwe Episcopalian priest during the turbulent 1800s is not a book I set out to write. Indeed, as a retired man who is certainly not Ojibwe, I felt self-conscious about taking on this subject. Yet the history of Enmegahbowh has intersected with my life, and I have been prompted by Ojibwe friends to put forth the results of years of research into a book. My prayer for the future is that Ojibwe authors will build upon this work and offer their perspectives on the primary documents. I also intend to give my part of the proceeds from this book to the Department of Indian Work at the Episcopal Diocese of Minnesota. By coauthoring this book, I have already received my reward.

I first encountered Enmegahbowh while attending Cass Lake Episcopal Camp (CLEC), located on the Leech Lake Reservation, where I spent time each summer from junior high through college. About one-third of the campers at CLEC and about half of its staff were Ojibwe. Alice and Edna Gear were summer staff who told me stories about their grandfather Ezekiel Gear, a priest who served Ojibwe communities in the 1850s and 1860s. The camp also introduced me to Fr. George Smith, an Ojibwe priest who led storytelling at campfires, and to George Whitebird, an Ojibwe layperson who became a priest later in life. The camp cooks, Sarah and Susan Whitebird, also shared stories and crafts during those summers.

It was at CLEC where I was first introduced to "Enmegahbowh's Story," a pamphlet consisting of letters Enmegahbowh wrote about the Hole in the Day uprising in northern Minnesota in 1862. In time, I also became aware of Bishop Henry Benjamin Whipple's writings about Enmegahbowh and of Reverend George C. Tanner's *History of the Diocese of Minnesota 1857–1907,* which includes sections detailing Enmegahbowh's missionary work as well as some of his writings.

PREFACE

I eventually became a priest in the Episcopal Church, and in 1980 I was called to be the rector of St. Paul's Episcopal Church in Brainerd, Minnesota. I was amazed to discover how little my congregation knew of the Ojibwe Episcopalians who were in the area from 1852 to 1868. Yet my own education on this history was still developing. Local Brainerd, Minnesota, historians Pete Humphrey and Carl Zapffe introduced me to the local historical Ojibwe sites. Shortly thereafter, I began to conduct retreats and pilgrimages to these sites for youth groups from the metro area and for some of my Ojibwe and Dakota friends studying for holy orders and licensed ministry in the church; these retreats and pilgrimages continue to this day. I owe a vote of thanks to Juanita Palmerhall and Coke Smith, Ojibwe priests who served at White Earth Reservation and who have assisted me with many of these events, and to Coke's son Rick Smith, who is a great Ojibwe storyteller, and Juanita's daughter Mary Kautzky, who is a hit with the youth introducing Ojibwe games.

In the early 1980s, I was responsible for reprinting "Enmegahbowh's Story," which now has undergone three reprints with some additions. I also introduced a resolution to the Episcopal Diocesan Convention in 1981 proposing that Enmegahbowh be considered as a saint of the church. The resolution passed, and since 1986, Enmegahbowh has been celebrated in the Episcopal calendar on June 12. This action is one way the Episcopal Church recognizes a saint of the church.

Father George Schulenberg was a priest at White Earth who collected articles written by Enmegahbowh in church publications. Reading through his collection spurred my interest in learning more about Enmegahbowh and trying to locate more of his writings. His letters have inspired me and deepened my spirituality. I was intent on compiling letters and articles concerning Enmegahbowh to preserve his legacy. As I began building my own collection, I wondered what would eventually become of it, but my main focus was on retaining this history before it became lost. My Ojibwe friends encouraged me to write a book about what I was learning, and while I slowly began to warm up to the idea, I also knew that research was my passion, not writing. When George retired, I hoped he would be the one to write a book, but instead he decided to pass his research on to me; this added to my collection of historical documents and increased the pressure to publish.

I was nearly set to pass my collection on to the Humphrey Center for American Indian Studies at the Central Lakes College library, in the hopes that someone else would write a history using my research. But then I met my friend Verne Pickering, and together we decided to write and compile this book—the first major work about Enmegahbowh to be published.

PREFACE
by Verne Pickering

Years ago, I was asked to write a history of Episcopal Community Services (ECS), a charity branch of the Episcopal Church of Minnesota, which was liquidated in 2011. After I completed a draft of the history, Steve, a fellow board member of ECS, invited me to lunch to discuss it. Over lunch, Steve mentioned that he needed someone to transcribe some original historical papers he had been collecting over the past twenty-five years. History being an interest of mine, I said "sure."

I quickly learned that the papers were all related to Enmegahbowh. The name and the history were unfamiliar to me at the time. But as I began sorting through the first box of letters—letters from the collections of the Minnesota Historical Society, the Newberry Library, the Library of Congress, the Wisconsin Historical Society, and other sources—I began to piece together the life of a very interesting and influential Ojibwe man. Over and over, I read about how Enmegahbowh, which means He Who Stands Before His People, put the meaning of his name into action during his life, which spanned from about 1813 to 1902.

Steve's collection was much larger than I had expected. It wasn't just one box, but many, plus much loose material. In addition to letters, it contained articles, pamphlets, and excerpts from books. I learned that Enmegahbowh was not only literate in English but also well connected and quite prolific as a writer. Of the approximately one thousand items in the computer archive I created, about two hundred were letters written by Enmegahbowh. They were sent to important historical figures, such as the first Episcopal bishop of Minnesota, Henry Whipple; Henry Sibley, the first governor of Minnesota; officials in the Bureau of Indian Affairs; and Senator Henry Rice. Enmegahbowh not only voiced his opinions to these figures but also was actively involved in Ojibwe-US government relations during this critical juncture in history. He attended treaty negotiations and traveled to Washington to discuss land acquisition for distribution to settlers and administration of treaty provisions.

Over the time it took to transcribe and organize Steve's research, it became clear to me that there was a story here, and I knew we had the base documentation from which to write it. Once we made the decision to move forward with the project, Steve furnished many books about the Ojibwe as background material, and I conducted additional research to fill in the gaps. I did this primarily at the Minnesota Historical Society Gale Library, and at the White Bear Lake Branch of the Ramsey County Library, which was able to have delivered to their doorstep a historical reference book of which only seven copies are known to be in existence. The result of our collaboration, aided by the contributions of many others, is this biographical history of Enmegahbowh and the Ojibwe.

ACKNOWLEDGMENTS

With gratitude to Lynda Halbert, John Lefevre, Jeanette Bakke, and Carol Murkowski, who were early readers of the manuscript and who gave encouragement.

The following institutions aided us in the publication of *Stands Before His People*.

The National Archives, Washington, DC

The Minnesota Historical Society, St. Paul, MN

St. Columba Episcopal Church, White Earth, MN

White Earth Tribal Office, White Earth, MN

The Episcopal Church in Minnesota, Minneapolis, MN

St. Paul's Episcopal Church, Brainerd, MN

Crow Wing State Park, Brainerd, MN

Pete Humphrey Library Central Lakes College, Brainerd, MN

Friends of Old Crow Wing, Brainerd, MN

Camp Ripley Museum, Little Falls, MN

Mille Lacs Indian Museum and Trading Post, Onamia, MN

Traverse des Sioux Treaty Site Park, St. Peter, MN

The Newberry Library, Chicago, IL

The *Jacksonville Journal-Courior*, Jacksonville, IL

Heritage Cultural Museum, Jacksonville, IL

Ebenezer United Methodist Church, Jacksonville, IL

MacMurry College Library, Jacksonville, IL

McKendree University Library, Lebanon, IL

Wisconsin Historical Society, Madison, WI

Lac Courte Oreilles Tribal Library, Hayward, WI

Hayward Area Historical Society, Hayward, WI

Ft. Crawford Museum, Prairie du Chien, WI

Copper Harbor Lighthouse, Copper Harbor, MI

Astor House Museum, Copper Harbor, MI

Trent University Library, Peterborough, ON, CA

Hiawatha First Nation Tribal Office, Rice Lake, ON, CA

STANDS BEFORE HIS PEOPLE

INTRODUCTION

Enmegahbowh was one of the few Native American Christian missionaries who lived during an era of great transition in our country's history. He witnessed—and experienced—the shift away from an Ojibwe semi-nomadic hunter-gatherer way of living to the restricted life on reservations, with the expectation that the Ojibwe become farmers of individually owned plots. He was both a man who desired to share Christianity with the Ojibwe and who represented the Ojibwe to the Bureau of Indian Affairs in Washington as an interpreter, an advocate during treaty negotiations, and an Ojibwe himself, who lived among his people. He was first educated by Christian mentors in an English-speaking school, which led to his eventual entry into missionary work and the white man's world. In his long life, he served first the Methodist Church and then the Episcopal Church, playing a pivotal role in building churches and congregations in northern Minnesota. Relationships were important to him. He had a wife and children of his own, and he built deep relationships with church leaders and Indian agents of the region. He was also a man who left a rare gift for future generations—an extensive written record of his unique life experience.

In his early adult life, Enmegahbowh was baptized as John Johnson, but the name he took seriously was the spiritual one given to him by his grandfather. The name Enmegahbowh means "Stands Before His People." He carried out this charge by becoming the first Native American Episcopal priest in 1869 and continuing to faithfully serve his people until his death in 1902.

Enmegahbowh was born near Peterborough, Ontario, Canada, and was brought up as a child of the forest. In those early years, he received some schooling, including learning English from Anglican and Methodist missionaries, after which he joined missions that operated in Wisconsin and Michigan along with George Copway, a cousin, and Peter Marksman, an Ojibwe from the St. Louis River valley. He interpreted and taught for two years, and when asked to become a full-time missionary, he replied that he did not feel educated enough. Along with Copway and Marksman, he underwent two years of training at a Methodist academy in Jacksonville, Illinois. Enmegahbowh then worked with Methodist missionaries to the Ojibwe in Minnesota and married an Ojibwe woman. His career as a Methodist missionary ended after an altercation with a person of mixed race; this incident also brought an end to the Methodist mission in Minnesota. For the next several years, Enmegahbowh lived the traditional Ojibwe way of life.

Yet Enmegahbowh did not forget his Christian faith, and when Reverend Ezekiel Gear introduced him to James Lloyd Breck, a zealous Episcopal priest who had come to St. Paul, Enmegahbowh soon found his way back to missionary work. Breck and Enmegahbowh formed a mission, St. Columba, to the Ojibwe at Gull Lake, where Enmegahbowh participated fully as a missionary and interpreter. After Breck left the Gull Lake mission to start another mission at Leech Lake, Bishop Jackson Kemper kept the Gull Lake mission active. When Henry Whipple became Episcopal Bishop of Minnesota in 1859, he visited St. Columba at Gull Lake, and he and Enmegahbowh formed a friendship, religious affinity, and political alliance that lasted until their deaths.

In 1862 the state was focusing on the Sioux uprising in southern Minnesota, but there was also a northern uprising. In his youth at Cass Lake Camp, Stephen Schaitberger heard stories from Ojibwe oral tradition about the Ojibwe northern uprising. According to these stories of Ojibwe oral tradition, Hole in the Day (the Younger) and Little Crow met at Fort Snelling in the summer of 1862 and agreed to attack the frontier forts of Fort Ripley and Fort Ridgley. It was to be a coordinated attack the day after the Dark of the August moon, which they called Mad Dog Rising because Native Americans in Minnesota were mad as dogs about government failures to honor treaty promises. Hole in the Day (the Younger) was unable to convince many beyond his own warriors to attack Fort Ripley. Most agreed with Enmegahbowh that a diplomatic approach focusing on treaty rights was a better path to justice. Enmegahbowh and others warned Fort Ripley about the intended attack, and when Hole in the Day (the Younger) saw that the fort was prepared, he withdrew his warriors. There was looting in the area at this time.

The frontier between the Ojibwe and whites passed through northern Minnesota from 1850 to 1880. The period was like the Wild West with murders, lawlessness, and lynchings. In the eyes of the US government, when Ojibwe murdered each other, it was considered an Ojibwe matter, while the killing of Ojibwe by whites could not lead to a conviction by white jury.

The White Earth Reservation, formed through an 1867 treaty, was situated on valuable land at a great distance from the "bad influences" of whiskey traders. It was to be a reservation to replace all other Ojibwe reservations, and the government expected that the Ojibwe moving there would become Christian farmers. Enmegahbowh himself settled in White Earth and proved to be an ideal Christian agrarian. The last large land transfer from the Red Lake Ojibwe in Minnesota took place by legislative action in 1889. However, whites continued to acquire land on the reservation through provisions of the Dawes Act and the Nelson Act. Many of the transactions that took place under these laws were fraudulent, resulting in long-standing landownership conflicts.

This is a story of transformation. It recounts how the Ojibwe were forced to abandon their semi-nomadic lifestyle as hunter-gatherers—as people of independent nations—and become "wards" of the US government encouraged to live on reservations administered by agents, an evolution that not incidentally opened up land in Michigan, Wisconsin, Minnesota, and North Dakota to lumbering and settlers. Enmegahbowh is central to this story by his participation in the religious, temporal, and political histories of the era—indeed, he was one of the few Ojibwe from this time who spoke both Ojibwe and English and who left a written record of his experiences. This is also a personal biography of Enmegahbowh, who was one of the most successful Protestant missionaries among all the Indian populations of the United States in the 1800s.

CHAPTER 1

Enmegahbowh Raised as a Native and Educated by Armour and Evans, 1813 to 1834

A son was born to an Anishinaabe chief and his wife in about 1813. The family lived on the north shore of Rice Lake, which is eighteen miles south of Peterborough, Ontario, Canada, in a band of Mississauga Ojibwe.[1] The Ojibwe, the Potawatomi, and the Odawa speak related languages and *Anishinaabe* is the word they used to describe themselves. The original home of the Anishinaabe was near the mouth of the St. Lawrence River. As the Europeans came to America and settled along the Atlantic coast, the Anishinaabe began to move westward.

The geography of the Mississauga area is often referred to as "the land between," as it lies north of Lake Ontario and south of the rocky northern woodlands. The terrain includes natural prairies, pine forests, lakes, streams, hardwood forests, and rolling hills. Travel for great distances was possible in birchbark canoes, with little need for portaging. Hunting and fishing were excellent and Rice Lake, which was shallow, provided much wild rice (*mahnomen*). It was the kind of environment in which the newborn child would feel at home for the rest of his life.

It was usual for a person to be given a spirit name by the elders before reaching adulthood. Elders chose the name after determining the person's spiritual and emotional demeanor. Parents and grandparents, along with other helpers, were all included in the naming process, which could take months or years. After the name was selected, the naming ceremony was conducted. Before the gathered people, the name was presented to the grandfather spirits in four directions, and all the participants in the ceremony repeated the name. The ceremony was followed by a feast and a giveaway. Elders suggested that the recipient repeat the name in four directions every morning for one year.

The son underwent *Kchitwaa nooz winkewin*, the naming ceremony, which was important to the Anishinaabe. The child was given the name Enmegahbowh, which means "He that stands before his people," by his grandfather.[2]

Enmegahbowh was raised in the Midewiwin (Grand Medicine) tradition and eventually became a member of the Grand Medicine Lodge. As a child, he went with his family on their seasonal round of hunting, trapping, fishing, and gathering. When he was perhaps ten years old, he was given a bow and arrows and became adept at using them.

CEDING RICE LAKE

In 1818, the Mississauga Ojibwe ceded 55,000 acres, including the area of Rice Lake, to Canada. The Native Americans thought that in this transaction they had retained the islands in Rice Lake, but the written treaty included no such exception. The agreed-upon price for the land was 522 English pounds annually in perpetuity, to be paid to the Ojibwe in goods, shared equally. Some land reserves were retained by the Ojibwe, but the Canadian government soon began selling much of the acquired land for development. Within two years of the treaty, settlers began coming to the area, and in 1825 Peter Robinson led two thousand Irishmen to settle around Peterborough.[3] As a result of the land cessation and the subsequent influx of settlers, the Ojibwe lifestyle of hunting and gathering began to change.

Samuel Armour, who had taught and been headmaster in the Old Blue School in Toronto until 1823,[4] moved to Peterborough in 1827 with his large family. Enmegahbowh's and Armour's families met, which resulted in Enmegahbowh's first brush with the English language at around age fourteen or fifteen. Enmegahbowh related this experience:[5]

> The custom of my father was to start out in the autumn of each year, with his family—and perhaps four or five families together—roaming from place to place. At this season, otters, fishers, martins and beavers were plentiful, and the furs were valuable. At the time of which I now speak, our fourth encampment brought us near the village of Peterborough, and many men and women came to see us. We had often camped near this village, and my parents knew Mr. Armour, an Episcopal clergyman. Mr. Armour and his wife came to see us. They looked at me very much and talked together while doing so. I said to my mother, "The black coat and his wife look at me all the time." She said, "Well, my son, what of that? Perhaps they pity you because you are ugly."

On the third day both came again to our wigwam and brought us bread and ko-kash (pork), and an interpreter. Mr. Armour said to my father, "Can you not leave your son with me during hunting?" My father said, "He is too small to leave with strangers. He would be lonely, take sick and die." Mr. Armour said, "I have two boys the same age. They would play and go to school together." My father was half willing, but my mother had no idea of leaving me in a stranger's hands, although she knew Mr. Armour was a good man.

After they had gone away, my father asked me what I thought of staying with Mr. Armour. I said I would like it. On the fourth day Mr. Armour came again with his two boys, and again asked my parents to leave me with him that I could go to school with his boys. They then consented. I took my bow and arrows to begin life anew. My clothing was changed, and I dressed like Mr. Armour's boys.

The first two days I felt homesick. I was punctual and always ready for school hours. I soon learned letters and figures and began to understand a little English. Mr. Armour taught me the Lord's Prayer, Creed, and Ten Commandments. At a certain hour of the night, a homesick fever tempted me to run away. I could not control the idea; go I must. The break of day was the appointed hour to depart. The hour came, and with my book in my bosom, and bow and arrows in hand, I traveled two days and reached the wigwam of my father. They were surprised to see me. I had been with Mr. Armour three months, had learned considerable English, and was a tolerable good reader. My foolish act even now gives me sorrow. I might have been a greatly educated man and would have been a greater help to my people.

MIDEWIWIN

Enmegahbowh was initiated into the Grand Medicine lodge of the Midewiwin tradition. Upon being trained and accepted as a candidate, he underwent six months of ritual, which included his parents' participation.[6] A large sacred Grand Medicine lodge was then erected with a doorway facing east. Four Midewiwin elders led the ceremony and for four evenings they began the ceremony by walking around the lodge four times, then inside four times following the direction of the sun's movement. There was then singing, drumming, and dancing in the lodge. On the fifth day, after a similar ceremony, all who could crowd into the large lodge heard the elders speak on the doctrine and history of Midewiwin. The ceremony ended with a blessing and then all took part in a feast.

The Midewiwin belief system is centered on nature. Each natural item, animal, plant, and stone is thought to have a spirit. According to the belief, upon death, an individual's spirit goes westward and joins dead relatives and friends. Their origin story involves the Gitchi Manidoo (Great Spirit). The Midewiwin tradition includes many stories of Nanabozho, a trickster and changeling, who despite his magical powers shares human triumphs and failings and seems to represent fate. The Mide, usually referred to in English as *medicine man*, performed seasonal ceremonies, rites of passage, healings, and rites for other occasions. Mide training was an apprenticeship to an older Midi and proceeded by degrees. In his medicine pack, the Mide carried white sage, tobacco, white cedar, and sweet grass along with other herbs and remedies. The medicine men also kept the history and lore of the Anishinaabe. Pictograph descriptions of some of the lore were recorded on birchbark scrolls.

Late in his life, Enmegahbowh wrote of the experience:[7]

> In the Grand Medicine Lodge are some things that are very perplexing and not easily understood by those who know not [its] teachings. For instance, when one is ready to enter the Grand Medicine Lodge, he goes to the Grand Medicine-man and tells him that he wants to be initiated. He is accepted, and a certain month a year hence is named for the event. The time of year arrives; six days before admittance to the Lodge, the beating of drums is carried on by the head Medicine-men while the applicant is undergoing instructions. What is the meaning [of] drum-beating for six days? This is a puzzle for one who knows nothing of the Grand Medicine religion. I can answer all questions about this religion because I have been in it, and it has been a help during my missionary work when my heathen people have confronted me with questions as to why the Christian religion is better.

A CHANGING LANDSCAPE

The area around Rice Lake began rapidly changing with the incursion of white settlers after the 1818 cession to Canada. In a generation, disease had reduced the Mississauga Ojibwe population from five hundred to two hundred by 1825. Liquor became readily available and many Ojibwe imbibed. Peter Jones came to the Rice Lake area in 1827 with a message of Methodism and abstinence.[8] Peter was born in 1802, the son of Augustus Jones, a farmer and surveyor, and an Ojibwe woman. He was raised by his mother with the Ojibwe until, at age fourteen, he went to live with his father on a large farm near Hamilton, Ontario. Upon learning to read, he read the Bible and was partially converted to Christianity.[9] However, he remained somewhat skeptical of Christianity due to the actions of white Christians that did not correspond to Bible teachings. Eventually, association with the Methodists alleviated his skepticism and he became a Methodist preacher. Enmegahbowh and his family may have heard their first message of Christianity and abstinence from Peter Jones.

In 1828, the Methodist Episcopal Church in Canada opened a missionary school north of Rice Lake on the Otonabee River.[10] The school was funded by an English missionary society. After the first year, James Evans, an Englishman, taught forty to fifty Anishinaabe children at the school until 1831. Reading, writing, arithmetic, and religion were taught in the school in both English and Ojibwe. School was interrupted by seasonal pursuits when families went into the wilderness to hunt, fish, and gather. Students also learned about music, which was a favorite subject. Enmegahbowh might have attended this school from 1828 to 1834 when he was between the ages of fifteen and twenty. Part of Enmegahbowh's education was in the Methodist faith, and during Evan's tenure he was baptized and given the name John Johnson Enmegahbowh. Kah-ge-ga-gah-bowh (meaning Standing Firm), a cousin and classmate of Enmegahbowh, was baptized as George Copway. In his autobiography, Copway recognized Ojibwe principles such as "Never pass a hungry person without giving him something to eat," "Help orphans," and "Help the aged" as being equivalent to the Christian Golden Rule.[11] Enmegahbowh and Copway would be associated closely for the next five years.

Enmegahbowh's lifelong abstinence and opposition to alcohol consumption was rooted in his early Methodist education. John Sunday, an Ojibwe chief whose Ojibwe name was Shawundais, had become a Methodist and had worked as a missionary in Sault Ste. Marie. He visited Rice

George Copway

Lake and introduced the idea of missions to the two hundred Mississauga Ojibwe in the area.[12]

In June 1834, the educational progress of the students at the missionary school was sufficient that when John Evans received a request from the Reverend John Clark, superintendent of Indian missions at Sault Ste. Marie, for two native teachers and two native interpreters, his selection included both Enmegahbowh and Copway.[13]

Enmegahbowh's parents were very reluctant to let their only child move away. "They asked me what I thought of going to heathen cannibals. They added cannibals to frighten me."[14] Evans asked the parents a second time to let their son go on a mission trip. "My mother spoke out and said, 'Mr. Evans, will you promise in writing that my son comes again in one year?' "He promised," said Enmegahbowh. "On the second day I said farewell to my dear parents for the last time. I never saw them again. My mother's weeping almost turned me back. Tears blinded my eyes as I went forth to an unknown heathen country."[15]

CHAPTER 2

Methodist Missionaries in the Lake Superior Region

John Clark's Methodist mission at Sault Ste. Marie had previously attracted several Ojibwe missionaries from Rice Lake and Credit River, Ontario. Peter Jones, John Sunday, John Taunchey, and John Cahbeach had all been converted in Canada and then baptized and ordained in the Methodist Church a generation before Enmegahbowh and Copway. Taunchey was an uncle of George Copway.[16] Clark had built a mission at Sault Ste. Marie and at L'Anse in Kewawenon Bay. Each mission consisted of a church, also used as the school, and a residence, built of logs.[17]

The assignment for Enmegahbowh and Copway under Clark in 1834 was to Sault Ste. Marie, on the south shore of Lake Superior, about five hundred miles from Rice Lake as a crow flies. The mission group consisted of Taunchey, Cahbeach, Enmegahbowh, and George Copway.[18] The trip commenced on July 14, 1834, with a one-day canoe trip on Lake Ontario to Toronto. The next leg was over land for about seventy miles from Toronto to Fort Pententuguishing[19] (present-day Penetanguishene) on Georgian Bay of Lake Huron. There were two routes to Sault Ste. Marie from Pententuguishing, one shorter and more hazardous and the other longer and safer. The long route was along the shore of Georgian Bay, while the short route entailed a twenty-mile stretch of open water. The men took the shorter but hazardous route, traveling in a large canoe. A high wind caused waves large enough that they could have swamped the canoe. One of the men used a red cloth, a chant, and tobacco on the waters to calm the waves. The party arrived in Sault Ste. Marie in late July or early August.[20] Enmegahbowh stayed three months in Sault Ste. Marie, working as an assistant and interpreter to Reverend Clark.

John Cahbeach, Peter Marksman, and Enmegahbowh then spent the winter of 1834–1835 in Ke-che-we-kwa-doong near Grand Traverse Bay, Michigan.[21] Marksman was a young Ojibwe convert in the Sault Ste. Marie mission, who "appeared" on an island in the St. Croix River in 1815.[22] He migrated with his family to Sault Ste. Marie in 1830, became interested in Christianity, and was baptized in 1833 by Peter Jones. His English name corresponded to his Ojibwe name, which meant a good aimer. For several years, Enmegahbowh, Copway, and Marksman would be closely related in their education and missionary endeavors. The following winter of 1835–1836, Enmegahbowh and Copway accompanied Clark to Madeline Island.[23] Madeline Island was the focal point of the Ojibwe migration to the west and to the south. Several bands lived on the island. It was also the western Lake Superior region's major trading post, which was owned by the American Fur Company.

Copway and Enmegahbowh lived at the La Pointe Mission with the Reverend Sherman Hall, who worked for the American Board of Commissioners for Foreign Missions (ABCFM), the Presbyterian mission board. Over the winter, the group translated the Gospel of Luke and the Acts of the Apostles into Ojibwe.[24]

Enmegahbowh, Copway, and Marksman spent the summer of 1836 teaching at Ottawa Lake, now named Lac Courte Oreilles, in present-day Wisconsin. The first leg of the trip to Lac Courte Oreilles was across Chequamegon Bay to the Bad River. The Bad River leg was a struggle, with much time spent in the water pushing canoes over rapids. This was followed by a nine-mile portage.[25] At Lac Courte Oreilles, the three men built a house and taught until late in the season. Enmegahbowh and Marksman then wintered in La Pointe while Copway stayed in Lac Courte Oreilles and continued to teach.[26] Enmegahbowh and Marksman rejoined Copway in the spring of 1837.

Before the 1836 Methodist Fall Conference, held in Rushville, Illinois, Copway, Marksman, and Enmegahbowh must have discussed the level of their education among themselves and with their supervisors. The three were encouraged to become permanent missionaries. Enmegahbowh had expressed that he did not know enough to counter arguments against Christianity.[27] At the conference, Alfred Brunson, a Methodist missionary, met Peter Cartwright, an educator and missionary, and Peter Akers, another educator and missionary, and made arrangements for the further education of Copway, Marksman, and Enmegahbowh.[28]

The three Ojibwe missionaries were assigned to attend the Ebenezer Manual Labor Training School, a Methodist seminary which Akers had founded in Jacksonville, Illinois.

In a letter to Lewis Cass, Brunson stated the purpose of his mission to the Ojibwe:[29]

We intend to throw ourselves among them, learn their language as soon as possible, converse with them by their firesides, sleep in their wigwams, hold the plow, the axe, the hoe, the scythe with them and preach Christ Jesus to them as the way of salvation, by way of precept, raise the barbarians into improved citizens.

THE TRIP TO PRAIRIE DU CHIEN AND KAPOSIA

The three Ojibwe canoed down the Chippewa and Mississippi Rivers, arriving at Prairie du Chien in mid-July 1837.[30] Just before they reached Prairie du Chien, they passed through Dakota territory, likely on the Mississippi River, were captured by the Dakota, and held for three days.[31] They were released when an interpreter was found and related that they were missionaries. Luckily or by appointment, they found Brunson, who was procuring supplies in Prairie du Chien for his mission to the Dakota, which was located ten miles down the Mississippi River from Fort Snelling at Kaposia. The four men then canoed the Mississippi River to Kaposia, where the three Ojibwe helped Brunson build a school and church. Brunson was proud of their work and used it as an example of what could be accomplished by educating Indians.

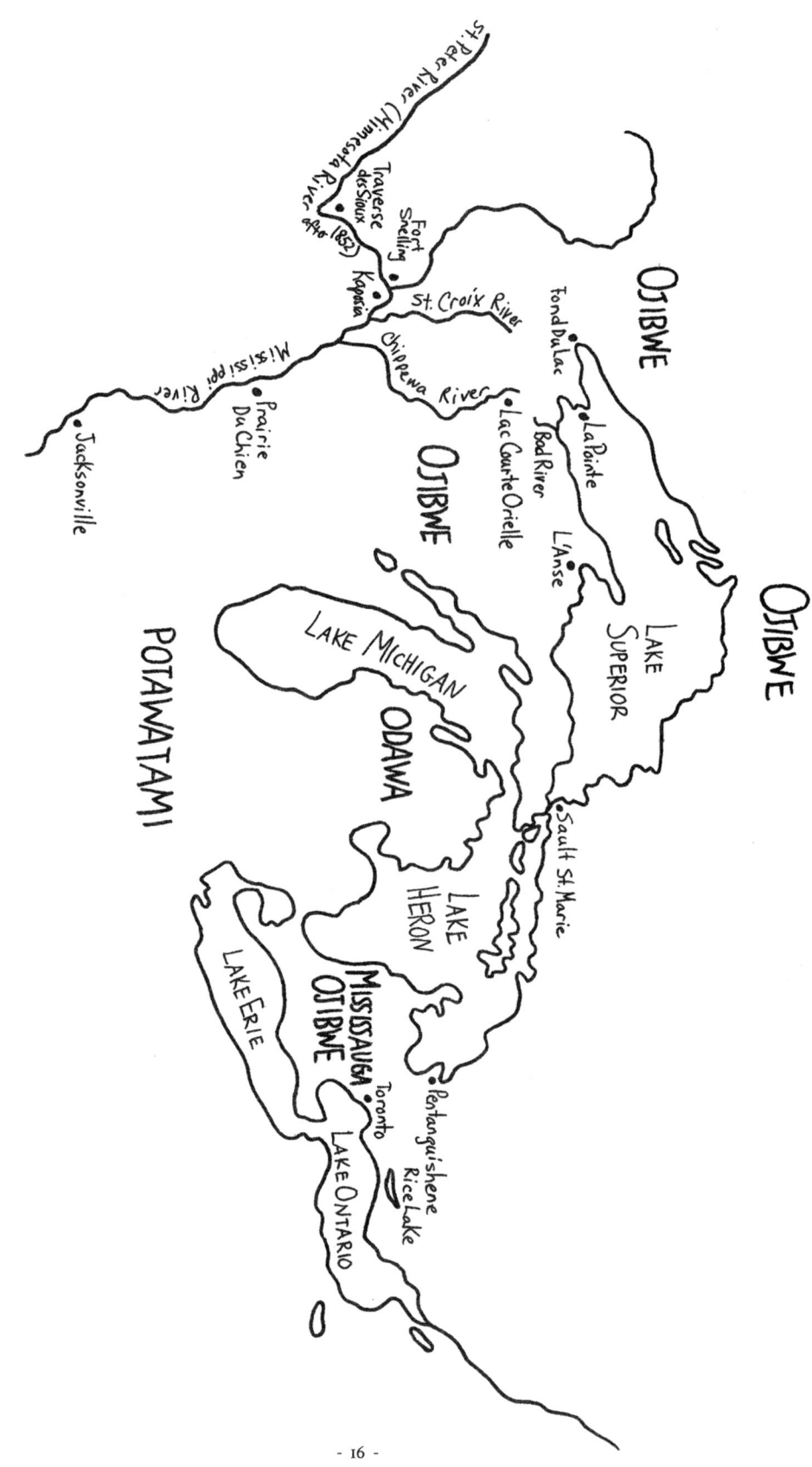

ANISHINAABE TERRITORY VISITED BY ENMEGAHBOWH, COPWAY, AND MARKSMAN, 1834 TO 1849

CHAPTER 3

The Ojibwe and the Americans until 1830

The Ojibwe and the Americans each had a distinct culture and history in the Lake Superior area where they would interact during the nineteenth century. Neither culture understood the other, which led to conflicts and contradictions that to an extent are present even today. This chapter presents the history and culture of the Ojibwe and Americans, which were to come into conflict in the remainder of the nineteenth century.

HISTORY AND CULTURE OF THE OJIBWE

By 1700, the Anishinaabe had moved from their original home at the mouth of the St. Lawrence River to the north shore of Lake Ontario and westward into Canada. The Potawatomi settled in southern Michigan and Indiana. The Odawa populated Michigan below Mackinaw. The Ojibwe migrated farther west of Sault Ste. Marie on both north and south shores of Lake Superior.[32] La Pointe on Madeline Island had become an Ojibwe stronghold by 1700. A hundred years later, the Ojibwe occupied land from Sault Ste. Marie, across northern Michigan, northern Wisconsin, northern Minnesota, and into North Dakota. Although there were also Ojibwe in Canada, their history is beyond the scope of this book.

The preferred habitat of the Anishinaabe was the northern woods with lakes and rivers. They lived by hunting, fishing, and gathering in somewhat isolated bands, seldom exceeding two hundred people. Their homes were wigwams built of bent poles covered with animal skins, mats, or bark. Birchbark canoes were used to navigate nearby lakes and rivers.

Within the bands, the society was cooperative and sharing. Leaders were civil chiefs, war chiefs, and Midis (medicine men). The civil chiefs were generally older men who were thoughtful and had speaking ability. War leaders were generally younger, more volatile men. Leaders led by their persuasiveness and did not rule. Consensus was a goal in band politics. Heredity played a role in the succession of chiefs but was not definitive. The custom in normal social contact and in council was to allow people to express their thoughts completely without interruption.

Work was differentiated by sex. The women cared for the household and gardens, and the men hunted, trapped, engaged in war with the Dakota, and built canoes. Ricing, maple sugar making, and fishing were often shared projects. In general, the Ojibwe centered their lives around the cycle of seasons, with activities of gathering wild rice, hunting, fishing, trapping, making maple sugar, and picking berries; indeed, nature provided for the people in their uncrowded environment. Sharing and reciprocity was a part of the Native American communal lifestyle, as food was perishable and there was no way to store it. The Ojibwe held mutual beliefs and practices that were satisfactory to them. Their primary motivations were survival in their environment, practicing their traditions, and engaging in battles with the hostile Dakota and some recreational games and gambling.

Ojibwe were born into the *dodem* (clans) of their fathers. Common names for clans were bullhead, crane, bear, martin, lynx, and wolf. Marriage between a man and a woman belonging to the same clan was taboo.[33] After 1800, clans became a less important cultural symbol.

Most marriages were monogamous. Marriage was by mutual consent and was usually a lifetime commitment acknowledged by the band. Divorces were possible, but not common.

Relationships external to the band were either friendly or antagonistic. Upon meeting, there was either mutuality—including the exchange of gifts resulting in friendship—or the contact was regarded as an enemy.

The Ojibwe and the Dakota were traditional enemies, and they fought over the territory they occupied and hunted in, grounds reaching from Michigan through Wisconsin and into the Dakotas. While their society was internally egalitarian and peaceful, Ojibwe warriors were honored for their battle skills, bravery, and the number of scalps they collected. The Ojibwe were well armed with guns; the Dakota had fewer guns.[34] The Dakota and the

Ojibwe continued to be enemies until after 1870, and they had many skirmishes along a line roughly from modern-day Stillwater, Minnesota, to Fargo, North Dakota.

A decisive battle between the Dakota and the Ojibwe took place in 1768 at the confluence of the Crow Wing and Mississippi Rivers. A Dakota party of four or five hundred had canoed up the Mississippi River and raided the Ojibwe camp at Sandy Lake.[35] Prisoners were taken. Although the Ojibwe had detected the upstream passage of the Dakota by their still warm campfires, they did not pursue them to Sandy Lake. Before the Dakota returned down the Mississippi River, the Ojibwe rallied warriors at Crow Wing and dug trenches along the river. When the Dakota passed, the Ojibwe decimated them with gunfire. The Ojibwe captives aboard the canoes overturned them and the Dakota were decisively defeated.

Fur trapping had been an important part of the Ojibwe economy since about 1600, during the French possession of Canada. Traders went into the lake regions and lived among the natives, often living with or marrying Ojibwe women and having children. They bartered with the Ojibwe, trading rifles, ammunition, traps, steel knives, iron pots, blankets, alcohol (which the Ojibwe called firewater), and other items for furs. When Great Britain defeated the French in 1763 and took Canada, the channels of fur trading remained largely in the hands of French traders, although they now traded through the English North West Company. The North West Company merged with the Hudson's Bay Company in 1821.[36] The merger was detrimental to the Ojibwe, as it made the Hudson's Bay Company a monopoly.

The children of the traders and other white men who either lived with or married Ojibwe women were labeled "mixed bloods." Often these children spoke French or English as well as Ojibwe and were generally more aware of the ways of their white fathers. Some lived near the Canadian border and spoke a language that was a mixture of French and Ojibwe called Métis French. They tended to favor the Catholic religion of their fathers.

The principal Minnesota Ojibwe bands were the Pembina of the Red River, Red Lake, Leech Lake, Mille Lacs, Gull Lake, St. Croix River, Sandy Lake, Fond du Lac, and Grand Portage. In Wisconsin, beside the base of Ojibwe at La Pointe, the main bands were the Lac du Flambeau and Lac Courte Oreilles.

Ceremonies were held for rites of passage, going to war with the Dakota, naming, and other occasions. Part of many ceremonies were traditional dances.

Land was possessed only to the extent that it was occupied by a band or hunting party. The future was the next season, and the Ojibwe did not aspire for more possessions. With these values and way of life, the Ojibwe had difficulty understanding the lifestyle of whites, who acted individually and who were possessive of land and property, had varied national and economic backgrounds, and held various religious beliefs, either Catholic, Protestant, or nonbeliever.

AMERICANS TAKE OVER THE OLD NORTHWEST AFTER THE WAR OF 1812

Although the United States gained the title of what would become Michigan, Wisconsin, and part of Minnesota in the peace treaty after the Revolutionary War, and what would become the rest of Minnesota in the Louisiana Purchase in 1803, the lucrative fur trade continued through the British Hudson's Bay Company until well after the War of 1812. Mackinac Island and Sault Ste. Marie were the main gateways to Lake Superior, northern Michigan, Wisconsin, Minnesota, and beyond. La Pointe on Madeline Island was a major trading post. A major route into the interior of Minnesota was up the St. Louis River to the Savanna Portage, then to Sandy Lake and the Mississippi River. The rapids of the St. Louis River required a major portage. A second route of trade involved a canoe trip up the Brule River from Lake Superior in Wisconsin and a portage to the St. Croix River. The third access to Minnesota, from the Great Lakes, was through the Fox River from Green Bay on Lake Michigan, a portage to the Wisconsin River and downriver to Prairie du Chien, then up the Mississippi to individual trading posts. The Fox River Portage became less important when steamboats regularly navigated to Fort Snelling after 1830.

THE NORTHWEST ORDINANCE

In 1787, the Congress, under the newly minted United States of America, passed the Northwest Ordinance, which defined how the area west of the Allegheny Mountains and north of the Ohio River would be administered. It defined the future subdivision of the old northwest and succession to statehood. The ordinance remained the pattern for expansion beyond the old northwest.

Regarding Native Americans, it stated in section eight: (The governor) "shall lay out parts of the district in which the Indian titles shall have been extinguished, into counties and townships . . ." Section three states:[37]

> The utmost good faith shall always be observed towards the Indians; their lands

and property shall always be observed; their lands and property shall never be taken from them without their consent; and, in their property right, and liberty, they shall never be invaded or disturbed, unless in just and lawful wars authorized by Congress; but laws founded in justice and humanity, shall from time to time be made for preventing wrongs being done to them, and for preserving peace and friendship with them.

The first effort to establish American sovereignty in Minnesota was made in 1805 by Lieutenant Zebulon Pike under orders from General James Wilkinson.[38] Pike and twenty soldiers propelled a keelboat from St. Louis to Prairie du Chien and then took bateaus to Pike Island at the mouth of the St. Peter (now Minnesota) River. There they met Little Crow (grandfather of the later, more renowned Little Crow of the Dakota uprising in 1862) and negotiated land cessation nine miles wide on each side of the Mississippi, from the confluence with the St. Peter River to St. Anthony Falls, plus another cessation at the confluence of the St. Croix and Mississippi for $2,000 in merchandise.[39] Pike continued up the Mississippi River and visited Leech Lake and Cass Lake, where he lectured the British trader to pay American duty on trade goods and shot down the British flag. The treaty for land cessation at the confluence of the Mississippi and St. Peter Rivers was ratified by the US senate in 1808; however, the transaction remained incomplete in that the $2,000 in trade goods was not paid at the time.

Prairie du Chien, near the confluence of the Mississippi and Wisconsin Rivers, while designated as US territory by the Treaty of Paris in 1783, continued to be occupied by the British. The United States attempted to build Fort Shelby there, but a British siege captured it in July 1814 during the War of 1812. The peace treaty ending the war reestablished American sovereignty, and Fort Crawford was built at Prairie du Chien in 1816 to assure possession.

In 1816, Congress passed a law that only US citizens could receive licenses for fur trading in American territory.[40] John Jacob Astor's American Fur Company took over much of the trade south of the Canadian border. This law also led a number of young, aggressive Americans to become traders, including Henry Sibley and Henry Rice. At the same time, the former Hudson's Bay traders Rolette, Renville, Faribault, Bailly, Provencalle, and Laframboise quickly became citizens.[41]

After the US government decided to build a fort at the junction of the Mississippi River and St. Peter (later Minnesota) River in 1819, the delinquent payment for the land, to the Dakota, was recognized; after fourteen years, $2,000 of goods and liquor were distributed to the current resident chiefs.[42] The fort was built in 1820 to 1824 and subsequently named after its builder, Colonel Josiah Snelling. The establishment of Fort Snelling was a decisive step in extending American power in the territory that would become Minnesota. The first steamboat to reach Fort Snelling, the *Virginia*, arrived in 1823.[43]

TREATY OF 1825

The first major treaty with the Ojibwe was made in 1825 in Prairie du Chien; it involved both the Dakota and the Ojibwe who recognized United States sovereignty and pledged to be peaceful.[44] The treaty drew a dividing line from approximately present-day Stillwater to present-day Fargo that would separate the Dakota and the Ojibwe. In the years that followed, the Dakota and the Ojibwe skirmished regularly over the line dividing them, even after it was delineated by markers; the only real effect of the treaty was to establish a line upon which the 1837 treaty negotiations would eventually proceed.

Major Lawrence Taliaferro was appointed Indian agent to both the Dakota and the Ojibwe in 1820. In 1827, the Indian agency for the Ojibwe was transferred from Taliaferro at Fort Snelling to another agent at Sault Ste. Marie.[45] The announcement of this change was made at a chance meeting of Ojibwe and Dakota at Fort Snelling. As the Dakota left the meeting, they turned and shot into the Ojibwe crowd. The extent of injury or killing of Ojibwe was not recorded, nor is there indication that those who fired the shots were punished.

THE FUR TRADE

John Jacob Astor had traded in furs since 1780 and established the American Fur Company in 1808. It began to compete with Hudson's Bay Company in 1814. By 1817, the company had a practical monopoly on the fur trade in the United States. Principal locations of its trading empire in the Midwest after the War of 1812 were La Pointe, Prairie du Chien, Mackinac, and Grand Portage. Trading reached its peak in 1830, at which point Astor sold his interest in the American Fur Company.

In 1826, Joseph Rolette Sr. of Prairie du Chien controlled the northern trading posts of the American Fur Company, which did business with both the Ojibwe and Dakota of the upper Mississippi River. Ojibwe posts were at Crow Wing, the mouth of the Chippewa River, St. Croix Falls, Leech Lake, Red Lake, Red Cedar Lake (Chetek, WI), and Sandy Lake. Dakota posts were at Lac qui Parle, Lac Traverse, Upper Sandy Hills, Traverse des Sioux, Mendota, Leaf Lake, Devils Lake, Big Stone Lake, Little Rapids (on the St. Peter River, now the Minnesota River), and the second fork of the Des Moines River.

No cash was involved in the fur trade,

only manufactured goods. Credit was extended to Native Americans in the fall and in the spring; when the furs were brought to traders, the value of the furs was credited on traders books against Indian debt.[46] Goods were typically marked up 100 percent to 400 percent. Trade goods were transported through Green Bay, up the Fox River, portaged to the Wisconsin River, and warehoused in Prairie du Chien. From there, the goods were assembled into packs for individual sites and transported up the Mississippi, Chippewa, Minnesota, and St. Croix Rivers. In the spring, furs were transported down the rivers and through the same route as trade goods moved, but in the opposite direction. After establishment of steamboat traffic on the Mississippi, trade was transacted from St. Louis. In 1835, the value of furs in Henry Sibley's Sioux area of trade was over $59,000.[47] The most valuable fur was muskrat, of which 289,388 were valued at $44,702. Other fur traded included 1,027 otters for $5,135; 1,039 buffalo robes for $4,157; 3,243 deerskins for $972; 609 fishers for $913; and 252 beavers for $900.

In 1830, few white Americans were living in what was Ojibwe territory. Traders were either living near Fort Snelling or they were dispersed from northern Michigan through northern Wisconsin, northern Minnesota, and North Dakota. That would soon change, as the Americans would act on their desire to settle on the westward land and use it for farming and lumbering.

CHAPTER 4

The Treaty of 1837, the Pine Tree Treaty, Ceding Land in Wisconsin and Minnesota

In September 1837, Brunson, Enmegahbowh, Copway, and Marksman continued their journey up the Mississippi from Kaposia to Fort Snelling where negotiations took place for the Treaty of 1837 between the Ojibwe and the United States. The treaty resulted in the Ojibwe ceding the triangle between the Mississippi and the St. Croix Rivers and ceding land in Wisconsin extending beyond the Wisconsin River. Enmegahbowh, Copway, and Marksman were informal interpreters during the negotiations, although they are not listed as such on the treaty.[48] Enmegahbowh later described the meeting:[49]

> The first treaty my people made was the most imposing gathering I have witnessed. The chief of each band wore the colors of his rank. His suit of clothing was made of the best dressed skins and furs, generously decorated. His firm step and independent demeanor indicated his strength and purity.

Brunson commented thus on the proceedings:[50]

> The whites showed their skill in making a good bargain. The traders who usually controlled the Indians in their treaties were on the alert to get as good a price out of the government for the Indian lands as possible, but always having an eye to the payment of their claims against the Indians, some of which it was said by those who presumed to know, had been paid two or three times already.

Chapter 4

Fort Snelling

And further:

This council was held at night, their traders being present and telling them what to do. The traders advised them to sell, of course, that being their only chance to get their pay from them. Then each trader presents his claim, some honest, and some dishonest; the whole is added together, with a wide margin for additions and the Indians are told to ask as much for their lands, with so much goods, so much in cash, and so much to be paid to their traders for their old debts. If the Indians object to the amount of debts to be paid, he is told to pay it, or they will leave the country, and they shall have no trade and especially no more credit. After disputation over the amount, the Indians not knowing what else to do, yield to the proposition, and the next day their answer is given. The amounts are usually cut down more or less, for the commissioner's credit as the seat of government depends greatly upon his good bargains with poor natives. When all these preliminaries are settled, the treaty is made out and signed.

Brunson was very proud of his three Ojibwe missionaries and commented thus:[51]

> The whites, also, who had doubted the practicability of Christianizing and civilizing Indians were much shaken in those doubts; for here were men before them who were taken wild from the smoky wigwam, now "clothed in their right minds;" their skins almost as white as the whitest, and quite as white as some of the dark complexions. Their speaking and interpretations indicated credible talents and intelligence, and to add to the moral effect, there were respectable traders from Chippewa country who indorsed the good characters and conduct of our native converts. Governor Dodge, especially expressed his high satisfaction in seeing and conversing with them, saying, "They are the first fruits of Christian missions that he had ever seen among the aborigines."

The impetus for the Treaty of 1837 for the US government was the lack of pine timber to build the rapidly expanding economy on the Mississippi River and in cities like Chicago. All the land east of the Mississippi River had been organized as states, except Florida, Wisconsin, and Michigan. Michigan would attain statehood in 1837. Meanwhile, settlers were streaming across the Mississippi River and into western lands. The Mississippi and Ohio Rivers had become a great channel for commerce and had the capacity for moving large volumes of timber and lumber. Lumber was greatly needed for building cities, homes, and farm buildings. There had already been intrusions into the area by lumbermen cutting timber for mills built on the St. Croix and Chippewa Rivers. Hercules Dousman had built a mill on the Chippewa River for which he compensated some Ojibwe, but an opposing group of Ojibwe had destroyed the mill. Before the treaty, timber for building material came from sources in Michigan and farther east, entailing high transportation costs.

THE CHANGING FUR TRADE

At the time of Enmegahbowh's birth around 1813, the Ojibwe were already involved in an established fur trade. However, the situation changed greatly by 1836, a few years after the peak year in the fur trade, 1830.[52] At this time, demand for furs decreased due to shifts in fashion from beaver hats to silk hats. Further, stocks of fur-bearing animals were also being greatly depleted. For the Ojibwe, these changes meant the loss of income from the fur trade. That loss, along with the desire for trade goods, was the inducement, upon the urging of the traders, to trade land for future benefits.

Henry Dodge, governor of the Wisconsin Territory, was appointed commissioner to negotiate a treaty with the Ojibwe in March 1837.[53] Bands of Ojibwe from the upper Mississippi, the St. Croix, and those associated with La Pointe were invited to the convocation to be held near Fort Snelling on August 20. One thousand Ojibwe men, women, and children attended the meeting.[54] Bands represented at the meeting were from Leech Lake, Gull Lake, Mille Lacs, Sandy Lake, St. Croix River, Snake River, Red Lake, and Fond du Lac in Minnesota, and Lac Courte Oreilles, La Pointe, Red Cedar Lake, and Lac du Flambeau in Wisconsin.[55] The treaty negotiations took place from August 20 to August 29 and were generally conducted without acrimony but for Lyman Warren's claim for $25,000 for bad debts of the Ojibwe.[56] Warren was supported by a boisterous band of Leech Lake Ojibwe. The disturbance prompted Taliaferro, the agent, to threaten to shoot Warren, and Hole in the Day (the Elder) urged him to do so. Dodge cooled the dispute and Warren got his money.

The Treaty of 1837 was a simple document with many ambiguities. The land ceded in Minnesota was located between the Mississippi River and the St. Croix River, extending nearly to the north shore of Mille Lacs, excluding that defined in the 1825 treaty as being Dakota territory.

The land ceded in Wisconsin extended from the Minnesota border to twenty miles beyond the Wisconsin River, south to nearly Eau Claire, and north to near Hayward. The area encompassed one-sixth of Wisconsin and was estimated by Dodge to be "nine or ten millions of acres abounding in pine timber."[57] The Ojibwe were to receive annually for twenty years the following: $9,000 cash, $19,000 goods, $3,000 blacksmiths and iron, $2,000 provisions, and $500 tobacco. Those of mixed race were to receive $100,000 in one payment. The traders were to receive $70,000 in payments for goods received previously by Ojibwe, specifically: William Aitkin of Sandy Lake, $25,000; Lyman W. Warren of La Pointe, $25,000; and Hercules Dousman of Prairie du Chien, $5,000.

The 1837 treaty did not specify the time and place of delivery of the yearly distribution of goods to the Ojibwe; therefore the US government decided when and where the delivery of goods and money would take place. At first, the delivery point was La Pointe on Madeline Island at an arbitrary time in the fall. Hole in the Day (the Elder) dictated a letter to Indian agent Taliaferro and Fort Snelling Commander Plimpton from Little Elk River in June 1839 protesting this location for the distribution of goods and stating that Fort Snelling was his preferred distribution point.[58] Hole in the Day (the Elder) said he "would rather die first" than go to La Pointe for his annuity. The Ojibwe bands lived 50 to 250 miles from La Pointe, a trip involving much canoeing and portaging. Also, the time of disbursement might have been during the fall hunt. The logistics of carrying the goods home was considerable and many items were simply abandoned at the distribution site. Hole in the Day (the Elder) also complained about the selection of goods.

An accounting of the Ojibwe debts was not mentioned in the treaty, and it is unlikely that any record can be found of such debts. Given the round number figures, it appears they were just pulled out of a hat. The traders had operated for years with enormous margins; any unpaid debts were amply covered by the high margins and would be considered a normal cost of doing business. The treaty provisions awarding money to traders was a windfall, making the traders rich men. The $70,000 allotted the traders would represent $1.4 million of purchasing power today.

Late in his life, Enmegahbowh revealed a loophole in this and subsequent treaties, whereby mixed-race Indians were allotted a onetime lump sum payment but the designation of mixed race was left undefined.[59] The onetime payment made to those of mixed race was soon spent.

Enmegahbowh continued: "The next pay came & all the mixed-bloods come to the payment & ask their grandfathers, uncles & nephews to have pity on them, that they were poor & spent all the money given them. The sympathizing grandfathers, uncles and cousins had too big hearts to refuse his grandsons & daughters. And put down their names in the roll to share with them again & again from that day to the present."

During the negotiations, the Ojibwe made plain that they would allow the cutting of pine trees but objected to cutting maple trees. No removal was stated in the treaty, and Ojibwe hunting and fishing rights and rice gathering rights were retained, subject to termination by the president. The treaty was signed with an "X" by forty-seven Ojibwe as representatives of bands from Red Lake, Gull Lake, Mille Lacs, Lac Courte Oreilles, Lac du Flambeau, La Pointe, Sandy Lake, Snake River, and Leech Lake. Being illiterate, the Ojibwe could not be certain that their desires were represented except as they were told by an official interpreter. They had no power to enforce the terms of the treaty nor did they speak the same language of the US government, which would have allowed them to determine whether the United States actually complied with the terms of the treaty.

For the United States, the signers of the treaty were nineteen men including the trader Henry Hastings Sibley and the Indian agent Lawrence Taliaferro.

HENRY HASTINGS SIBLEY

Henry Hastings Sibley was born in 1811 in Detroit to parents who came from the East. He was well educated, including having trained for two years to become a lawyer.[60] However, in 1834 he was offered a post as a trader with the Dakota by Dousman and Rolette of Prairie du Chien. After establishing the post, he built a house in Mendota in 1836. In the winter of 1839–1840, Sibley married *à la façon du pays* (that is, in the manner of the country) Red Blanket Woman, a Dakota[61]. She gave birth to a daughter, Helen Hastings, whose Dakota name was Wahkiyee ("Bird") in August 1841. Sibley abandoned Red Blanket Woman and she subsequently married a Dakota man and died before 1873. Sibley then arranged for Helen to be adopted by William and Martha Brown, a farming couple. Sibley married a white woman, Sarah Jane Steele, in 1843. Sibley continued to support and socialize with his daughter, and he paid for her education at a boarding school in the East. Helen married an American doctor in 1859 and died in 1860 of scarlet fever after giving birth to a daughter, who also died within days. Sibley would later become the first governor of the State of Minnesota.

At the time of the signing of the 1837 treaty, the only white residents in what would become Minnesota either lived on the Fort Snelling land cession or were traders scattered throughout Minnesota. Some whiskey traders and refugees resided illegally across the Minnesota River.[62]

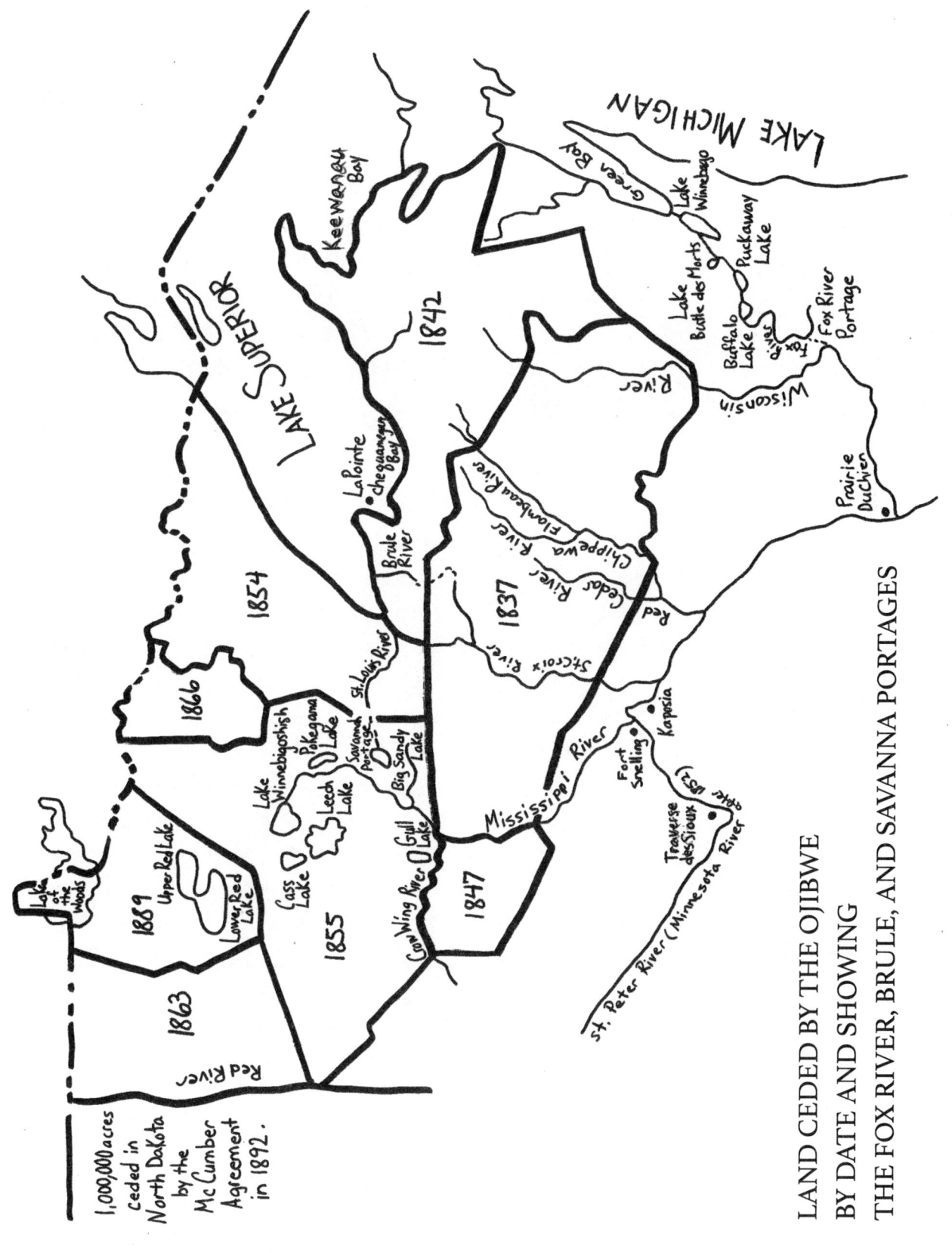

LAND CEDED BY THE OJIBWE
BY DATE AND SHOWING
THE FOX RIVER, BRULE, AND SAVANNA PORTAGES

CHAPTER 5

Enmegahbowh's Education as a Missionary and Service in Minnesota, 1837 to 1850

After the 1837 treaty was completed, Brunson led his three protégés down the Mississippi in a canoe toward Jacksonville, Illinois, where the Methodist conference was to be held in October; Jacksonville was also the site of the Methodist seminary. They camped on shore, on islands, or lodged with friends of Brunson.[63] Upon reaching the vicinity of Burlington, Iowa, they were discouraged by headwinds, so they sold their canoe and camping equipment and hired a hack to take them overland to Jacksonville.

The school to which the three Ojibwe missionaries were assigned was the Methodist seminary Ebenezer Manual Labor Training School in Jacksonville. The Reverend Peter Akers had petitioned the Methodist Conference to establish this seminary for frontier missionaries, intending to pair white and Indian students together so they could teach each other aspects of each culture.[64] (Enmegahbowh, Copway, and Marksman were paired with Allan Huddleston, Samuel Spates, and George Weatherford.) Akers's plan was approved, and the school was opened in 1835 with Akers heading up the faculty. The seminary, located two miles north of Jacksonville, was intergenerational, vocational, and self-sustaining.[65] Faculty and students cooperated on raising crops, tending cattle, and building shelter. Reverend Clark and Peter Burien had raised $3,000 to educate Enmegahbowh, Copway, and Marksman at the seminary.[66]

Peter Akers

Jacksonville was a remarkable choice for the Ebenezer Manual Labor Training School. In 1837 the city was larger than Chicago and was a hub of westward movement. Besides western settlers, the Mormons moved through Jacksonville from Ohio to Nauvoo. Indeed, the city was a center for education on the frontier. Both the Presbyterians and Methodists established colleges here. There was a small mill but no railroad, thus the industrial base was weak. Education and ideas found a ready acceptance. Jacksonville was a day's journey by horse carriage from the new state capital of Springfield, and many legislators had homes in the city, including Stephen Douglas. The issues of the day were center stage: slavery, states' rights, and equality for all.

While Enmegahbowh was enrolled in school at Jacksonville the Potawatomi Indians traveled through Jacksonville on their Trail of Death to Kansas. A plaque in Jacksonville placed by the Morgan County Historical Society and the Peoria Area Native American Fellowship reads, "On October 1, 1838, about 800 members of the Potawatomi nation, having been forced from their homeland in Indiana, camped here on their march to Kansas. A girl of Chief Meteah's Family fell under the wheels of a wagon and was crushed to death."

As a Methodist seminary, the Ebenezer Manual Labor Training School offered appropriate religious courses. When it came to learning Latin, Hebrew, and Greek, Enmegahbowh opted out, successfully arguing that dead languages would not be useful when teaching Indians in still another language. The three Ojibwe attended Ebenezer for two years. The seminary apparently had a congenial mix of races, temperaments, and personalities. Camp meetings and quarterly meetings were held. Reflecting on his time there, Copway relates, "At this institution I spent some of the happiest seasons of my life."[67]

The Methodist Church, having educated the three Ojibwe and others, made assignments for the graduates to teach at missions. In 1839, the new superintendent of missions to the Ojibwe, replacing Alfred Brunson, was the Reverend B. T. Kavenaugh.[68] He took with him Rev. Samuel Spates, Rev. Huddleston, Rev. John Johnson (Enmegahbowh), and Rev. Peter Marksman[69] and traveled up the Mississippi to Little Elk River north of Little Falls, Minnesota, where the elder Hole in the Day (the Elder) and some of his people were camped. Huddleston died of dysentery on December 30, 1839, and was buried at Little Elk River. Stones were placed on his grave by Hole in the Day (the Elder) with the words, "To mark the place where a good man lies, who came to bless us."[70]

Hole in the Day (the Elder), Puk-O-Nay-Keshig,[71] was a war chief who received fame first as a peacemaker, until 1837, and then as a fighter against the Dakota in the area south of Crow Wing. He was born around 1800. His son called Boy was born in 1825 and took the name of his father upon his father's death in 1847.[72]

George Copway did not join any of the missions immediately upon graduating from the Ebenezer Manual Labor Training School. Instead, he traveled east and in Toronto courted and married Elizabeth Howell, a white woman. They spent two years as missionaries, mostly at Fond du Lac in Minnesota.[73] Copway was present at La Pointe when the Treaty of 1842 ceding the south shore of Lake Superior was negotiated. Then returning to Canada, he worked with the Methodist minister Peter Jones and incurred unpaid debts for which he served time in prison. At this time, Copway had two sons and a newborn daughter.[74] His autobiography, *The Life, History, and Travels of Kah ge ga gah bowh,* was published in January 1847.[75] He did considerable lecturing through 1849. In 1850, Copway submitted a proposal to Congress on creating an Indian territory east of the Missouri River for Midwest Indians, away from the bad influences of white men. He called it *Kahgega*, meaning Ever to Be. Perhaps the idea for White Earth originated here. Other memorable events in Copway's life included taking a trip to Europe and meeting with Henry Wadsworth Longfellow. Copway died in 1869.[76]

The missionary group under Kavenaugh went to the Rock River, Illinois, Methodist Conference in the fall of 1840 and when they returned to northern Minnesota, they found that all the Ojibwe had departed from Little Elk River, having been attacked by the Dakota.[77] Kavenaugh then established his base at Sandy Lake, with subsidiary bases on Whitefish Lake and Fond du Lac, near Duluth. Spates and Enmegahbowh built a house and school at Sandy Lake, where they opened a mission.[78] Enmegahbowh was in charge and taught at Whitefish Lake for a year, but he was lonely and did not find teaching to be enjoyable. Kavenaugh visited Enmegahbowh at Whitefish Lake and apparently perceived his sorrow. Enmegahbowh relates the following, which happened in 1841:[79]

About this time the Rev. Mr. [B. T.] Kavenaugh, with his party came to see me if I were living or dead. He found me at Crossing Sky's reservation in a very sour condition . . . a deep insubordination had imprinted on my heart. Dr. Kavenaugh asked me to accompany him as far as Sandy Lake and then return. Before reaching the noted Pine River, we made two encampments, reaching the mouth at noon of the third day. Here was a large settlement of Indians.

We waited, however, for Dr. Kavenaugh to preach to the people, and afterward he said to me: "Did you see the beautiful maiden who sat next to the old blind woman covered in silver broaches?" Mr. Fostrum, the pilot, said, "I know the family well. She belongs to the family of Hole in the Day and Strong Ground; they are her uncles." Dr. Kavenaugh advised me to ask her hand. He said, "I am sure she would make a good companion." Mr. Fostrum spoke out and said, "She would make a good companion, but it is doubtful if she would consent. I have known many young chiefs and warriors who have tried to make a match, but it is always no! no!"

Dr. Kavenaugh said: "You are from a far country and may succeed. Try, for I am sure she will make a good companion." Hence, we entered the wigwam, and Mr. Fostrum said to the maiden: "I come with my young friend, En-me-gah-bowh, to ask if you will take his hand and live as man and wife?"

The father said, "Your friend is a stranger. We do not know him. If we give our consent, he may stay with us a while and then take her away to his country. She has never been away from us." The mother asked what I would do if they consented. I said I would remain in their country as long as we both should live. With this promise, both parents consented. I then had a hard question to ask them, whether they would both allow their child Christian baptism before the marriage took place. The father said, "We have *given you our only child to protect and make happy. If your Christian baptism would make her happy, do what would be for her good." Dr. Kavenaugh said he would baptize her the next morning; I was much afraid that some of the old Grand Medicine men would object. . . . When the hour arrived, chiefs and the Grand Medicine men had come to see this wonderful baptism and were seated in a circle. During the night, she had been instructed as to baptism. Dr. Kavenaugh, with cup in hand, asked her to come forward. Her name Charlotte was given her by the daughter of Allen Morrison, one of the Indian traders on the frontier. Before all the Grand Medicine men Charlotte knelt and answered all the questions of the holy rite. Then came marriage, and so all the Christian religious ceremonies came to an end. . . . Here the party left me, after a blessing and many kind words.*

> Allen Morrison had Canadian roots before coming to Minnesota. His daughter was named Charlotte. Names are very important in Ojibwe culture, and the name Charlotte was as popular to Canadians as Sacagawea was to Americans. In Canada, Charlotte Small was the daughter of a Cree mother and a North West Company investor-trader, Patrick Small. Charlotte Small was married to Canadian explorer and mapmaker David Thompson for fifty-eight years and bore thirteen children.[80] She traveled with her husband on most of his extensive travels. Enmegahbowh's wife, Charlotte Johnson, would also have many children and would also accompany her husband, thus extending the proud legacy of the name "Charlotte."

The date of their marriage was July 4, 1841.[81] Enmegahbowh continued his work at Whitefish Lake, now accompanied by Charlotte, to whom he referred as his dear companion.

There continued to be Dakota raids and threats, which caused Hole in the Day (the Elder)'s band to flee the area. In 1842, the Methodist Church ordained Enmegah-

Charlotte

bowh as a deacon. In August of that same year, Enmegahbowh reported to his superiors that after a year and a half of teaching, children "are now able to spell four or five syllables and are advancing in figures."[82] He indicated an inclination of his students to settle down and cultivate the soil, a few of them having planted potatoes and corn. He lauded the trader as being very supportive. The year 1842 also brought the birth of Enmegahbowh and Charlotte's first child, Martha; their second child, Alfred, was born in 1844.[83] Sandy Lake was the Methodist mission base for the upper Mississippi area in the years 1842 through 1844, with occasional missions to Leech Lake, Cass Lake, and Red Lake.

Then in 1844, an incident involving Enmegahbowh and his wife precipitated the end of Methodist Ojibwe missions in Sandy Lake and throughout Minnesota. Apparently, Charlotte was insulted by James Turner, who was of mixed race. Enmegahbowh responded by knocking Turner to the ground and holding him there while Charlotte gave him a beating. Soon afterward, Enmegahbowh was removed from the mission ministry, and Methodist missions in Minnesota were terminated.

Afterward, Enmegahbowh and Charlotte went to live in the Rabbit River tribe of Charlotte's uncle Strong Ground.[84] Years later, Enmegahbowh reflected on his time with the Methodists as an interpreter and missionary and concluded that "they failed to meet the wants of the Indians and failed to secure a single convert."[85]

Enmegahbowh said:[86]

The missionaries understood the Indian language so as to preach to the people. Did their work bear fruit to the conversion of souls? I am sorry to say it totally failed. Why? Were they unfaithful in their work? No; there were never more faithful workers than these men. After considering and weighing the whole matter of their work, and seeing no fruit, concluded to leave their several fields of labor. I saw them when they sailed down on the Father of Rivers. I stood and [thought]—I feel very lonesome to see them leaving and deserting the Indian.

By July of 1844, Enmegahbowh was discouraged and longed to see his parents and his old home at Rice Lake in Ontario. His unsuccessful efforts to get to Ontario constitute his "Jonah experience," which his own writing best describes:[87]

I heard that white missionaries were discouraged and were about to leave the country. It made my heart sorrowful and made me think very seriously. I said, "If these men of learning have failed to teach these heathen, who can succeed? And what am I that I should attempt to train my people? If I remain in this country, my days and years will become a failure and a sorrow. But I promised my dear companion in the presence of noted heathen men that I would never desert her country nor make her, and so long as we shall live."

Enmegahbowh finally yielded, however, to the impulse to go back to his Canadian birthplace, and taking his wife with him, he started the long journey. It is unknown whether their daughter, two-year-old Martha, accompanied them. Since the exact date of Alfred's birth in 1844 is unknown, he may have been a newborn or still in the mother's womb at the time of the trip. At La Pointe, on Madeline Island, Enmegahbowh found a sailing vessel about to leave for Sault Ste. Marie, the *John Jacob Astor*. As soon as the wind was favorable, the captain put out; but when they got in the lake, clear of the islands, the ship encountered high winds, and the captain headed back to La Pointe. Enmegahbowh's description of the trip continues[88]:

With difficulty, we reached the harbor. Before leaving the vessel, my companion talked to me thus: "I must say a few words, Enmegahbowh. I believe, as I believe in God, that we are the cause of almost perishing in the deep waters. I believe that although poor, God wanted you to do something for our dying people. What you said to me is true, that this is a great heathen country full of darkness and idolatry."

I said: "I fully agree with your words that I am the cause of our disaster." I had thought this to myself, but to tame down my conscience I said: "To be recognized by my Heavenly Father and to be impeded on my journey to the rising sun, I am too small! Too poor! It is impossible!" But to her I repeated my argument that the white missionaries with means, education, experience, had found it useless, and had deserted, and what were we that we should set ourselves to do this work. My companion said quietly: "Do you still mean to go?" I said: "Yes." "I will follow you," was her answer.

THE LESSON OF JONAH

Again, the captain put out when the wind was right, and again the ship ran into a gale. Enmegahbowh gave a vivid description of the storm, undoubtedly allowing his imagination to color his recollection:

The heavens were of ink blackness; there was a great roaring and booming, and the lightning seemed to rend the heavens. The wind increased, and the vessel could not make headway. The captain ran here and there talking to his sailors. . . . I was sure that he would summon his mariners and say to them: "Come, let us cast lots that we may know for whose cause of this evil upon us." If they had cast lots, it would have fallen upon the guilty Enmegahbowh. . . . They would have asked me who had caused the storm, and would have discovered who I was, my occupation and my country. Would I have been bold enough to tell all this? If my faith in God was real, certainly I could have said: "My friends, I have been a missionary; I believe there is a God in Heaven; that I am the sole cause of this great wind, for I have sinned against God. I have taken the inclination of my heart and have run away from my work."

Here Mr. Jonah came before me and said: "Ah, my friend Enmegahbowh, I know you. You are a fugitive. You have sinned and disobeyed God. Instead of going to the city of Nineveh, where God sent you to spread his word to the people, you started to go, and then turned aside. You are now on your way to the city of Tarshish, congenial to your cowardly soul. The consequences of your sin and disobedience are upon you. God is great. He knows of your every step. He governs the elements of the world and He has sent this wind to tell you that you cannot escape His notice. Enmegahbowh, I pity you. The only way you can find mercy is in deep repentance of your sin. Let me tell you an incident of my life which took place many thousands of years ago."

Enmegahbowh then paraphrases in his inimitable way the story of Jonah and continues Jonah's direct address to him:

"My friend . . . your position is precisely like mine. You have run away from your work.... The Lord has dealt with you as He dealt with me. Had you faith to say as I did: 'Take me up and throw me in the sea?' If so, where is the big fish to swallow you? There is no whale in this lake, no fish big enough for your huge body. Hence, if they cast you in, it is the end of you. Your dear companion is watching your movements. She was persuaded that you were the cause of the evil, and warned you after the first disaster.... Just one word or two more.... You must go to the Lord and tell him of your great repentance! Only contrition shall save you. Farewell! Farewell! May the Great Spirit pardon you and bring you to dry land. In saying so he departed from my sight."

It was a profound experience for Enmegahbowh, and much later he told Bishop Henry Whipple that the images he related took place in his brain, not in his eyesight. Nonetheless, the experience strengthened his mission spirit, and he returned to his life's work. On this trip, Enmegahbowh and his family did not reach Canada to see his parents; by the time he did make it back, years later, his parents had died.

In less than a month after the Enmegahbowhs left the ship, the *John Jacob Astor* capsized and sank in Copper Harbor, Michigan, on September 1, 1844, and yet occupies its watery grave.

ENMEGAHBOWH AND CHARLOTTE'S EARLY MARRIED LIFE

Other than his travels, little information can be found about the life of Enmegahbowh between his being evicted from the Methodist mission in 1844 and his contact with the Episcopal Church. What is known is that he and his wife adopted the life of her relatives with its yearly round of maple sugaring, hunting, fishing, and rice gathering at Rabbit Lake. In a letter datelined "Sandy Lake, June 6, 1846," Enmegahbowh related to the Indian sub-agent that during the fall and winter hunts, he taught children and observed "gradual improvement in industry, morality and religion."[89] He also assisted the agency farmer, tending his garden for sustenance as well as for an example of civilized living, repaired the schoolhouse, and distributed twenty-three bushels of seed potatoes.

In 1849, Enmegahbowh and his family, together with Hole in the Day (the Younger), established a village, on the east shore of Gull Lake.[90]

Enmegahbowh and Charlotte's family also continued to grow during these years. Their third child, Gaius, was born in 1848 and their fourth child, George, was born in 1851.[91]

THE OJIBWE POPULATION

The first head count of the Ojibwe was made in 1843 by the sub-agency at La Pointe.[92] The lists appear to be incomplete, as the Otter Tail, Turtle Lake, and Pembina bands are not included. The total number of Ojibwe tabulated is 8,180. The bands were divided into two groups: those receiving annuities, numbering 5,195, and those not receiving annuities, numbering 2,985. The number of bands is only available for the annuity Ojibwe, and the average number of Ojibwe per annuity band is 137. The Hunter's Island band could not be located. Of the annuity bands, 15 percent were of mixed race. A high percentage of mixed-race Indians in bands indicated long-term mingling with traders. The differentiation between full blood and mixed race was and is a subjective judgment.

OJIBWE BANDS[429]
BANDS WITH ANNUITIES IN 1844

State	Location	Number of Bands	Full Breed	Mixed Race	Totals
Michigan					
	Montreal River	1	12	4	16
	Keeweenaw	1	304	33	337
	Ontonogon	1	87	28	115
	Lac Vieux Desert	1	202	11	213
	Michigan Total	4	605	76	681
Wisconsin					
	LaPointe	3	390	218	608
	Chippewa River	2	325	47	372
	Trout Lake	1	82	0	82
	Lac Courte Oreilles	2	209	10	219
	Lac du Flambeau	1	198	76	274
	Wisconsin River	1	328	18	346
	Lake Chetek	2	289	42	331
	Pelican Lake	1	134	0	134
	St. Croix Lake	1	71	8	79
	Red Cedar Lake	1	131	0	131

	Yellow Lake	1	126	7	133
	Wisconsin Total	16	2283	426	2709
Minnesota Annuity					
	Fond du Lac	3	322	123	445
	Crow Wing	4	399	30	429
	Gull Lake	1	59	0	59
	Pokegama	2	151	22	173
	Sandy Lake	2	199	79	278
	Snake River	1	168	4	172
	Mille Lacs	2	151	0	151
	Rice River	1	132	0	132
	Minnesota Annuity Total	16	1581	258	1839
Total Annuity Ojibwe, 1844		36	4469	760	5229

NON-ANNUITY BANDS IN 1844
RECOGNIZED BY THE BUREAU OF INDIAN AFFAIRS

Non-Treaty Ojibwe, Estimated		
Minnesota	Leech Lake	1000
	Winnibigoshish	200
	Cass Lake	300
	Red Lake	315
	Rainy Lake	325
	Vermilion Lake	200
	Hunter's Island*	500
	Grand Portage	145
Minnesota Non-Annuity Total		2985
Minnesota Ojibwe Total		4824
Ojibwe in Michigan, Wisconsin, & Minnesota		7782

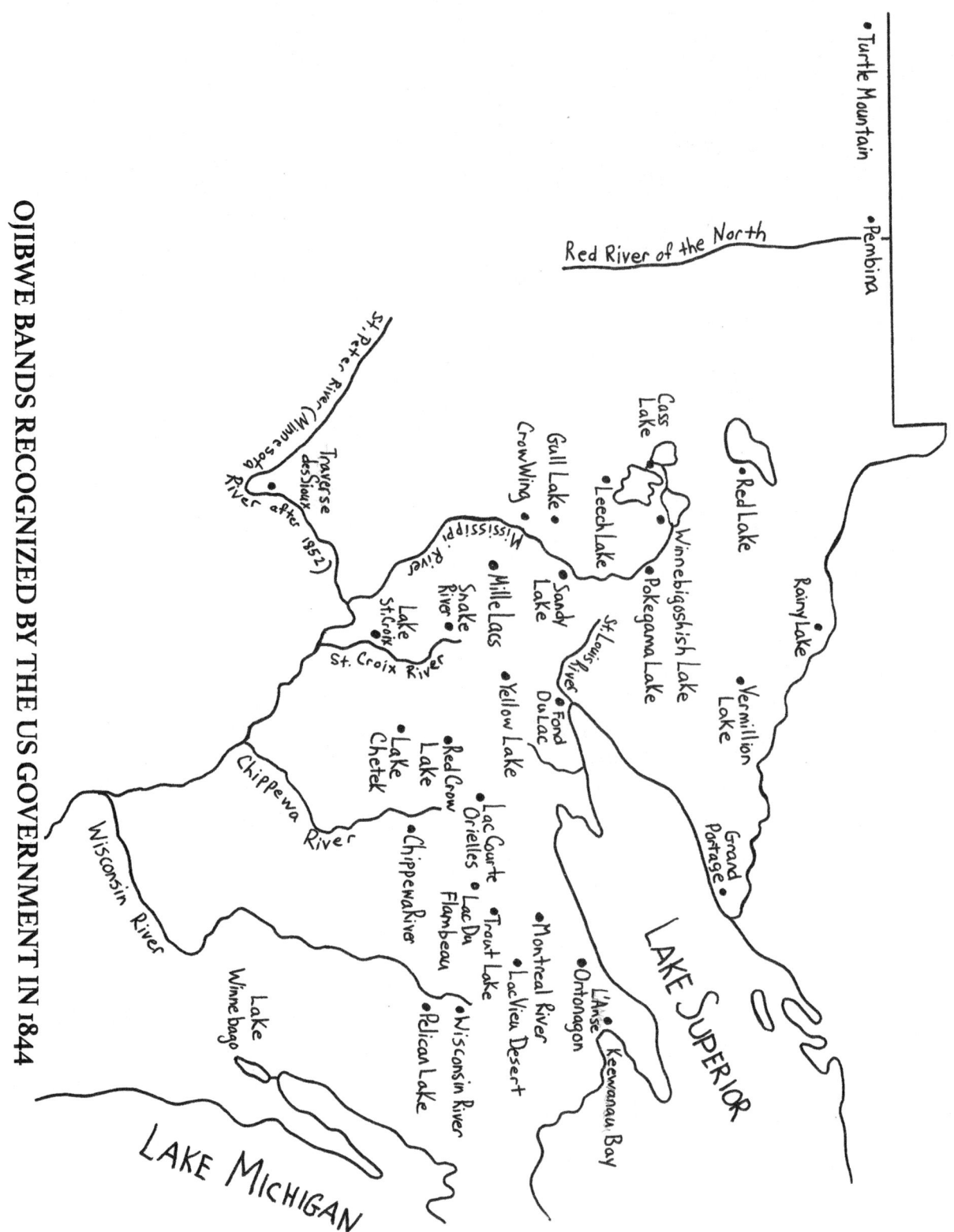

CHAPTER 6

Ceding the South Shore of Lake Superior, 1842, and Central Minnesota, 1847

On December 6, 1830, President Andrew Jackson gave a speech to Congress calling for the relocation of all Indians to lands west of the Mississippi River. Earlier that year, in May, Congress had passed the Indian Removal Act, which Jackson signed into law. By 1843, most Indians who had resided east of the Mississippi River, except those in Wisconsin and Michigan, had been removed to Indian Territory west of the Mississippi. East of the Mississippi River, all states except for Wisconsin and Florida had been incorporated into the union. West of the Mississippi, Louisiana, Arkansas and Missouri had joined the union.

Land in northern Wisconsin and northern Michigan became the next target for cession when copper and other mineral deposits were discovered in the Keweenaw Peninsula. The treaty involving those lands, negotiated in La Pointe, is important in two respects. The acting commissioner of Indian affairs Robert Stuart, who negotiated the treaty, deemed that the Ojibwe of Michigan, Wisconsin, and Minnesota were one nation. This meant that the Ojibwe of Minnesota, who were not ceding land, would become recipients of the annual payment negotiated. The US expected that the Ojibwe from Michigan and Wisconsin would be removed to Minnesota. These treaty negotiations were more acrimonious than were those for previous treaties. The Wisconsin Ojibwe were against ceding their land, which bordered Lake Superior and extended east. They were, however, outnumbered by the Minnesota Ojibwe, who had nothing to lose by the transaction. The Michigan Ojibwe also were willing to exchange land for annuities. Stuart implied to the Ojibwe that the removal would not be immediate but would rather occur far into the indefinite future. When Buffalo, an old chief from La Pointe, asked for an explicit date, Stuart is recorded to have answered, "As long as we behaved well & are peaceable with our grandfather [in Washington] & his white children."[93]

The articles of the 1842 treaty are summarized as following:

- Article 1 defines the ceded area in Wisconsin and Michigan. (See map on page 31)
- Article 2 allows occupancy by Ojibwe of the ceded land until removal is required by the president.
- Article 3 states that eventual removal will be to Minnesota Ojibwe lands.
- Article 4 is a schedule of payments: $41,200 per year for twenty-five years consisting of money and service; $5,000 to a fund for the War Department; $75,000 to traders for debts; and $10,000 to those of mixed race.
- Article 5 stipulates that half of the $41,200 per year is to go to Mississippi Ojibwe and half is to go to Lake Superior Ojibwe.
- Article 6 states that Ojibwe in the copper district are subject to removal by order of the president.
- Article 7 states that the treaty becomes active when ratified by the president and the Senate.
- Article 8 states that the Ho-Chunk (formerly Winnebago) were to be removed from Iowa when it was to become a state in 1842.

A list of Ojibwe debts to traders was appended to the treaty.

After it was determined that Isle Royale was US territory by the Webster-Ashburton Treaty with Britain in 1842, Isle Royale was appended to the Lake Superior land ceded.

Alfred Brunson, the former Methodist missionary and then sub-agent under Stuart, argued against the harshness of the treaty before it was ratified; he was fired for his effort.[94] Brunson pointed out that the treaty paid only seven cents per acre, that the 1837 treaty had paid eight cents per acre, and that the Copper Treaty ceded valuable copper and harbors. Stuart's retort said that Brunson was "not only deficient in head but deprived in heart" for making "false and absurd observations."[95]

THE TREATY OF 1847 CEDING CENTRAL MINNESOTA LAND

FOR WINNEBAGO AND MENOMINEE TRIBES

The Winnebago (now Ho-Chunk) Indians of Wisconsin were ordered in 1832 to be removed to Iowa and southeast Minnesota "neutral ground," but many of the tribe wandered or lingered. They ceded their last Wisconsin land in 1842, but again wandered to Minnesota and Iowa or remained in Wisconsin. The Winnebago chose Henry Rice, a trader, to select land for their "permanent" settlement. Another objective of the 1847 treaty was to provide a place for removal of the Menominee Indians from Wisconsin. Rice selected an area west of the Mississippi and south of the Crow Wing Rivers[96] (see map on page 31). He then negotiated a treaty in Fond du Lac, Minnesota, on August 2, 1847, with the Mississippi and Superior bands of Ojibwe to cede 890,700 acres to accommodate the Ho-Chunk and Menomonie.

The 1847 treaty benefits were to be distributed two-thirds to the Lake Superior Ojibwe and one-third to the Mississippi Ojibwe. The Mississippi and Superior Ojibwe tribes were each to receive $17,000; the Mississippi Ojibwe were to receive an additional $1,000 for forty years to be spent on teachers and blacksmiths. The distribution points for the payments were specified as being L'Anse, La Pointe, Grand Portage, and the St. Louis River. The Bois Forte Ojibwe were to be paid $10,000 plus $10,000 in goods for five years and received the right to select their reservation, subject to approval by the president.

The Menominee were to be removed "permanently" to the western half of an area in central Minnesota, bound on the south by the Long Prairie River and on the north by the Leaf River. However, the Menominee declined to move as directed and so received a reservation on the Wolf River in Wisconsin instead.[97]

The wandering Winnebago from Iowa were to be removed to the eastern half of the area. Some Winnebago came to the reservation at Long Prairie where the annuities were paid, but many wandered to where alcohol was more available. Henry Rice was then contracted to remove Winnebago to the new reservation at seventy dollars per head. By 1849, Rice had succeeded in moving 323 Winnebago to the new reservation. Reason, then force, was used to move some of the Winnebago to their new reservation. Some Winnebago were loaded on boats in the Mississippi by troops, to be taken to the new reservation, but many abandoned their transport along the river. Henry Sibley protested the contract and the two Henrys became political enemies, neither of whom triumphed before a congressional committee reviewing the removal. However, the commissioner of Indian affairs was discredited, and he resigned. The Winnebago who had moved to the reservation roamed back to Wisconsin or went farther west.

In 1849, Fort Gaines (later renamed Fort Ripley) was established ten miles south of Crow Wing on the Mississippi River. The fort was designed to project power into the region and protect the expected settlers, lumbermen, land speculators, and merchants. However, the stated purpose was to keep the peace between the Ojibwe, who previously had occupied the land, and the Menominee and Winnebago, who were to be removed to the land. Since neither the Winnebago nor the Menominee occupied the land, the former Winnebago and Menominee reservations were opened to white settlement in 1855.

Hole in the Day (the Elder) died in 1847. His son took the name Hole in the Day (the Younger) as well as leadership of his father's Mississippi band.

Fort Ripley

CHAPTER 7
The Sandy Lake Tragedy, Late Fall 1850

Removal of all Native Americans east of the Mississippi River was a current topic in the 1840s among the general population and among government entities. George Copway, Enmegahbowh's co-scholar in Illinois, wrote an extensive paper on creating one large reservation for all Indians between the Missouri and James Rivers in the Dakota Territory to be isolated from the bad influences of white frontiersmen.[98] Among its supporters was Alexander Ramsey, the territorial governor.

Wisconsin became a state in 1848. After that, in 1849, the Territory of Minnesota was organized on part of the land remaining from the Wisconsin Territory, and Alexander Ramsey was appointed governor. A census was taken in 1849, which showed that there were 4,680 white people—more men than women—residing in the Minnesota Territory. Population centers were St. Paul, 840; St. Anthony and Little Canada, 571; and Stillwater, 609. Outlying settlements were Pembina and Crow Wing. The people of Minnesota came primarily from the east, except for the northern Selkirk settlement, which was largely inhabited by people who came from Scotland via Canada.

The annuity payment of goods and money to Ojibwe who were a party to the 1837 and 1842 treaties took place at La Pointe on Madeline Island during the years 1843–1849. It must have been an arduous journey for Minnesota Ojibwe to travel to La Pointe, especially since it is assumed that each family member had to be present to qualify for payment. In 1848, the Lake Superior Ojibwe sent a delegation to Congress to obtain twenty-four sections of land in seven locations where bands could reside "as a permanent home." The sections requested were at Vieux Desert, Trout Lake, Lac Courte Oreilles, La Pointe, Ontonagon, L'Anse, and Pequaming. The delegation was well received, and Congress even agreed to finance their return trip.[99] Governor Dodge of Wisconsin helped finance their return from Green Bay to their homes and commented favorably on their desire. Despite this reception, Congress took no action regarding a permanent home for the Ojibwe.

On February 6, 1850, President Zachary Taylor ordered the removal of the Lake Superior Ojibwe to Minnesota.[100] There was much confusion in the Lake Superior region about this order. A letter to the commissioner of Indian affairs in April 1850 states that the Ojibwe were to be removed to Fond du Lac, Minnesota.[101] Another letter indicated that removal was to take place in the summer of 1850. The Lake Superior Ojibwe were alerted be ready to move and to not plant gardens, as gardens would be planted for them at their intended removal destination.[102]

After 1849, the distribution of annuity payments was moved from La Pointe to Sandy Lake, Minnesota. Thomas Ewing, secretary of the interior, Governor Ramsey of the Minnesota Territory, and John Watrous, head of the Ojibwe Indian Agency, planned the next distribution for October 25, 1850. Ramsey boasted that the removal plan "fully matured" in his office.[103] Moving the distribution point to Sandy Lake has been interpreted as an attempt to lure the Lake Superior Ojibwe to Minnesota and then strand them there by the onset of winter. Watrous is quoted as saying, "This is a new and ingeniously contrived way of effecting the removal of the natives."[104]

Four thousand Ojibwe from Wisconsin, Michigan, and Minnesota congregated at Sandy Lake on or shortly after the 1850 annuity distribution date.[105] The Indian agent had gone to St. Louis to get money and supplies for the distribution, but he returned with few supplies. Meanwhile, survival depended on gathering local supplies, which were meager, and on what credit could be extended by traders. Winter weather then arrived, and Ojibwe began dying of exposure, hunger, dysentery, and measles. Much of the pork and flour that had been made available to them was in inedible condition or, if eaten, caused sickness. Within days of the Ojibwe's arrival, a foot of snow was on the ground, lakes and rivers were frozen, and canoes had been abandoned. Enmegahbowh, who was present with his family, commented on the conditions:[106]

The Indians from all the Mississippi lands, Mille Lacs, Gull Lake, Leech Lake, and Pokegama were present. The old

Sandy Point was covered with wigwams. The first day they received their beautiful well-colored flour hard with lumps, and pork heavily perfumed. The old chief brought me some of both and said, "Is it fit to eat?" I said, "No, it is not fit to eat." But the Indians were hungry, and they ate it. About ten o'clock at night the first gun was fired. You well know, Bishop, that the Indians fire a gun when a death occurs. An hour after another gun was fired, and then another, until it seemed death was in every home. That night, twenty children died, and the next day as many more, and so for five days and five nights the deaths went on. Oh, it was dreadful! Weeping and wailing everywhere! I and my companion were dumb. All the time women were coming to ask if the disease was contagious. As the deaths increased, wigwams were deserted, and the inmates fled into the forest. They buried their dead in haste, often without clothing. The chief's prophecy was true: "A fatal treaty! Woe be to my people."

Within five days of the first deaths, wigwams were deserted, and the Ojibwe began their journey home with little provisions, no shelter, rivers frozen, and a foot of snow on the ground. The Ojibwe had varying distances to travel to reach their homes: those from northern Michigan had about 230 miles to go; the Wisconsin Ojibwe, an average of 140 miles; the Minnesota Ojibwe had about 45 miles. The Sandy Lake camp was cleared by December 3, thirty-eight days after the initiation date for the annuity payment distribution.[107]

Charlotte's mother had accompanied Enmegahbowh's family to Sandy Lake.[108] At some point on the family's return journey to Gull Lake, she became unable to continue on. A hole was dug, and she was placed in it in a traditional sitting position, facing west. The hole was covered with sticks to prevent wolves from eating her alive, and the rest of the family returned to their home.

It is estimated that 170 Ojibwe died at Sandy Lake that year, and 230 died on the return journey.[109] A full 10 percent of the Ojibwe who came to Sandy Lake died before reaching home. By some combination of planning and ineptness by Ramsey, Ewing, and Watrous, 400 Ojibwe were removed—permanently. The number of deaths was never enumerated accurately; the actual number of deaths could be many more or many less. Flat Mouth, a chief at Leech Lake, dictated a letter outlining his grievances with Governor Ramsey about how the deadly handling of the distribution, which reads as follows:[110]

Dec. 5, 1850
Speech of Flat Mount

My friend,

When I saw the Governor last spring in our own country, I listened attentively to all he said and believed he would make his words true. He saw our makeup and watched us and promised he would help us. But now, I'm called upon to mediate. We have been called here and made to suffer by sickness, by death, by hunger and cold. I lay it all on him. I charge it all to our Great Father, the Governor. It is because we listened to his words that we have suffered so much. We were poor before, but we are now poorer now because we have been called here to receive the small annuity of a blanket or so apiece to cover _____ up. We have been taken from our country at the most valuable season of the year for hunting and fishing, and if we had _____ at home we should have been far better off than we now are with our small annuity. I am not one that speak of another behind his back. I say to his face all that I desire to do at all, and I would say to the Governor if he were here, all that I say to you. I want you to write down the words I speak and carry them to him. Tell him I blame him for the children we have lost, for the sickness we have suffered and for the cold and snow that we have suffered. The fault rests on his shoulders. [Blurred sentence]

Why were we brought here to be made a laughing stock among the Indians? Tell him I blame him for this. Also charge all that has happened to us to him. I told him last spring that we got nothing to eat from our

Great Father when we came to payment but had to depend upon the charity from our fellow Chippewas: of this we have been accused and made a laughing stock _____. I have always been friendly to the whites. I see nothing behind me to cause angst. I have always said what I thought and kept nothing back: It is for this reason I am not ask him. I speak to no Great Father at a distance: tho words that you now hear will be aimed to him. When I saw him, he spoke to me about farms and other matters of interest to us. I believed his words would be _____ in this respect, but instead of this they have been falsified. And I blame him for this. My friend, it makes our hearts _____ to look at the losses we have sustained while at Sandy Lake. You call us your children. If we were, we would be white. You are not our Father and I think you call on your children only in mocking. This earth is our Father and I will never call you so. The reason we call the earth our Father is because it resembles us in _____. We call the sky our Grandfather. We do not call the _____ to our Grandfather. We give it to him in order that he might follow our example and be liberal to us. I told the Gov. at Crow Wing that we had not rec'd an equivalent for our land and that we wanted more. As much again as we have, and if he had been here, I should have called upon him to secure our annuity. When I saw him at Fort Gaines, others heard what he said. He promised to get us more. Will he do it? If he will, let him add one half to our present payment. If he will do this we will again come to our annuities, but if not, we will not come. Our people will not come if I tell them not to. I have matched the policy of the whites for a long time, and I see that somehow, they make up their minds to do something, they do it. They now listen to that policy of the Indians whom it comes in contact with them. I am much like them. I have great influence with the _____ Indians, and when I put words into this heart they are not soon forgotten nor lightly regarded. Now we ask, and we require, and we demand that our payment be staged next year at Crow Wing. I speak as I do because I know it is a hard thing to get our request granted, but we demand it and I speak the demand. I want you to understand us perfectly. I call on our Grandfathers at St. Paul. I call on you to double our payment next year. I do not blame our Great Father because we were so badly _____ in the sale of our lands. It was the trader's fault. He put honey on his lips to deceive us, and if our annuity cannot be doubled next year we will not come for it. Set the annuity that is due to us for the two coming years be put together. It is not worth the time we spent to get it in when we receive only one year's dues. I have said enough on that subject. Now I will ask you a question. Does our Great Father intend to call us to a summit early next summer? If he does not, I want to go out of the country, but if he does, I will wait for him.

Delivered at Sandy Lake to the Chip-a Agent, J. S. Watrous, December 3rd 1850
And _____ as it was interpreted by [name obscured] J. G.

Flat Mouth

In late summer in 1851 three Ojibwe chiefs, two warriors, and Enmegahbowh decided to go to Washington to relate to the government the hardships of their threatened removal. The trip would involve walking to St. Paul, taking a steamboat to a railhead on the Mississippi, and then taking a train to Washington. Somehow, they secured enough money to finance part of the trip. Enmegahbowh stated the trip was to "ask the government to have pity on us."[111] Enmegahbowh later wrote about the trip:[112]

Before we started, I became acquainted with Rev. Dr. Gear, Chaplain of Fort Snelling, and knows all about my movements. On our way to Washington we stopped at Philadelphia for three or four days to replenish our exhausted pockets. We did not pretend to deceive the whites to gather the dimes, but represented ourselves as we really are, by making war whoops and waving war clubs before vast audiences. In those days it was quite a curiosity to see the two-legged animals. We met the once celebrated Jenny Lind in the state. She invited us to her own room and made us sing the war songs. After singing for us one of her beautiful tunes, she turned to me and asked how much we need and assistance in the way of money. I said, "My friend, whatever you feel disposed to assist us, whether a little or much, we shall be grateful." No, that will not do. I must name the sum, and whatever it may be, she will give it. When I refused positively to name the sum—here we sat like dumb animals. Here I was. I was afraid to say too much or too little. At last I made up my mind to say five hundred dollars. "Five hundred dollars," she added, "all right." She said, "Another five hundred dollars is added to you which makes one thousand dollars." This gave us victory. Another war song and a spiritual one too, and to the end of the song made another war whoop. Before we started from Philadelphia, the chiefs said, "In receiving money from unexpected sources, a good sign, a very good omen for our effort," and was just as sure that our errand shall come to pass, and before we reached

Washington a letter overtook us in the city of Philadelphia from Dr. Gear of Minnesota, advising me not to disturb ourselves about white missionary, that a missionary was on the ground already, willing to go with me just as soon as I returned from Washington. The news was like a flash of lightning. Let us give thanks by singing another war song. I can never forget the incidents which took place amongst us. In the far land among strangers. I believed the Great Spirit looked upon us with His pitying eyes and heard our prayers and desires.

Despite securing the money they needed to fund the rest of the trip, they ran into trouble soon afterward. A letter from R. P. Dawden to the secretary of war tells of John Johnson, interpreter, and five chiefs who left a railroad car on September 1, 1851, and were about to find rest for the night in woods near Bladensburg, Maryland, which is ten miles from Washington.[113] Their guide, a Mr. Whiter, had left them. Could they have been robbed of their gains in Philadelphia and been too ashamed of being gullible to tell about it? Dawden took them into his home and fed them supper and breakfast, then transported them to Washington. Their intent was to see President Millard Fillmore. The letter requested payment by the Bureau of Indian Affairs for the food and lodging. No report was found of the meeting.

A letter from Enmegahbowh written on August 4, 1851, was received on September 5, 1851, by Commissioner Lee of the Bureau of Indian Affairs.[114] Enmegahbowh apparently wrote the letter while in Washington to address the concerns of the chiefs who were with him. They requested an interview to clarify removal intentions of the government and to request that they be left alone in their schools, shops, and homes. They also protested that their annuities had been reduced by agents who were bribed by traders presenting fraudulent debts. He volunteered to discuss the evils present in the Ojibwe area he knew and the efforts being made to improve the condition of the Christian Ojibwe. Finally, he asked for money to make the appearance of chiefs more presentable; a note by a clerk indicates that $20 was expended for that purpose.

Although the federal government was moving to relocate Ojibwe, considerable support for nonremoval of Ojibwe from Wisconsin was developing in Wisconsin and nationally. Cyrus Mendenhall, a copper entrepreneur associated with the Methodist Episcopal Mission Society, created a petition signed by "ministers, phy-

Buffalo

sicians, local officials, merchants, mine foremen, lumbermen, and other influential citizens opposing removal."[115] Newspapers in Sault Ste. Marie and Detroit opposed removal, as did the *New York Times*. Chief Buffalo did a survey of the Ojibwe to determine if any hostile action to whites had occurred; he found none. Some in Minnesota continued to support removal, contending that it would improve the Ojibwe in the arts of civilization.[116]

Efforts to remove the Ojibwe from Wisconsin were suspended. In June 1852, Chief Buffalo led an unauthorized group of five fellow chiefs to Washington with Benjamin Armstrong as an interpreter. As a result of their efforts, the removal order was rescinded (although no record of this action was found), and payments were resumed in La Pointe.[117]

CHIPPEWA INDIAN AGENCY

In 1851, a Chippewa Indian Agency was established for Minnesota on the north shore of the Crow Wing River near its confluence with the Mississippi River.[118] John Watrous was the first agent, followed by David Harriman in 1853 and Joseph Lynde in 1858.

The agency compound at Crow Wing consisted of residences for the agent and staff and warehouses for goods to be distributed.

CHAPTER 8

Ceding the North Shore of Lake Superior, 1854, and Mississippi Headwaters, 1855

The issues resulting in the 1854 treaty were permanent reservations for the Ojibwe and ceded land on the north shore of Lake Superior. The US government hoped that the Lake Superior north shore contained minerals, although none had been discovered at the time. When negotiations with Commissioner Henry Gilbert got acrimonious, Chief Buffalo insisted that he have an interpreter friendly to the Ojibwe. The ensuing negotiations resulted in a treaty that established reservations at Bad River and Red Cliff in Wisconsin. In 1856, President Franklin Pierce issued an executive order establishing additional Wisconsin reservations at Lac du Flambeau and Lac Courte Oreilles. Reservations were also established in Minnesota at Fond du Lac and Grand Portage.

The 1854 treaty ceded Ojibwe land that extended from the shore of Lake Superior and the St. Louis River to the border with Canada.[119] Payment terms for the land was $5,000 in coins; $8,000 in goods; $3,000 in tools, cattle, and buildings; $3,000 in education for twenty years; plus $90,000 to the chiefs designated to pay present bills, $6,000 to those of mixed race, and $1,000 of men's clothes. Liquor was prohibited on the reservations but was generally available, as traders who sold it could not be convicted by a white jury. Drunkenness among the Ojibwe was sporadic, depending on supply and funds to pay for it.

The negotiations for the 1854 treaty were somewhat more businesslike than previous negotiations, in that the Ojibwe and particularly Chief Buffalo were clear about their aims: they insisted on their own interpreter; they communicated that they wanted reservations within the area they presently lived; and they insisted that the distribution points for money and goods be specified. Land was allocated at L'Anse and Vieux Desert in Michigan; Lac du Flambeau and Lac Courte Oreilles in Wisconsin; and at Grand Portage and Fond du Lac in Minnesota, all of which became reservations. In general, after a year, the Wisconsin white and Ojibwe populations were favorable to the treaty. The St. Croix Ojibwe and the Sakaogan Ojibwe were not included in the treaty, and they continued to roam their traditional territory pursuing their traditional way of life.[120]

Despite their general satisfaction with the treaty, the Ojibwe found that the small reservations boxed them in, making their traditional way of life difficult and ensuring their dependence on the US government for a meager living. Also, the government's record of making the annuity payments outlined in the treaty was spotty.

THE TREATY OF 1855

The object of the Treaty of 1855 with the Ojibwe was pine lands near the headwaters of the Mississippi. David Harriman, under commissioner of Indian affairs George Manypenny, led the negotiations. Traders, who often influenced negotiations, were led by Henry Rice, who, having found the fur trade dwindling, looked to profits in timberlands. A group of Ojibwe leaders was invited to Washington to discuss an unknown agenda. The invited Ojibwe leaders were from the Mississippi bands, excluding the Mille Lacs, the Pillagers of Leech Lake, and the Lake Winnibigoshish band. Chiefs Hole in the Day (the Younger), Buffalo, and Bad Boy were present. That Washington was chosen as the venue for negotiations limited the number of Ojibwe participants, which was probably intentional.[121] Although the Mille Lacs Ojibwe were not invited, they nonetheless sent a delegation that may not have arrived in time for the negotiations. Regardless, the terms of the treaty applied to them. The land ceded as a result of the treaty encompassed most of the Mississippi River drainage area north of Crow Wing and west to the Minnesota border.

Reservations were specified at Mille Lacs, Rabbit Lake, Gull Lake, Pokegama, and Sandy Lake for the Mississippi bands and at Leech Lake for the Pillager and Winnibigoshish bands.[122] The Mississippi Ojibwe were to be compensated with $10,000 in goods, $50,000 to pay debts to traders, and $20,000 annually for twenty years. The Pillagers and the Winnibigoshish Ojibwe were to receive $10,000 in goods and services, $40,000 to settle current obligations, and $10,666 annually for thirty years. Money was also designated for ammunition and tobacco, a road to Mille Lacs, and miscellaneous services.

The Mississippi bands were to be paid at their reservations, and Pillagers and

Winnibigoshish were to be paid at Leech Lake. Hole in the Day, Bad Boy, Buffalo, and eleven other Ojibwe signed for the Mississippi bands, and three Ojibwe signed for the Pillager and Winnibigoshish bands. Henry Rice, a presumed white beneficiary of the treaty, signed the treaty as well.

Given the lax legal language in the treaty, the treaty being written in a language not understood by the Ojibwe, the Ojibwe having no reading skills, the poor records of traders, and the greediness of the traders and bureaucrats, there was a large area in which fraud could be committed. It appears that the annuity system worked on a first-come, first-served basis. Congress did not always fully fund the annuity payments. Perhaps the bureaucrats who arranged cash payments and contracted suppliers (with possible kickbacks) got their share of the money. Then the traders, in collusion with the agents, inflated the debts of the annuitants. Perhaps some of the cash to be distributed stuck to the hands of the agents. Records of money transfers were apparently slim or nonexistent. Enmegahbowh wrote a letter to a Mr. Whiting, presumably in the Bureau of Indian Affairs, dated September 1855 complaining that he had expected $120 for the annuity for his six family members but received only $18.[123] He further outlined how traders were generously paid in several treaties for the debts of the Ojibwe and how additional money is deducted from each annuity payment and put in the trader's box.[124]

Here is an excerpt from that letter:

The first payment was made at Crow Wing according to the last treaty ---(was) twenty dollars a head was to be given him besides the goods. And when the person or persons are called to come forward the nine dollars was taken out of the twenty dollars and put in the trader's box for several traders. I and my family consisted of six in number, according to the treaty my portion would have been in money one hundred and twenty dollars. Instead of receiving it, the whole amount, we received only $18 in all. I had no single shilling in debt to no one. I can name several others treated in the same manner. Last year at La Pointe, Lake Superior, another treaty was made and in this treaty another claim against Indians is brought which I believed the Indians *consented to pay the old debt. At Washington I was not present when the treaty was made there. I believe another large sum was reserved especially for the old debt as it was called. Mr. Whiting, sir, there have been five different treaties made and at different times and places and of these different treaties claims were made again with adjustments to meet them. The Indians are always ready to meet any just claims even now at the present time. Mr. Shallor, who has been trading now over twenty years among my people, have positively informed me before others, that he knows an old claim that has been paid at two different times and places and that the very same claim and the very same old claim is again presented to have it paid.*

Less aware Ojibwe would have been even more susceptible to fraud than literate and numerate Enmegahbowh. He also wrote of the confusion of payments made under several treaties that applied to the Mississippi Ojibwe. A cursory reading of the treaties would indicate that these Ojibwe could be owed money under the 1837 treaty, the 1847 treaty, and the 1854 treaty. When multiplied by the thousands of Ojibwe capable of being defrauded, the take by agents, traders, politicians, and bribed chiefs would have been enormous.

After the signing of the 1855 treaty, speculators came to Crow Wing and beyond to appraise and obtain timberland. They were followed by loggers and some settlers. Crow Wing was booming, and the increased population made whiskey more available. Hunting and gathering lands began to be cut over and logging road activities scared game away. Traditional hunting and gathering became more difficult for the Ojibwe, and poverty increased.

CHAPTER 9
The Breck Mission to the Ojibwe, 1852 to 1858

In the 1850s, the Reverend James Lloyd Breck's path was to cross that of Enmegahbowh. Breck had formerly headed the Nashotah House, a Benedictine Episcopal seminary near Milwaukee with a large farm worked by the students. He left Milwaukee and headed to Minnesota as a missionary. Breck traveled with the Reverend Timothy Wilcoxson by railroad to Janesville, to Galena by stage, and to Fort Snelling by steamboat between June 9, 1850, and June 30, 1850.[125] He met the chaplain at Fort Snelling, the Reverend Ezekiel Gear, and afterward built a building in St. Paul, which became the headquarters of his mission and the home of Wilcoxson and Breck.

When Breck arrived in St. Paul, there were settlements in St. Paul, St. Anthony, and Stillwater and scattered settlers at Cottage Grove, Point Douglas, Arcola Mills, Marine Mills, and St. Croix Falls. Breck and Wilcoxson walked to each of these locations to hold services. Overall, the white population of the Minnesota Territory in 1850 was about 5,000. St. Paul was the head of navigation on the Mississippi River. Much of the trade in St. Paul derived from the ox cart transport from Pembina. Two-wheel wooden ox carts hauled furs southward and trade goods northward and were driven by the Métis of Pembina. Much of the St. Paul population was Catholic, including new arrivals from Ireland.[126] The most northern settlement in Minnesota was Sauk Rapids, to which Breck and Wilcoxson also walked. Wilcoxson formed and became rector of Christ Church in St. Paul, the first Episcopal Church in Minnesota.

James Lloyd Breck

Breck envisioned his establishment in St. Paul as "a second Nashota,"[127] an Episcopal seminary that would operate as a self-sustained monastery. Yet his vision for such a seminary was rejected by territorial Bishop Kemper, who claimed there would be too much competition with Nashotah in Wisconsin. By early 1852, the mission house had ten rooms and a primary schoolhouse; it was also a residence for ten "brothers." They had gardens for both vegetables and decoration.[128] The mission house helped start Episcopalian churches in St. Paul, Stillwater, and St. Anthony. Breck's mission to Minnesota was financially dependent on freewill offerings from the people to which they ministered. No support came from the church's domestic board.[129]

When Enmegahbowh traveled to Fort Snelling in the fall of 1851 to collect his annual annuity payment, he met Ezekiel Gear, the fort chaplain. Gear wrote of his encounter with Enmegahbowh:

A native Chippeway, well qualified to act as interpreter, catechist, schoolmaster, translator, and teacher of the language is on the ground, willing and anxious to cooperate with us. He is decidedly of the opinion that our services are better calculated to impress and interest the Indians than any other. I gave him a Prayer Book when I first became acquainted with him, and he informs me that he has translated some portions of it into the language and could readily prepare it for the press.[130]

Ezekiel Gear

The first indication of a connection between James Lloyd Breck and Enmegahbowh is found in a letter Breck wrote to his brother. In it, he mentions that in September 1851 "two Chippeway youth" will become residents of the St Paul mission house.[131] Further, he identifies the father of one of the boys as "a partially educated Chippeway" or Ojibwe who was brought up as a Methodist,[132] residing 150 miles north. The boy was Enmegahbowh and Charlotte's seven-year-old son, Alfred. Enmegahbowh had written a letter requesting a missionary and teachers who had "a better way." That he had found Breck and written was very important to Breck. Soon Breck envisioned establishing a school at Gull Lake for boys and girls from the ages of seven to twelve. Besides English and religion, the school would teach domestic skills to the girls and farming skills to the boys. According to Breck's plan, the Ojibwe would abandon the blanket, cut their hair, and adapt to the clothing of the white man. It excited Breck that the school was to be located on the site of the Ojibwe village.[133]

Breck and Stephen Hayward walked from St. Paul to Gull Lake in February 1852 to visit Hole in the Day, a war chief who deemed himself a leader of the Mississippi Ojibwe and who had sustained potentially mortal wounds.[134] (Earlier, Hole in the Day had been approached by the Catholics, but he rejected them, as his father before him had rejected Catholicism.) It is presumed that Enmegahbowh was present at the meeting between Hole in the Day and Breck and Hayward; however, no record was found to confirm this. Hole in the Day seems to have more acquiesced than agreed to the coming of Breck to civilize and Christianize the Ojibwe.

Chapter 9

Hole in the Day (the Younger)

In April 1852, Breck, with his colleagues Captain Craig, Stephen Hayward, Halstead, and Theodore Holcombe, walked to St. Anthony, took a small steamboat to Sauk Rapids, and then rode a stagecoach to Fort Ripley.[135] They were hosted overnight by the Reverend Solon Manney, the fort chaplain. Next, they rode a wagon or buggy to Crow Wing where they met Enmegahbowh, who informed them that Hole in the Day was at government farm rather than at Gull Lake as they had thought. He advised them that it was still wise to meet with Hole in the Day again, because he was important in the Ojibwe hierarchy. The group traveled on and spent several days with Hole in the Day, who was not too pleased with the intent of Breck. At Gull Lake they received a warmer reception by the chiefs Bad Boy and White Eagle, who called a council that approved building a mission.

Bad Boy, in addition to being a chief, was a canoe builder.[136] He built three during the summer of 1852, and the only help he received was from a group of women who gathered supplies and wove the strong gunnels. Holcombe describes Bad Boy and White Eagle as being "men of intelligence and serenity—They would scorn a mean or shady act as beneath their dignity."[137] Bad Boy first attended St. Columba in 1854 and continued his attendance. He took a temperance pledge, which he kept.[138]

Work on the mission began at Gull Lake. First, a log house was built for the missionaries, completed by the end of August 1852. All work was done by hand, and any lumber used was whipsawed. Shingles were hand hewn. A second building, twice the size of the first, was also similarly constructed, and a corridor was built between them. A room was used

Bad Boy

St. Columba Mission in 1855

as a church, school, library, dining room, and kitchen. In October, Mrs. Eliza Wells joined the group as matron. She was housed on the second floor of the mission house, which also served as a dormitory for girls. [139]

The church cornerstone was laid in late 1852, and the church was completed in the summer of 1853. St. Columba Church was consecrated on August 7, 1853, by Bishop Kemper.[140] An additional twelve-by-fourteen mission house of hewn logs was built by the end of 1853. At the school, girls were taught sewing, and boys participated in building and farming. Students were also taught reading and writing along with religion. Enmegahbowh and Breck were the real forces in the settlement. Enmegahbowh's role was as an interpreter, relating Ojibwe ideas to the missionaries and missionary ideas to the Ojibwe. Breck's enthusiasm and energy were boundless. He even envisioned that Hole in the Day would convert to Christianity and separate from two of his three wives, something that never happened.

The missionary and school staff included several men and women engaged in teaching, including a Miss Mills who arrived in early March 1853.[141] Through Breck's connections in the East, he pro-

St. Columba Church

cured donations of money and clothes. All work at the mission on buildings and gardens was done in cooperation with the Ojibwe as object lessons in civilization. Theodore Holcombe, an early member of Breck's staff, identified Enmegahbowh as "the Providential Man"[142] who enabled the mission to be formed and who was a guide, laborer, and mediator, without whom the mission would have been impossible. He also praised Charlotte as "an effective helpmeet" who had learned to read and write English.

Holcombe also admired qualities of Breck:

> Dr. Breck excelled not only in possessing the courage of his convictions, but in his power to enkindle the souls of others with a devotion similar to his own. Of this power, I think he was always conscious. As in this year of trial he stood in the presence of an empty larder, so often in times past he had faced similar conditions undismayed. Even when there was discoverable only a little in the bottom of the barrel with which to feed his large and dependent family, there was no outward sign of worry or anxiety. . . .
>
> [Letters received regularly] were white-winged messengers of peace and relief to the strong soul who could both work and wait with equal serenity, for like the great Apostle, he might truly say: "In all things I have learned both to be filled and to be hungry, both to abound and to be in want. I can do all things through Him that strengthened me."

Wautaub, Enmegahbowh, and Breck

ENMEGAHBOWH'S FAMILY

A great celebration in Enmegahbowh's family occurred on February 27, 1853, at St. Columba Church when four of his children were baptized by Breck and the parents were accepted into the Episcopal Church.[143] The children were Martha, Alfred, Gaius, and George. William Augustus (Gus), born April 27, 1852, was baptized on August 10, 1854. Eliza was born on February 27, 1854, and baptized on May 27, 1854. Jane Maria was born in 1856 and baptized the same year.

Among several Ojibwe who came to observe the Gull Lake mission was Flat Mouth, a chief at Leech Lake, seventy miles north of Gull Lake.[144] As reported by Tanner, he said:

> "I have come a distance to see you. I hear that you love the Red man. We know you seek our good, and we desire our children to grow up in the religion and ways of the white man. I ask you come and help us, for we have no other who care for us and our children."

Although there was no road to Leech Lake, during the winter of 1853 Breck, with Captain Todd and Chaplain Manney, used a "train"—a toboggan towed by a horse—to go to Leech Lake so they could meet Flat Mouth and examine a mission site.[145] During the trip, they were housed in George Bonga's log house.

GEORGE BONGA

George Bonga was described as a forty-six-year-old coal-black Afro-Ojibwe married to an Ojibwe woman. He spoke English, French, and Ojibwe. Bonga was the grandson of a black man indentured to a British officer.[146] The officer had brought his servant to Mackinac during the Revolutionary War, and at the officer's death, Jean Bonga became a free man. Jean and his Ojibwe wife had a son, Pierre, who became a fairly prosperous trader near Duluth. Pierre also married an Ojibwe woman, Ashwinn in 1842, and they had two sons, George (who was born in 1802) and Stephen. George was sent to Montreal to be educated. He, too, became a trader and traveled extensively in Ojibwe country. George Sr. was six feet and four inches tall and could carry large packs over portages.

In 1898, Enmegahbowh recalled an incident that can be attributed to this period involving a black man, probably an offspring of George Bonga.[147] As a friend,

George Bonga

he consulted with Enmegahbowh about his problems in finding a wife among the Ojibwe. He first asked Enmegahbowh for a "love powder," and though Enmegahbowh had heard of such a potion among white people, he had no source of it. The black man, who had received a good sum in a payment provided by a recent treaty, then bought two large brass kettles, two large iron kettles, and two large tin kettles and brought them to his wigwam. He stated, "Now girls & you second-hand squaws stirred up with your lukewarmness & refusal to marry me. If any color can do it, I know my brass, iron and tin kettles will do it." He then invited the parents of his intended to his wigwam to show them his offer of sugar kettles for the hand of their daughter. The mother consented but doubted that her daughter would accept his proposal. The mother argued to her daughter that color was of small consequence and that the offered gifts would not turn black and that the love he showed could become mutual. She reluctantly accepted, they married, and they subsequently raised a large family of sons.

ST. COLUMBA GROWS

As Breck began to see the results of his endeavors at the Gull Lake mission, he thought more broadly about expanding the Gull Lake program further among Ojibwe bands. In June 1853, Breck and Rev. Solon Manney, accompanied by George Bonga, took a canoe trip to Otter Tail Lake to scout out new missionary sites.[148] The group ascended Crow Wing River in a twenty-foot canoe with George Bonga leading the way. Here, Breck reached an agreement with the resident chief for a mission at Otter Tail Lake.

Meanwhile, St. Columba continued with its work. By 1855 there were fifteen people on the staff of the mission, and several Ojibwe children also lived in the complex.[149] While Breck diligently labored to lead and finance the mission, younger members of the staff spent some leisure time enjoying the scenery, swimming, and canoeing.[150] Holcombe described the atmosphere at Gull Lake:

It was not a great while after this that the usual troubles began. The propinquity, the social dependence, the exhilarating atmosphere of *kahgee-ashkoon se kaga*, the beauty of the moonlight, the daily associations. All these good things as the good doctor writes to his Bishop, "threatens love. This bringing together of a number of unmarried missionaries, both male and female is more than I can manage. I have determined to marry them off as fast as I can. There is no mending the matter in any other way." A most philosophical conclusion, nor was Dr. Breck himself free from suspicion of honorable intention towards the sex he had heretofore declined to consider matrimonially, and this may account for his rapid acquisition in the desires of others who like himself had waited and hoped in vain. It was not, however until sometime later that the morning papers had this announcement: "Married on Saturday, August 11, 1855 in the church of St. Columba near Fort Ripley, by the Rev. E. G. Gear, chaplain U. S. A., The Rev. James Lloyd Breck, missionary to the Chippeways, and Miss Jane Maria Mills, daughter of the late William R. Mills Esq. of Argyle, New York."

Jane Maria Mills had worked for two years as a teacher at Gull Lake.[151]

Territorial Governor Willis A Gorman, in the second year of operation of the Gull Lake mission, had $500 per year assigned to its operation. The Indian agent David Herriman had the amount designated for education in the reservation assigned to the mission. However, on September 29, 1855, the grant ceased, as a provision in the 1855 treaty allotted the school money to Hole in the Day, who wanted to hire his own teachers.[152] In 1855, Henry Rice procured government money amounting to $3,000 per year for the mission. In addition, Breck's extensive network of contributors helped with the mission's expenses.

In January 1855, Breck described his mission at Gull Lake:[153]

The following are Missionaries: Mr. John Johnson (Ojibwe), interpreter; Mr. John Parker, carpenter and overseer of Indians at work; Mr. Charles Selkirig, curator; Mr. Jonathon Edwards, farmer; Miss Jane M. Mills, head of the school department; Miss Richardson, assistant teacher; Mrs. Parker, housekeeper. These teach civilization in all its varied branches, in the house and in the field. We have no white servants. The Indians perform all the cooking, washing, ironing, baking, and making butter, under direction of the ladies. There are few now who cannot sew and make their own clothes, which applies to women in the wigwam as well as in the Mission House. All kinds of gardening and farming are taught as well as house-building. During the year, about four hundred different natives work under our direction, frequently for weeks together, averaging thirty a day in both field and the house.

A summary of work at the Gull Lake mission for three years ending in August 1856 included the following:

- adults baptized, 30; children baptized, 49; total 79
- adult Romanists received by public profession of faith, 3
- confirmations, 21
- communicants, 8
- marriages, 6
- deaths, 3
- present number of Ojibwe communicants, 98[154]

Breck described the beginning of a service in 1857 at Gull Lake with pride in his success:[155]

> The church bell had been ringing for some time, and the natives are gathering in groups about the mission house . . . The children have assembled in their schoolroom, all neatly dressed in uniform. The boy's long hair had been cut off. Their blankets had been laid aside, and nice coats substituted for them. The girls, likewise, with their well-padded hoods for winter and white bonnets for summer . . . look very pretty and neat.

Breck's pride in Gull Lake did not necessarily mean life was easy for the Ojibwe who lived there. With the annuity as their only source of income, the people of the Gull Lake village lived as the Ojibwe had in the past by hunting, fishing, trapping, gathering wild rice, and making maple sugar.

A CLASH OF CULTURES

The white race confused the Ojibwe mightily. The Ojibwe were of one Medewiwin belief. The whites whom the Ojibwe met appeared to be of many different beliefs: Roman Catholicism, Episcopalism, paganism and assorted groups of Protestantism. Many of the pagan whites sold alcohol to the Indians and may have been perceived as immoral. The Roman Catholics (referred to by the Episcopalians as Romans) primarily taught their Christian religion. The Episcopalians taught their religion plus civilization skills. These differences in teaching and example greatly perplexed the Ojibwe.

LEECH LAKE MISSION

Breck envisioned an Indian mission at Leech Lake and selected a site at Onigum, where the Ojibwe would be taught Christianity and white civilization.

Breck was summoned by the Ojibwe of Leech Lake to meet with the agent. This was the band of which Flat Mouth was a chief; with a population of 1,100, the band was known as the Pillagers. In February 1856, Henry Rice, territorial representative, informed Breck that the government would pay for the new educational program at Leech Lake.[156] Land was selected, and buildings were planned. Breck embraced the idea and planned to go to Leech Lake.

Meanwhile, a man was needed to take Breck's place at Gull Lake, and the Reverend E. Steele Peake, a Nashotah alumnus, accepted the position. To get to Gull Lake from the east, the reverend and his wife took a train to Galena, Illinois, then a steamboat for four days up the Mississippi River to St. Paul.[157] Mrs. Peake described St. Paul as a "mere hamlet." From St. Paul, they took a stage appropriately called a "mud wagon" and rode, with appropriate stops to refresh horses and people, from 5:00 a.m. until 2:00 a.m. the next day to reach Watab, ten miles beyond St. Cloud. They slept there a few hours, then resumed their journey and reached Crow Wing that evening. In Crow Wing, Allen Morrison, a longtime trader, hosted them in his comfortable home. The Morrisons and Peakes became lifelong friends. From Crow Wing, it was a half-day trip to Gull Lake during which the Ojibwe agency was passed and noted.

E. Steele Peake

Peake and his wife finally arrived at Gull Lake on November 12, 1856.[158] Mrs. Peake found everything in order at the mission, except that the chinking of the logs of buildings had been poorly done. The lack of chinking caused much discomfort during the winter.

On the same day that the Peakes arrived, Breck started his journey to Leech Lake. Fortunately, a sixty-mile road had been completed between Gull Lake and Leech Lake, as stipulated in the 1855 treaty, at a cost of $14,000. Further, Breck had received a team of horses and a wagon, costing the Bureau of Indian Affairs $400.[159] Sherman Hall, a candidate for holy orders, and John Parker, a carpenter, went with Breck. A plan for the facility at Leech Lake included a two-story school with kitchen and quarters for staff and students, a two-story farmer's house, a stable, and the Church of the Good Shepard.[160] The buildings were built by January 1857 at Onigum on Leech Lake. The lumber for the buildings was either whipsawed or hauled sixty miles.[161]

An interesting map showing the state of land transportation was published in the *Minnesota Advertiser* in 1857.[162] It shows a Chicago and St. Anthony railroad to St. Anthony and a railroad from Winona to St. Peter and to St. Cloud. No roads are shown beyond Crow Wing. The condition of the roads would probably better be described as trails with little grading and few bridges.

The original contingent at Leech Lake besides Breck, his wife, and their new baby included. Tom Reese, the mission farmer, his wife, and their five children. Sixteen Ojibwe children were housed, taught, and fed in the government buildings.

Everything went well until the Ojibwe hunters returned from their winter hunt and got their yearly allotment. Alcohol was readily available at Crow Wing (also known as Whiskey City), and apparently, much alcohol was moved to Leech Lake. The resulting revelry with drinking lasted six weeks, and the lives of the missionaries were threatened by Ojibwe wielding knives.[163] The Brecks decided that continuing their mission at Leech Lake was too hazardous and retreated to Gull Lake. The Peakes were awakened by the ringing of the church bell, announcing the emergency arrival of the Leech Lake missionaries. The retreating party consisted of the Brecks, the Reeses, and the teacher, Miss Heron. Mrs. Peake attributed the uprising among the Leech Lake Ojibwe to the influence of jealous whites who resented Breck's control of government money and who roused the natives.[164] There were no police or troops from Fort Ripley to enforce the peace. Feeling that their lives were threatened, Breck decided to abandon the Leech Lake mission entirely. The mission at Leech Lake lasted from November 12, 1856, to July 16, 1857.[165] Perhaps if the mission had included a native liaison like Enmegahbowh, a different outcome could have been achieved.

UNREST AND FRONTIER JUSTICE

Beyond Fort Ripley, frontier justice prevailed in an area that was rapidly being populated by white settlers. On August 19, 1857, two Ojibwe women reported to Enmegahbowh of a murder at nearby Round Lake.[166] He went to the lake, dug in the sandy shore where the women indicated, and found a body. The victim, Fritz, a hapless German wanderer, had been either stoned to death or drowned. Three drunken Ojibwe—Charles Gigabish, James Shambo, and Jo Shambo (the alleged perpetrators)—were soon apprehended by members of the Gull Lake Mission and taken to Fort Ripley. However, there were no troops to incarcerate them, so they were moved to Little Falls and put in jail by the sheriff. They were charged with murder and the next day were being transported to St. Paul, where they could be properly incarcerated and tried for murder. The group got as far as the Platte River when the prisoners were apprehended by vigilantes and lynched. Soon afterward, the fathers and uncles of the lynched men threatened Enmegahbowh and Peake for their part in the investigation. A rebellion was threatened by the Ojibwe, who believed that three lives for one was out of proportion. Peake and Enmegahbowh, before retreating to Fort Ripley through a hostile Ojibwe community, consulted Bad Boy, a friendly chief. He suggested that they wait until morning when the ten gallons of whiskey would have been consumed and the exhausted Ojibwe would be asleep. Manney, the Fort Ripley chaplain, along with Tom Reese, arrived at Gull Lake late at night, having perceived the danger. All of the mission personnel and their families boarded the wagon and, with four armed men beside them, made their way to Fort Ripley.

Enmegahbowh and his family returned to Gull Lake after a month. Enmegahbowh would remain at St. Columba and keep the mission open.

It was August of 1858 when the Peakes moved to Crow Wing because food was scarce at the fort.[167] A cow kept by the Peakes for milk had been killed and eaten by the Ojibwe. Regardless of the danger, Reverend Peake continued offering weekly services, alternating between Gull Lake, Crow Wing, and Little Falls. He joined the army as a chaplain in 1862.[168]

THE CROW WING AREA

Crow Wing during this period was becoming a metropolis of the north. The location at the junction of the Mississippi and the Crow Wing Rivers was advantageous. It had been established as a trading post in 1823 by Allen Morrison, a Canadian with the American Fur Company.[169] He eventually became the namesake of Morrison County. Sometime later, he was joined at the trading post by his brother, William.

Other traders to follow Morrison were John Fairbanks, Paul Beaulieu, and Clement Beaulieu.

Crow Wing also became an important route of travel. By 1845, the Woodland Trail through Crow Wing, which crossed the Mississippi, became the preferred route for the ox carts of the Métis going between Pembina and St. Paul, as the Dakota had made the Prairie Trail along the Red River and Minnesota River more hazardous. Besides Clement Beaulieu's post, there were seven whiskey shops in Crow Wing in 1858 (which explains how the settlement earned the nickname, Whiskey City). Mrs. Peake characterized the town as "one of the most wicked places there has ever been in Minnesota or the Northwest."[170] The population grew to eight hundred people, consisting of Ojibwe, traders, those of mixed race, lumbermen, and settlers. A ferry was maintained across the Mississippi. The west bank ferry station had trails to Leech Lake and Pembina. The best homes in the town were those of Robert Fairbanks, the Chapmans, the Clement Beaulieus, and the Morrisons. Other prominent white residents were William Aitkin, John Fairbanks, Peter Roys, Tom Cathcart, and W. W. Hartley.[171] A Catholic church was led by Father Francis Pierz.

Crow Wing

Hole in the Day had a fine house located near the agency on the Crow Wing River that was financed by the US government through treaty negotiations.

In 1858, Minnesota became a state and Henry Sibley was elected governor. The unrest on the frontier prompted him to send soldiers to Fort Ripley, which had been largely evacuated when troops moved south to assist with troubles arising prior to the Civil War.

Enmegahbowh and Isaac Manitowab, a Christian chief, represented the St. Columba mission at the Diocesan Convention on July 6, 1859. Just a few days earlier, on July 3, 1859, at Faribault, Bishop Kemper ordained Enmegahbowh as a deacon in the Episcopal Church.[172] Becoming a deacon increased the scope of Enmegahbowh's ministry, though it did not allow him to preside at rites such as communion.

THE FARIBAULT SEMINARY

Breck was not idle after leaving Gull Lake. He traveled east, talked to people and clergymen, and, upon his return to Minnesota, procured land in Faribault to develop a school for prophets. He named the school Seabury University in honor of the first Episcopal bishop in the United States, Samuel Seabury.[173] By October 18, 1858, there were six divinity students and fifty-five day students in attendance. Among the first students were three Ojibwe from Gull Lake—Charles Wright Nashotah, Fred Smith Kadawabide, and George Johnson, Enmegahbowh's son. Later, the son of Chief Shay-Day-Ence, Samuel Madison, also received two years of schooling, including English, at Breck's school in Faribault. These men later became deacons in the Episcopal Church. Space for the school and resident scholars was rented until a building could be constructed.

CHAPTER 10
Henry Whipple Becomes Bishop of Minnesota, 1859

Henry Benjamin Whipple was elected Episcopal bishop of Minnesota on June 19, 1859. Born in Adams, New York, in 1822, he was the son of a merchant. He was educated for a few years at Oberlin College, but his education was interrupted in 1840 by a respiratory condition (which persisted throughout his life). He returned to Adams and worked for his father and in 1842 married Cornelia Wright. His wife involved him in the Episcopal Church. After the birth of their first child, Sarah, he suffered another respiratory infection and was sent alone to St. Augustine, Florida, to recover. The journey back to Adams in 1844 was by way of New Orleans, the Mississippi River, the Ohio River, Philadelphia, and Washington. Business and politics engaged Whipple until 1848. Meanwhile, two more daughters, Cornelia and Jane, were added to his family. He began studying for the Episcopal priesthood in 1848 under Rev. W. D. Wilson and was ordained in 1850. Zion Church in Rome, New York, was Whipple's first parish; the family's fourth child, Frances, was born there. Cornelia became ill with typhoid soon after Frances was born and, as a result, a sojourn to Florida was recommended. The family spent six months in St. Augustine, where Henry became interim rector of Trinity Church. Afterward, the evangelical spirit of Whipple attracted him to answer a call to a new "free" (no pew rental) church in Chicago named Church of the Holy Communion in 1856.[174] He also preached as a guest in St. Ansgarius Church, a Swedish church.[175]

In 1859, a convention to elect a Minnesota bishop was held in St. Paul's Church in St. Paul.[176] The represented churches were St. Mark's of Minneapolis, Christ Church of Red Wing, Trinity Church of Stockholm, Wisconsin, St. John's Church of Minneapolis, Church of the Good Shepherd of Faribault, Trinity Church of Orono, and Trinity Church of Anoka. After two ballots, then a speech for Whipple by Rev. Manney, the clergy elected Whipple as the bishop for Minnesota. A vote by the laity confirmed the clergy vote. The salary was to be $1,500 per year.

Bishop Henry Whipple

When Whipple was called to become the bishop of Minnesota, he consulted with other bishops. The conclusion was that it was his duty to accept this position, and he did so on July 12, 1859. He was consecrated as bishop of Minnesota on October 13, 1859, at St. James Church in Richmond, Virginia, by Bishop Jackson Kemper. The standing committee met its new bishop in St. Paul in early November. Whipple found out that his see consisted of four organized churches in Minneapolis–St. Paul, the St. Columba mission in Gull Lake, Breck's school in Faribault, and thirty-four mission churches, with seventeen of them having buildings. Whipple visited all of the priests in St. Paul, Minneapolis, and St. Anthony, and he also met Enmegahbowh, who invited him to Gull Lake.

By steamboat, buggy, and walking, Whipple went to Gull Lake in late November 1859 with Breck to visit Enmegahbowh's mission of St. Columba. There among the Ojibwe population he found poverty, disease, alcoholism, and hunger.[177] Of the experience, he reported the following:

> A few miles from St. Columba we came to a wigwam where half-naked children were crying from cold and hunger, and the mother was scraping the inner bark of the pine tree for pitch to give to her starving children.

> Our Indian affairs were at their worst; without government, without protection, without personal rights of property, subject to every evil influence and the prey of covetous, dishonest white men, while the firewater flowed in rivers of death.

At the church, Whipple conducted a communion service and sermon, which Enmegahbowh translated. He also visited wigwams. After the ten-day trip to Gull Lake, Whipple resolved to do what he could for the Native Americans.[178]

After a trip to New York to attend his father's funeral, Whipple returned to Minnesota and went to Faribault to become acquainted with Breck's school. Faribault in 1860 had a population of 1,520. The theology school had two students and two professors, and the elementary school had 134 students. Elementary students were taught by the theology students.

In his personal life, with six children and a low salary, Whipple had a problem of adequate housing. Alexander Faribault, a Catholic pioneer, made a generous offer to build Whipple a house if he made the town of Faribault the seat of his see. Whipple accepted. Faribault also donated land for a school.[179]

In March 1860, Whipple, Breck, Peake, and Enmegahbowh made a trip to "a new band of Indians near Lake Superior" (probably Fond du Lac) over frozen lakes and snowy ground.[180] For three nights they camped out. The chief they contacted indicated an interest in the improvement of his people.

At the turn of a decade, a snapshot of Minnesota is in order. In ten years, the white population had increased from less than 6,000 to 170,000. Most of the settlement took place in the southern half of the state, which was largely prairie and became farms. The northern half of the state was less settled and unorganized, and lumbering was the main activity. St. Paul had a population of 10,000 and Minneapolis had a population of 3,000. The Ojibwe population likely remained stable at around 10,000 but felt increased pressure from white settlement. No major progress had been made in Ojibwe education. Most of the Ojibwe remained hunters and gatherers, but on less land. Meanwhile, the St. Columba mission at Gull Lake continued to operate with Enmegahbowh on-site and with Peake journeying from Crow Wing to conduct services. Students were being taught at Gull Lake, and some were taken to Breck's school in Faribault for further religious education.

With the birth of Henry Whipple Johnson, born in December 1861, the family of Enmegahbowh and Charlotte now included eight children. Martha was nineteen, Alfred was seventeen, Gaius was thirteen, George was ten, William was nine, Eliza was seven, and Jane was five. Henry Whipple Johnson was baptized by Bishop Henry Whipple on August 1, 1862. Sarah Jamison was born to Enmegahbowh and Charlotte in June 1865. She was baptized on June 9 by Bishop Whipple.[181]

A letter from Enmegahbowh to Rev. and Mrs. Breck, dated January 23, 1862, is a good summary of the St. Columba mission:[182]

I have been wanting to write to you for some time. . . . It is no new thing to you to know how we are getting along here. More so at present by the recent visit of the Bishop as I have no doubt will tell you all about us and the poor injins here. Every christian ojibways you have signed them with the sign of the cross have expected you with our beloved Bishop and once more to hear you speaking to us from word of the great spirit, but were disappointed not finding you with the Bishop. The old Wa ge ma we shkong [Grand Medicine brother] was inquiring whether mister [meaning Mr. Breck] came up with the Bishop. I told him No and then he said he must have forgotten us. . . . Tell Mr. Breck that I have already given up all my children to be numbered with the christens Ojibways and I am happy to say they are doing well. You also tell Mr. Breck I am myself and by & by you will see me kneeling with you and praying with you in the church. You recollect old Wa ge ma we shkong is and has been one of the leading meda in the country and the only one that has any way opposed the Missionaries and the Christian religion here and now he comes with the language of Agrippa— almost thou pursuadist me to be a Christian— not merely to follow my children because they are Christians but to do with the uttermost of my ability the instruction you have been given. The old man means what he says, during the whole summer I have not seen him to have touched the ish kotawahboo. Kept himself away from the whiskey city. And his children are faithful members in the church.

Last night Bad Mouth came in and said that all old Wa ge ma we shkong children are at my house wanted you to give them the same talk you gave them night before. I told him to ring the bell and make good fire. For several nights past I have been reading and explaining to them on the catechism by & according Bp Brownell to the commentary on our prayer book. That is I told them that way.

We will have short service before commencing every night we meet. When the weather permits. This has been astonishing to see and so my members abound. For you would I know be pleased to hear the prayers offered every morning & evening according to liturgies of our prayers by your Ojibway Christian children.

Last fall before rice making I started to go over to Bad Mouth's house and see what time they are returning back. This was early in the morning. Just before opening the door I heard them repeated the Lord's Prayer. . . . As my poor heart leapt with joy and tears I went in and shook hands with them. I believe in my last I told you what Bad Mouth had said, that he was determined to be a Christian family, I believe the great spirit blesses him. I was telling Bro Peake Bad Mouth was very brave.

I know my encouragement in the work if I can only save one through my feeble efforts all will be well with me.

There were down periods at the Gull Lake mission, as Enmegahbowh discussed in his letter to Breck and his wife:

And then again I have my dark hours I really think none would stand against what I have passed through. My children did actually cried for food for several days, We have had nothing but potatoes. I did in actually make fire in the nights for weeks in order to keep us warm. We tell the agent or rather I went to make known to him our suffering. And ask me how many children and he gave us one blanket all round, two dresses for my wife and mother and the girls and two lbs flour and some pork. You ask brother Peake what we had from August to January 14—I did actually thought that it is treating your injin missionary like the Kentuckians. You white missionaries been living on the turkey and I the Crow. There is our church it is not fit to hold service in the cold weather and it is now nearly five months past and it is only once out of 5 months we have the sacrament administered to us here. The Bishop would say and has said to me it was all my fault being suffered. As poor Injin however dear you innocent you may have it with the poor injin. Injin all the time but no white man. The great stress and weapon used for the poor missionary is the war. War has been the great cause of this sufferings of all men. I admit for and not as much as suffering as I have already passed through. What has been done to the Indian helpers through out the Indian country in assisting the white missionaries among the Indians is like the Kentuckians to the Indians. There was here John Sunday, John Taunchey, Henry Blatchford all educated Christian men. They all left and they blame them much of doing so and I poor fellow still hang in not entirely without hope. I have strong hopes that the church will not treat me like the Kentuckians. But I must say I have already in past see, hear, smell, taste & feel it from every point. I have had dear Dr. evidence some situation in the government employ where I can easily command my six hundred dollars per year. If you understand me right I ask no more than my full support for my work no more so I cannot every now & then follow hunting & leave my work every now & then. I did actually think and still do think now that if you allowed me to beg abroad to friends to finish my church I believe I would have succeeded. And if I were succeeded going to my friends I am going to do it and I do think I can finish it off. Its becoming a good church if I say fairly. Even now I think I can do it although the war the war! We want a teacher here under your care. I do not wish to have any one under my roof because we serve him but I do like to have one here to teach & assist me in the work.

In his letter, Enmegahbowh further expressed concern as a father for his child Gaius, age thirteen:

A few words about little Gaius. I have some hope of him that he will be great service to and assistance to us. He is one of my best child of the whole. He is industrious in times of our near starvation he has hunted every day setting steal traps. He has killed 6 minks 2 foxes of which he bought one sac flour, 3 lbs pork, 2 caps, 3 pr mockesins and 2 shirts for himself. The flour he bought was just at the extreme point of our wants. To see the young Gaius going out every day with his young and I going to the other direction I am always sure wether I or Gaius would bring some game home with us.

The little fellow during the summer has work hard and has done a great deal of ploughing for us and the Indians. Ka kina waush ask him if he would plough his land for him in the spring—yes said he if you pay me I will plough all your land. If the Indians think that I am going to plough again for them this coming spring they are mistaken (said he). In the summer while he was making hay with the rest of the young men he cook one afternoon and there was an old Wa ge ma we shkong came where they were. After the dinner the old man asked the young men if they have any crumbs left. No one answered. The old man asked again the second time. Gaius said—yes. The crumbs are just as good to us as to any man that will work—He is the stingiest of the whole family—take good care of the cattle and milk the old cows. I am in the church with pleasant songs & responses loud and it is great assistance to me in every way both temporal and in assisting me in the church. It will be a lonesome to us should I ever send him to some white school. As I must in some way send him to such school. I am very anxious indeed that Alfred & Gaius both have some better English Education. <u>And be enabled to go through the world with ease as their father.</u> I have told you some of Gaius hunts and if I let him remain with me by & by he will do nothing but hunt. I want to get him away from our people. If I do not find him a place before spring or summer I shall prepare him for confirmation.

Now Dr. I must tell you one thing. During the whole winter he has not put it on a coat on his back. I had an old blanket coat that I worn last fall in my hunt that poor fellow had to put it on the coldest day and I feel for him. I say I am going to try very hard for him to go to school next summer or just as soon as I find a place for him. I told Gaius if the brethren are able to send my last quarter salary in full I will buy him a coat. You would be astonished to learn what we have to pay one for calico here. When you send us a check we are compelled to trade it here in goods. 25cents a yd calico at Crow Wing. That is the regular price. And so with the proportion of everything else either in goods or provisions etc.
Yours very truly
Enmegahbowh

In early 1862, Enmegahbowh was approached by two white men from St. Paul who asked for his help in recruiting young Ojibwe men to join the Union army as substitutes for drafted white men. As an inducement, $100 was offered for each recruit.[183] Enmegahbowh was skeptical and so was his wife. Two Ojibwe men from Leech Lake had already been recruited and taken to Fort Snelling. Their fathers came to Enmegahbowh in war paint and objected to the transaction. They stated an intent to kill Mr. Horn, the whiskey trader who made the transaction, but wanted to check before doing so. Enmegahbowh dissuaded them from doing so and said he would consult with Henry Sibley and Henry Rice to find out facts and return within seven days. His wife made him two new pairs of moccasins for the journey, and in two days he walked to St. Paul, where he consulted with Rice and Sibley. They did not support such recruitment. Sibley gave Enmegahbowh $25 to return home by stage, but he walked back and advised the fathers that recruitment could not be supported in any legal or moral sense.

On August 4, 1862, Bishop Whipple left Fort Ripley on a trip to Red Lake to visit the Ojibwe there.[184] He had already traveled 150 miles, probably by railroad from Faribault to St. Cloud and then to Fort Ripley. Mr. Spenser, the fort sutler, accompanied him, and at Crow Wing they were joined by Reverend Peake on their trek toward Leech Lake. After camping the night, they reached Leech Lake at 1:00 p.m. on August 6. They were joined by William Superior, who was of mixed race, Manitowab, and Enmegahbowh. The six men boarded two canoes. From the west lobe of Leech Lake, they proceeded to Cass Lake through marshes and a portage of two miles. Along the way, Enmegahbowh displayed his skills as a hunter and as a resourceful backwoodsman.

ENMEGAHBOWH AND WHIPPLE VISIT RED LAKE

Fr. Stephen Schaitberger recalls a story told about Enmegahbowh by his friends who are Indian concerning a Red Lake visit via canoe with Bishop Whipple and others from the national Episcopal Church.

On the journey, the entire expedition relied on Enmegahbowh's survival skills as a woodsman. Much game and plant life were required for sustenance. At one point in the canoe ride, a mother duck was seen with her brood trailing behind her. Bishop Whipple saw Enmegahbowh reach for his shotgun, and he called to Enmegahbowh not to shoot that mother duck with so many ducklings. Enmegahbowh stared intently at that duck and declared to Bishop Whipple that it was no mother duck but an imposter. And thus supper was provided.

They crossed the continental divide between the Mississippi River basin and the Hudson Bay basin on August 9. Another portage and a small lake brought them to a place where they left their canoes and baggage with William Aitkin, a trader. It was a difficult fifteen-mile land journey to their destination on Red Lake. Halfway there, the son of the French-Canadian trader Shubway appeared riding a pony and guided them to Red Lake. An agent of the American Fur Company, Shubway had been at Red Lake since 1823. He had a wife and seven children. There were about seven hundred Ojibwe in the Red Lake community and two hundred in the Pembina community, which was his trade area. Shubway did the usual trading of goods for furs but did not deal in alcohol.

A church service was held on Sunday, August 10, in a large room provided by Shubway. The room was filled to capacity with the Ojibwe, and those who couldn't fit in the room peered into the windows and doors. Whipple preached and Enmegahbowh translated.

Later, the Red Lake Ojibwe emphatically expressed that they did not want to enter a treaty with the United States and sell their land. Shubway stated that other traders estimated the band's debts at $150,000, but he felt they were more like $20,000. Mrs. Shubway was asked if she felt threatened when her husband was absent for more than two months during the summers. She reported that she felt no threat and said that chiefs checked with her frequently to see that things were all right.

The chief and the elders had talks with the visiting party. The Ojibwe stated that they felt they were poorer since the coming of the white man and they would like to have a school for their children.

The group began their return trip on August 10 along the same route by which they came. That afternoon, they reached the place where they had left their canoes and paddled and portaged their way back. On August 12, they were in Cass Lake, then Leech Lake, and then back to their homes.

The year 1862 also brought sorry tidings to James Lloyd Breck. His wife, Jane Marie Breck, died after a month-long illness that winter. She had been taken from Faribault to a St. Paul hospital in a sleigh and soon after perished.[185]

MANIFEST DESTINY

Within the white population of the United States, an idea took hold during the nineteenth century that they would occupy land "from sea to shining sea" and their culture would be dominant. Assimilation of any other culture into the dominant (Christian) culture was assumed. It was perceived that the American experience was a good example for the world. The use of land for agriculture was deemed best, and the clear-cutting of trees for lumber would result in more land for agriculture.

This set of ideas was called Manifest Destiny by John L. O'Sullivan, a Texas writer and editor in 1845 when he advocated for accepting Texas into the union as a state. Politically, the concept resulted in the Homestead Act of 1862, which awarded title for 160 acres of land to those who farmed the site for five years. This act increased people's desire, expressed to their representatives in Congress, to obtain Indian lands that could then be surveyed and made available to homesteaders.

FATHER FRANCIS PIERZ

Another religious pioneer and contemporary of Enmegahbowh in northern Minnesota was Francis Pierz. He was born in 1785 in Slovenia.[186] While serving as a parish priest in 1830 in Slovenia, then a part of the Austrian Empire, he was contacted by Father Fredric Baraga who informed him of the need for missionaries to the Ojibwe in the United States. In 1836, at the age of fifty-one, he came to Detroit and then was assigned successively to La Croix, Sault Ste. Marie, and Grand Portage from 1837 to 1839. He worked mostly among the Ojibwe, teaching religion and modern living. In 1839, Pierz was assigned to L'Arbre Croche (now Harbor Springs, Michigan) where he continued his program of Catholic religion and civilization among the Odawa until 1851.

The Catholic Diocese of St. Paul, which consisted then of the territory of Minnesota, was organized in 1851 under Bishop Cretin. Cretin, having heard of Pierz's accomplishments in the region, called him to become a missionary in his diocese, and Pierz arrived in Minnesota on June 18, 1852. Pierz established himself in Crow Wing and ministered to both the Ojibwe and the settlers. He established a church in Crow Wing dedicated to St. Francis Xavier and then churches in Belle Plaine and Sauk Rapids. He also visited German settlements in St. Cloud and St. Joseph. And, with great difficulty, at the age of sixty-seven, Pierz made trips to Sandy Lake and Mille Lacs.

By 1855, Pierz concluded that the work of the Catholic Church in northern Minnesota was too much for him, and he suggested that the Benedictine Fathers of Pennsylvania be called to assist in his ministry. The Benedictines arrived in Minnesota in 1856 and established themselves at St. Joseph; this would become the basis of St. John's Abbey and subsequently St. John's University. St. Benedict's Monestary at St. Joseph and the College of St. Benedict were also outgrowths of Pierz's influence.

After the arrival of the Benedictines, Pierz devoted himself to establishing missions at Sandy Lake, Mille Lacs, and Fond du Lac. In 1858, Father Lawrence Lautischar was paired with Pierz, and together they initiated a mission at Red Lake. Lautischar, left in charge at Red Lake, died in December 1858 on a return trip across Red Lake from attending an ailing Ojibwe.

In 1864, Pierz returned to his home country and recruited sixteen young men to come to America and be trained as priests to aid him in his labors. As a result, the priests Joseph Buh, John Zuzek, and Ignatius Tomazin came to Minnesota to help him.

While Enmegahbowh and Pierz shared goals of converting the Ojibwe to Christianity and making them into farmers, the authors could not locate any records of them meeting.

CHAPTER 11

The Hole in the Day Disturbance, 1862

The administration of President Abraham Lincoln, elected in 1860, brought in new faces throughout the Bureau of Indian Affairs. Within a year, the Civil War began and dominated the attention of Lincoln. William P. Dole became head of the Indian Commission, and Charles Mix of Minnesota was named the assistant commissioner.[187] C. W. Thompson was head of the northern regional agency, and Lucius Walker became the agent at the Mississippi Ojibwe agency on the Crow Wing River. All were political appointees, and there were many vying for all levels of positions, as the potential for financial gain had previously been proved to be enormous. The personnel changed with the new Republican administration, but the venality of the appointees remained the same. Indeed, corruption was prevalent throughout the administration of the Bureau of Indian Affairs in the western United States.

In Congress, Representative Cyrus Aldrich from Minnesota and Senator James Doolittle of Wisconsin perceived that the situation in the Midwest could lead to turmoil, and they recommended George E. H. Day "to use and recommend such measures as will most likely to promote peace between the Indians and the whites." Day, a St. Anthony attorney, was duly hired for that purpose by Indian Commissioner Dole;[188] Dole appointed him on August 10, 1861.[189] The sponsors and Day apparently interpreted the assignment differently. While the sponsors wanted simple measures to prevent turmoil, Day conceived the assignment to be to thoroughly investigate the Indian situation. His first finding upon interrogating Thompson was that there were no books, contracts, or vouchers recording the operations of the northern regional agency in Wisconsin, Minnesota, and the Dakota Territory.[190] In September and early October, Day traveled 1,800 miles by mule-drawn wagon to visit the Dakotas, the Ojibwe, and the Winnebago.

Afterward, Day recommended creating a voucher system and accounting to document annuity distributions. Day's disclosures did not sit well with administrators, who recommended that the report should be kept from department operatives below Dole. Dole in turn moved to limit the investigation. However, Day found an authorization for illegal timber cutting by Morrison on Indian land signed by Dole. Dole denied the authorization. Day found that Thompson, whose salary was $2,000 a year, had spent up to $200,000 personally over the last four years. Day also found that the assistant commissioner, Mix, contracted to supply pork for annuity payments at $16 to $18 a barrel but delivered spoiled meat only worth $3 a barrel. Since all of Day's findings were of fraud from top to bottom of the department, he decided to write Lincoln asking for $135 to travel to Washington and consult with the president.[191] He accused almost all the Indian agents, traders, and Senator Henry Rice of being corrupt and politically powerful. He stated in a letter to Lincoln that Superintendent Major Cullen had saved over $100,000 in four years on a salary of $2,000 a year.[192] The letter appealed to Lincoln personally to heed what was happening under Dole. Lincoln never answered the letter. Thompson voiced countercharges of corruption against Day, and Day's report was dismissed by the Indian Commission with no action. Presumably, Day had made a complete report of his travels, findings, and recommendations; however, no trace of such a document was found.

A letter to Thompson from Thomas Galbraith, a Dakota agent, illustrated the attitude held in the department when he stated that "the biggest swindle pleases the Interior Department best if they but have a share of it." Lucius Walker, the agent at Crow Wing reported to C. W. Thompson. Bishop Whipple, in a letter to Lincoln in March, stated that it was "a tradition on the border that an Indian Agent can retire upon an ample fortune in four years."[193]

ANNUAL PAYMENTS

The major trader in Crow Wing, Clement Beaulieu, made specific investigations into the distribution of annual payments in 1861.[194] He went to Washington and procured the payments payroll, for which he paid $50. In council with the various bands, he established their numbers and tabulated what they were paid in past distributions. A band that numbered seventy people was listed on the official payroll as having 120 members. A payment listed officially at $50 was actually $5, as reported by the recipient. Beaulieu's tabulation indicated that the agent Lucius Walker had stolen $8,000 from the enrolled Mississippi Ojibwe at the previous distribution. Walker had gotten word of Beaulieu's investigation, and a short time later, presumably as a result, Beaulieu's trader license was revoked on the charge that he was selling alcohol.

Clement Beaulieu

In early June 1862, Hole in the Day went, uninvited, to Washington to see Dole with a well-planned agenda. He addressed the short payments in 1861, requested simplified payments in 1862, and asked for the removal of Walker. Although Hole in the Day thanked Dole cordially by letter for his meeting, no real action resulted from the meeting.

ENMEGAHBOWH AND HOLE IN THE DAY (THE YOUNGER)

Charlotte, being Hole in the Day (the Elder)'s niece, made Enmegahbowh part of the family. The two men had wandered across Minnesota and were neighbors at Gull Lake. They were both aware of the Civil War taking many men to the southern battlefronts and that Fort Ripley was thinly manned. Their relationship had been friendly. Then, on about August 17, 1862, Enmegahbowh learned that Hole in the Day had called Pillager warriors at Leech Lake to take prisoners of whites and seize their horses and goods.[195] Enmegahbowh felt threatened by this action and attempted, with his wife and children, to drive his team of oxen to a white settlement. He was stopped by four warriors and told to go back, which he did. When the family returned home, war drums were beating, and he saw that preparations were being made to attack the agency on the Crow Wing River. In council, Enmegahbowh told Hole in the Day that attacking whites would mean much death among the Ojibwe, but Hole in the Day said he could no longer control the assembled warriors.[196] From Rabbit Lake, Chief Crossing Sky came to Enmegahbowh and told him the agency would be attacked in two days. An alarmed Mr. Yanknight, a resident of Crow Wing, also came to Enmegahbowh with a warning. Enmegahbowh went to the agency with a warning of imminent attack. On Saturday morning, Hole in the Day's warriors approached the agency, and scouts reported back that the agency was well prepared for an attack.[197]

Hole in the Day was made aware of Enmegahbowh's betrayal and sent two warriors to the mission house with orders to kill him. Enmegahbowh knew his life was in danger but felt that, as a cleric, he should not personally be violent. Instead, he armed Charlotte with his double-barreled shotgun.[198] When the two warriors appeared at the door, she shouted, "I know what you have come for, but the first one to show a weapon, I will shoot down like a dog." The men believed her and left.

Enmegahbowh then fled with his wife and children to Fort Ripley by canoe. William Superior, a mixed-race Christian, and his family accompanied Enmegahbowh. The distance to Fort Ripley from the mission was approximately twenty-five miles, half of it on the Gull River. The Gull River leg of the trip was particularly difficult, as the river was shallow. Enmegahbowh or his wife had to get out of the canoe and wade to get it over rough spots. They arrived at Fort Ripley in the afternoon and were hospitably given accommodations in the fort.[199] Two of the children, Alfred and Henry, had already been sick, and their condition worsened during the trip. Alfred, who was eighteen years old, died on November 9, and Henry, only one year old, died on November 14.

In retaliation for Enmegahbowh's betrayal, the warriors went to St. Columba mission and trashed everything they could. Enmegahbowh's two "horned horses" (oxen) were killed.[200] Lucius Walker, the agent, sent word to Fort Ripley of the events and asked for soldiers to be sent to arrest Hole in the Day. On August 19, twenty soldiers marched from Fort Ripley to Crow Wing; they saw Hole in the Day and some of his warriors on the west bank of the Mississippi near the agency. Shots were fired by both sides, but Hole in the Day escaped.[201]

THE DISTURBANCE

Upon receiving a message from Hole in the Day, some Pillagers from Leech Lake broke into buildings for supplies and held seven whites hostage temporarily.[202] After Hole in the Day exchanged shots with the soldiers, he became more belligerent and sent a message to Chief Buffalo of Leech Lake to kill the hostages. Yet shortly thereafter, the hostages were released.

On August 20, Walker perceived great danger to himself and his wife. She took the stage to St. Paul while he left for St. Cloud, where he met Indian Commissioner Dole, who was to go to Red Lake and negotiate a treaty.[203] Dole found Walker to be incoherent. Walker then rode a horse to Monticello, where he commandeered a ferry to cross to the east bank of the Mississippi. The ferryman demanded that the ferry be brought back to the west bank, but Walker refused, shouting that three hundred Indians were pursuing him. Several days later, a search party found Walker dead near Big Lake with a bullet in his head and a revolver by his side with one chamber empty.[204]

Dole Encamped in Minnesota

Dole called upon George Sweet to meet Hole in the Day, to which errand Sweet agreed.[205] Sweet proceeded to Crow Wing and persuaded Clement Beaulieu, who was known to be friendly to Hole in the Day, to accompany him to this meeting. Before reaching Hole in the Day's encampment, they were accosted by warriors who escorted them to Hole in the Day. After listening to Hole in the Day's complaints, Sweet arranged for the release of hostages, a four-day truce, and a meeting with Dole. Sweet then returned to St. Paul and communicated to Dole the results of his meeting. A meeting between Hole in the Day and Dole was arranged in Crow Wing on September 10. When Dole arrived, he was immediately surrounded by two hundred armed warriors. Dole's mood of belligerence at Fort Ripley was changed to being conciliatory at Crow Wing. Nothing resulted from the meeting, except that Dole appointed Ashley Morrill, the postmaster, as interim agent. Dole left for St. Paul on September 12.[206]

Dole then requested that Governor Ramsey send troops to Gull Lake to suppress any further aggressiveness by Hole in the Day. Instead, the state legislature convened a committee—whose members were Henry Rice, Judge David Cooper, E. A. Hatch, and Fredrick Ayer—which negotiated a "peace treaty'" with Hole in the Day.[207] This treaty was not recognized by the US government, as states did not have the right to make such a pact, but it did succeed in quieting the frontier. Dole, in a letter to Whipple, expressed chagrin that when he called for troops, he got a committee that made compromises that he refused to accept. Dole stated that the compromise he refused was "purchasing the good will of Hole in the Day while he and his people were in arms against the whites."[208]

That the Ojibwe disturbance coincided with the Sioux war being waged in southern Minnesota suggests that the attacks were coordinated. They may have been, as Little Crow and Hole in the Day had recently met; however, there is no documented evidence of their conspiracy.[209] The only evidence that any form of conspiracy may have existed between Hole in the Day and Little Crow were the words of Enmegahbowh who said, "He [Hole in the Day] had decided to assist his hereditary enemy to go forth to a war against the whites."[210]

CONSEQUENCES OF THE DISTURBANCE

The Hole in the Day uprising alarmed much of the white population of northern Minnesota. Volunteer militia were formed in Marine Mills, Taylors Falls, Stillwater, and Sunrise in response to the perceived threat. From Ramsey County, an armed militia moved northward. Fort Ripley was a refuge for local people.[211] Of course, the incident of Hole in the Day's belligerence was small news in comparison to the Civil War, which was not going well for Lincoln, and to the Dakota Uprising in southern Minnesota, which took on aspects of a real war.

The uprising under Hole in the Day resulted in three deaths. Enmegahbowh and Charlotte's children Alfred, age eighteen, and Henry, less than a year old, died of an existing illness and from exposure after their retreat to Fort Ripley. Agent Walker died by his own hand. However, the motivation for Hole in the Day's action was similar to the Dakota motivation for the attacks on Minnesota River valley settlements. The explanation for the outbreak, according to Clark Thompson, superintendent of Indian affairs of the north, was "difficulty between the late Agent Walker and Hole in the Day, and an old firm of traders."[212]

As a result of Hole in the Day's action, the St. Columba Mission was destroyed, Enmegahbowh's oxen were killed, and oxen at the agency were killed. On September 11, whites from Crow Wing burned Hole in the Day's home.[213]

Enmegahbowh was very much disheartened by the outbreak.[214] He called for Hole in the Day to be hanged, along with four of his henchmen.[215] Enmegahbowh wrote to John G. Nicolay, Lincoln's personal assistant, requesting that Peter Sutherland be appointed agent for the Mississippi Ojibwe.[216]

In time, Enmegahbowh and Hole in the Day again attended many councils together and listened to each other civilly. Enmegahbowh opposed Hole in the Day's militant stance, but it was Ojibwe custom to listen respectfully to the full ideas of others in council. The perceived betrayal of Hole in the Day by Enmegahbowh during the 1862 disturbance lingered in their relationship.

The feeling around Crow Wing was that there were good and bad Ojibwe. Bad Boy's Gull Lake band, the Mille Lacs band, and the Mississippi band of Ojibwe that did not follow Hole in the Day were considered good. The bad Ojibwe were those who followed Hole in the Day. This was an impression of both the Ojibwe and the whites. Both Enmegahbowh[217] and Peake[218] suggested that the "good" and "bad" should be separated. Both sides also agreed that the Ojibwe had been fleeced by the Indian agent, Walker, and through the entire administration of Indian affairs.

Enmegahbowh had a really hard time in the last months of 1862. He had no housing, no source of income, and his sons Alfred and Henry Whipple had died. Hole in the Day was still his enemy, yet he participated in councils with the chief. His wife was ill with a cough (probably tuberculosis, which eventually killed her and many of their children). Enmegahbowh told Whipple that he would probably have to live as a native Indian by hunting, but he would nonetheless faithfully pursue his ministry.[219]

LIFE CONTINUES AT CROW WING

In 1863, Enmegahbowh was living in Crow Wing and ministering to his people as a deacon. When in need, Enmegahbowh depended on the charity of Whipple. Enmegahbowh wrote to Breck and Whipple in February 1863 that the Ojibwe wanted to send a delegation to Washington to deter removal, especially out of state. He was remorseful and reluctant to serve as interpreter, as they had requested. His wife was reported as being sick, and he was still grieving the loss of two of his sons. The chiefs and Whipple nonetheless convinced Enmegahbowh to accompany the chiefs to Washington. Enmegahbowh wrote to Whipple from La Crosse on February 16 where he met the chiefs Bad Boy and Crossing Sky and two other Ojibwe. He reported that his wife was alone with their children, unwell, and without resources.

Among the Ojibwe, the biggest worry was out-of-state removal. Reverend Gear, of Fort Ripley, reported to Whipple that there was much drunkenness in Crow Wing during the preceding winter. In a letter to Whipple, Enmegahbowh reported thirty-three deaths in the Gull Lake band and twenty-five in the Mille Lacs band.[220]

Reverend Peake joined a Wisconsin regiment as a chaplain, as he felt there was a need for religious services to the Union troops.[221] In the absence of Peake, Reverend Gear volunteered to back up Enmegahbowh in the services held in Crow Wing.

CHAPTER 12

Treaties of 1863, 1864, 1866, and 1867

Five treaties were put into effect from 1863 to 1867. The treaties were negotiated with selected bands, but they eventually related to all the Ojibwe. The treaties in 1863, 1864 and 1867 related to north-central Minnesota bands and resulted in White Earth Reservation being established as the intended destination of all Minnesota Ojibwe. The Old Crossing Treaty of 1863 ceded land from Red Lake and Pembina bands. The Bois Forte Treaty of 1864 ceded land after a false discovery of gold.

THE 1863 TREATY WITH THE MISSISSIPPI, PILLAGER, AND LAKE WINNIBIGOSHISH BANDS

The intent by leaders in the Bureau of Indian Affairs for the 1863 treaty with the Mississippi, Pillager, and Winnibigoshish Ojibwe was to eliminate all reservations except Leech Lake and then establish a yet-to-be-determined reservation north of white civilization. The treaty was written largely by Henry Rice in Washington with the intent of selling it to the Ojibwe.[222] Enmegahbowh reported from Crow Wing to Whipple that a council was held on the subject of the treaty and was attended by chiefs, including Hole in the Day and a Sandy Lake chief.[223] The chiefs expressed hope that the contemplated removal would not be to an out-of-state location. Later, Enmegahbowh accompanied Bad Boy, Crossing Sky, and two other chiefs to Washington at the request of the northern superintendent of Indian affairs. George Bonga and Clement Beaulieu also wished to join but were denied permission. On March 13, Enmegahbowh reported from Washington that the treaty was concluded and signed by the chiefs.²²⁴ The treaty was amended by the Senate, and amendments signed by the chiefs were then passed by the Senate. It was proclaimed by Abraham Lincoln on March 19, 1863.

The treaty ceded land making up the Gull Lake, Mille Lacs, Rabbit Lake, Pokegama Lake, and Rice Lake Reservations to the United States. Annuity payments were to be extended by ten years, with a board of visitors specified to audit annuity payments. An additional $20,000 was to be paid for damages done during the 1862 disturbance. Provisions were made for building houses for the Ojibwe before removal, but a destination for removal was not addressed.

BOARD OF VISITORS

Whipple, J. L. Grace, and Thomas Williamson were appointed to the board of visitors, a committee charged with overseeing annuity payments to the Ojibwe, as specified in the 1863 treaty, in the autumn of 1863.²²⁵ In a letter to Commissioner Dole,²²⁶ they expressed their disappointment that Hole in the Day had not been punished for his leadership of the disturbance in August 1862. Most of the whites and many of the Ojibwe believed him guilty of conspiracy with the Sioux and that some penalty was deserved. Instead he remained at liberty and received almost double the amount of annuity that other chiefs received as a result of his frequent participation in previous treaty negotiations.

Whipple again wrote Dole to report his participation in the committee monitoring the fall annuity payment.²²⁷ He had witnessed the payment of the annuity and commented that he was not aware of any plan by the Bureau of Indian Affairs to affect the distribution and therefore could not judge whether it met conditions of the applicable treaty. He asked that such information be provided in future distribution. A permanent home was called for upon the anticipated removal of the Mississippi Ojibwe. He lamented that the primary beneficiaries of treaties were chiefs, traders, and interpreters and that Congress underfunded their obligations defined by treaties.

Williamson, as a member of the Board of Visitors, seconded Whipple's viewpoints in a letter to Dole.²²⁸ He agreed that manipulators peripheral to the bands had advocated for treaties and that they were the primary beneficiaries of such treaties.

Dole answered Whipple's letters in March 1864.²²⁹ He reported that he, in Minnesota, "had unflinchingly refused to compromise the honor of the Indian Dept." by negotiating with Hole in the

Day. He pointed out that he did not pay ransom to Hole in the Day and that there was no consensus opinion that Hole in the Day was guilty of any crime. When he called for troops, which were not available because of the Civil War and the larger insurrection in southern Minnesota, he got a committee that proceeded to make the very compromise he refused, by negotiating with Hole in the Day. He also said that the Dakota who were removed to a bend in the Missouri were not starving, as Whipple contended.

Later in 1864, Whipple reported on his service, along with Williamson, on the board of visitors.[230] Apparently, Dole took Whipple's suggestion to develop a plan for distributing cash annuities, and the next distribution proceeded according to plan. Cash was distributed in paper money, not coin as specified in the treaty. However, a plan for the distribution of trade goods was either absent or not followed. The distribution of annuities for the Mississippi bands was scheduled for October 20 but was delayed until October 27. The distribution included the following: 1,325 Ojibwe received $7, for a total of $9,275; twenty-three chiefs received a total of $1,333. No value could be placed on the trade goods distributed, as there were no invoices or other estimates of value, nor was the distribution seen as equitable. The able-bodied apparently took things from piles of goods on a first-come, first-served basis. At Leech Lake, the $7 payment was made on November 2 to 1,966 Ojibwe. There were complaints that larger items like guns and kettles could not be equitably distributed. Blankets and cloth and clothing were suggested as articles to be equitably distributed. The Mille Lacs bands received their annuities at Crow Wing on November 6. Here 675 Ojibwe received $7 each. The Leech Lake payment was $500 less than the stated treaty amount, and the Mississippi and Mille Lacs bands were paid $4626.44 less than the stated treaty amount. The treaty called for there to be no white people residing on reservations, but many instances were found of traders and employees living with Ojibwe women. Other reservations were not visited, and no evaluations were made on adherence to treaty provisions at those locations.

The board of visitors also made recommendations concerning administering the reservations. Their first concern was that the various bands did not constitute nations, as assumed by the treaties, and that there was no law that applied in the reservations. It was also recommended that annuity payments be made by September 20, which would enable normal scheduling of the fall hunt.

THE TREATY OF 1863 WITH THE PEMBINA AND RED LAKE OJIBWE, THE TREATY OF THE OLD CROSSING

Desirable agricultural land of the Red River valley was an object of cession from the Ojibwe to the United States for about "a dozen years."[231] Access was also desirable for railroads and riverboats. Ramsey was chosen as a commissioner to negotiate the cession. The negotiating party, which included sixty army supply wagons, thirteen wagons of trade goods, five passenger carriages, and three companies of mounted men, arrived at the Red Lake River crossing where the Pembina and Red Lake chiefs awaited them. The date was September 21, 1863. After protracted negotiations, a treaty was signed on October 2. The Ojibwe had ceded land on both sides of the Red River comprising approximately five million acres.

The Ojibwe tribes were scheduled to receive $20,000 a year for twenty years. Chiefs would receive $500 to build houses. A board of visitors was specified to monitor the distributions. Those of mixed race could apply to receive 160 acres of land.[232] The treaty became effective in October 1863 upon ratification by the Senate. As part of the treaty, Norman Kittson and James Hill were awarded $10,000 for damage to their steamboat by the Ojibwe, which occurred on the Red River.

Bishop Whipple called the approved treaty "a fraud from start to finish."[233] Over the previous two years, Bishop Whipple had administered his diocese, advocated for the interests of the Dakota and Ojibwe, and served on the board of visitors. All this activity was affecting his health to such a noticeable degree that fourteen of his clergy urged him to take a six-month respite.[234] He did that by renewing contact with friends and relatives in the East.

THE 1864 TREATY WITH THE LEECH LAKE AND MISSISSIPPI OJIBWE

The 1863 treaty was immediately considered bad by the whites and the Ojibwe, and further negotiations were initiated in Washington in March 1864 with both Hole in the Day and Enmegahbowh present.[235] A congressman provided Hole in the Day with liquor and a fight ensued. Hole in the Day cut the nose of one man, and a shot was fired that hit Hole in the Day on the right side of his neck and came out through his jaw. He was hospitalized and was thought near death, such that he told Enmegahbowh that he desired Whipple to keep and raise his children. He survived. George Bonga, who was also present at the 1864 negotiations, got to see Lincoln and shake his hand. Enmegahbowh was tired of being in Washington and desired that Whipple send some money to Charlotte. Through revision by the Senate and negotiation, the 1863 treaty was replaced with the 1864 treaty. Negotiations took place under Henry Rice. The new treaty changed some reservation boundaries and awarded Hole in the Day $5,000 and a half section—320 acres—of land. The board of visitors was given the power to determine the time and place of the annuity distribution.

THE BOIS FORTE TREATY OF 1866

In 1866, the Bois Forte (Strong Wood) band of Ojibwe entered a treaty with the United States that ceded most of their land and established a reservation on Nett Lake. The impetus for the treaty was a false report that gold had been discovered in the region.[236] This triggered a small gold rush with political pressure to give whites access to the area. Nine chiefs signed the treaty. In return for the land, the US government agreed to build and maintain a school and a blacksmith shop for the Bois Forte as well as provide annuities for twenty years.

THE 1867 TREATY WITH THE MISSISSIPPI AND LEECH LAKE OJIBWE CREATING THE WHITE EARTH RESERVATION

When white dissatisfaction with the 1864 treaty arose—probably because of the ill-defined removal destination and land not being cleared of Ojibwe for white settlement—a new treaty was demanded. Hole in the Day and nine other Ojibwe were once again called to Washington in early 1867. Enmegahbowh was obliged to go along and act as an interpreter. Joel Bassett, the designated leader of negotiations, wrote to Whipple prior to the meeting, outlining his ideas for the accord.[237] They included a definite reservation, annuities, and accommodations for the Ojibwe.

By January 24, 1867, Enmegahbowh was on his way to Washington.[238] The negotiations lasted into March and on the way home, according to a report by H. B. Batterson, Enmegahbowh gave a moving speech to five hundred children in Philadelphia.[239]

The Treaty of 1867 nullified the Treaty of 1864 and better defined some aspects of the language. One of the primary beneficiaries of the treaty was Bassett, the leader in the negotiations who had timber interests. Hole in the Day is listed as the first Ojibwe signer and nine other chiefs follow. Enmegahbowh signed the treaty using the name John Johnson. Removal was called for from the Mississippi reservations on which Ojibwe resided in Minnesota, including the Mille Lacs Ojibwe. The foreword to the treaty suggests the federal government's intent, as well as Bishop Whipple's, that there be one Ojibwe reservation in Minnesota, isolated from whites, on which the Ojibwe would become Christian agrarians. The foreword also states that Ojibwe bands would move from the poor agricultural land of Leech Lake to the good agricultural land of White Earth, and the land abandoned by the band at Leech Lake would be sold. The treaty ceded two million acres of land to the United States and established White Earth as a reservation consisting of thirty-six townships. Hole in the Day received an annuity of $1,000 plus a half section of land. Houses were to be built for Ojibwe settling in White Earth, ground was to be broken for crops, a blacksmith engaged, and oxen provided.

White Earth was unique among Indian reservations. No Ojibwe had previously lived in the area, though both the Dakota and the Ojibwe had hunted there. It was located on the dividing line between the fertile Red River valley and the northern boreal forest. Those who wrote the treaty anticipated that the remoteness of White Earth and a policy of limiting its population to Ojibwe residents only would prevent bad white influences of traders and whiskey sellers. At the time of the reservation's creation in 1867, it was remote from white civilization and from the habitation of most Ojibwe. The Treaty of 1867 was the last negotiated treaty between the United States and the Ojibwe.

The Red Lake Bands of Ojibwe continued to possess a large tract of land in Minnesota that contained much timber, which the government still desired to procure and exploit. The farm and forest land that the government had already procured through the treaties would quickly be utilized by anxious settlers and lumbermen. Henry Whipple, in a paper dated from 1866 and titled "Bishop Whipple's Report on the Moral and Temporal Condition of the Indian Tribes on Our Western Border," summarized his thoughts on the US government making and executing treaties with the Indians.[240] He was a qualified and involved observer of the process. Here is an excerpt from that paper:

> Our system is based on a falsehood; we recognize the wandering Indian tribe as an independent nation and make and ratify treaties as with all foreign powers. We do this with full knowledge that they are to send representatives to us, and we none to them; that they have no power to compel us to observe a treaty, and when every possible relation that can exist makes them simply

our wards. The Indian who sells his land must become civilized or perish. If we take away the means of savage subsistence by the chase, and give him nothing in its place, the end is death. Our own sense of justice, our pity for the helpless, and our fear of God, demand that the men who go to make this treaty shall be God-fearing men. It makes one ashamed and sick at heart to think of the history of Indian Treaties. The parties are a Christian nation, and a heathen people. The treaty is made ostensibly to extend civilization. It is often made in order to pay certain claims of traders and others against the Indians, to secure land for speculation, and to provide a new opportunity to fill some political plunderer's pocket. Every provision of the treaty is gauged as to the amount which can be stolen, and, if possible, some loop-hole left which will make way for a new treaty when the Indian can be used again as a key to unlock the nation's treasury. The Indian is credulous. The sad fate of other tribes has cast a gloom over the whole race. Old men talk of it in the council and wigwam, and any plan which offers a door of hope is gladly accepted by the Indian. The Indian is told that he has no houses, no oxen, no ploughs, no fire-horses, no fire-canoes, no schools, no churches. He does not know the way of the Great Spirit. These white men come as brothers and their ruler is to be his great father. If he sells his land, he will live and not die. He cannot read. He believes that every word and promise is in the treaty. Often the real parties to the treaties are ignorant of each other's views, for both of their heads are on the interpreter's shoulders, and he is the bribed agent of some cunning scoundrel, who has pecuniary interests to subserve. The treaty is made—then come deferred hopes. The robbery begins in the contract for removal. Even men of fair names and high honor are parties in the iniquitous ring to rob the savage of bread for himself and children. So profitable are these harvests of iniquity, that in a recent removal of the Chippewa over $200,000 were paid to secure the contract to provide rations for the Indians. The Agent is selected to reward him for political work done for a Congressional patron. The government sends him, knowing he will and must steal. His salary to support a family far away in the Indian country, where all supplies cost four-fold, is $1500. The other employees are selected from the same motives of reward for political service, and at half the salary good men could receive in a civilized country. What would follow but fraud in the contracts, pilfering of annuity goods, dishonesty in every form and shape? Such a system cannot gather around an agency of good men. The agency or some settlement near it, becomes the scene of whiskey traffic, profanity, gambling, adultery and drunkenness hold a carnival of death. Strange diseases, which mark the victim as accursed of God and shunned by man, reap a terrible harvest. At last the poor savage, writhing under a sense of wrong, on the first provocation, will enter a career of war, and the cry of murdered women and children is heard everywhere on the border. To these evils which uproot confidence, we add another less perilous—we leave the Indian without protection to property, person or life—we made the treaty on the hypothesis that we are dealing with an independent nation, and we carry it out by leaving them without law. The popular idea is, that the Indians have a patriarchal government of which the chief is the ruler head. The chief is simply the leader of a savage tribe. He has no power to make or execute law. His influence is simply that of advice and counsel. The influence he has with the tribe is often weakened or destroyed by the treaty; for unless he becomes a pliant tool of agents and traders, he will most likely be deposed, and a more pliant tool put in his place. The civilized and Christian Indian is pitiably helpless. His crops may be destroyed, his oxen killed, his wife and children treated with violence, and his only remedy is murder. The only law we administer is to pay a premium for crime. If an individual Indian steal from a white man, we deduct the value of the theft from the annuities of the tribe, and the thief always make a profit of his theft. We redress no wrongs that the Indians suffer from each other, and never punish white men for crimes committed against them.

CHAPTER 13

Enmegahbowh and Hole in the Day Coexist, 1863 to 1869

While not on trips to Washington, Enmegahbowh performed his religious duties as a deacon and participated in community life at Gull Lake, Crow Wing, and at Mille Lacs. There was an uneasy truce between Enmegahbowh and Hole in the Day, and they participated civilly in Ojibwe councils.

A CUTLERITE MORMON FRIENDSHIP

In mid-November 1864, Enmegahbowh was with a group of friends fishing about forty miles north of Crow Wing when he was approached by a man named Lewis Denna. The sequence of events leading to this rendezvous began with a thought before the death of Alpheus Cutler, a leader in the Mormon Church who told his followers of a "grassy place between two lakes in Minnesota."[241]

Alpheus Cutler had been fourth in the hierarchy of the Mormon Church and had been mandated by Joseph Smith, the prophet founder of the Mormon Church, to carry the Mormon gospel to the Lamanites, which were said to be a lost tribe of Israel deemed to be American Indians.[242] When Joseph Smith died and Brigham Young assumed Mormon leadership that led to migration to Utah, Cutler did not join him. Cutler was disfellowshipped from Brigham Young's Mormon Church in 1850. No longer under Brigham Young, he deemed his authority as a church leader came directly from Smith. When he died in June of 1864, Cutler was head of a group of four hundred followers. Chauncy Whiting assumed leadership of the Cutlerites in Manti, Iowa, after Cutler's death.

Chapter 13

Lewis Denna was an Oneida chief until 1840, and while in Nauvoo, Illinois, he was befriended by Mormons. Considered a Lamanite by the Mormons, he became an influential member of the Mormon Church. Denna then worked in Kansas bringing the Mormon message to other Indians.

Whiting wanted to move from Iowa, motivated by the rift with the Josephites, the proximity to the Civil War, and the thought of a mission to the Lamanites. Cutler's dream of a grassy place between two lakes also directed the Cutlerites toward Minnesota. Denna was chosen to find this place in the Minnesota wilderness. He had either previously met Enmegahbowh or had knowledge of Enmegahbowh's work in northern Minnesota. In late September 1864, Denna, four couples, and eleven children proceeded by covered wagon from Manti, Iowa, to Red Wing, Minnesota. The families settled for the winter in Red Wing and Denna, Sylvester Whiting, and Francis Whiting proceeded to Crow Wing. Upon being informed of Enmegahbowh's fishing trip, Denna went alone to find Enmegahbowh. The two men returned together to Crow Wing and had a congenial meeting with the Whiting brothers. Denna and the Whitings then returned to their families in Red Wing for the winter.

In February 1865, Enmegahbowh met again with Denna and Sylvester Whiting to further discuss a destination for the Cutlerites. Similarities of Enmegahbowh's and Denna's backgrounds and the communal attitudes of the Cutlerites cemented their relationship. Ojibwe chiefs, Enmegahbowh, and the Cutlerite leaders met in Mille Lacs and made an accord of friendship, which was signed. It is likely that Enmegahbowh suggested they settle in Otter Tail County. Upon arrival in Otter Tail County, they viewed several sites, and after much praying, the group settled on a site on Clitherall Lake, which met the requirement of "a grassy place between two lakes," the second lake being Battle Lake to the north. The date was May 6, 1865. They were the first white settlement in Otter Tail County. The remaining Cutlerites in Manti, Iowa, were divided about whether to journey north to the new settlement of Clitherall. Twenty-five families ultimately decided to go and started on May 31, 1865, in thirty-five covered wagons along with herds of cows and sheep. Upon arrival and greeting the original settlers, they had to work hard to prepare for the coming winter. Log cabins were built, and grass was harvested for hay. The hardships of the winter were great, and during the next summer several families returned to Manti, Iowa. Twenty-five households remained, forming the core of the new settlement. Within a few years, the community had a church and a school and survived on the frontier.

Enmegahbowh continued his friendship with the community through correspondence and infrequent visits. In a letter to Breck, Enmegahbowh told of an offer by the Cutlerites for him to become a high priest in their church.[243] Desiring that his son be educated among the white population, in the winter of 1866, Enmegahbowh sent his fifteen-year-old son, George, to Clitherall, where he was housed with Mr. Sherman, a Cutlerite Mormon leader.[244] George soon got homesick and returned home. Eight letters from Enmegahbowh to Chauncy Whiting, Denna, and Sherman exist between 1865 and 1886. A note attributed to Chauncy Whiting, probably written in 1869, records the good feelings that existed after Enmegahbowh visited Clitherall.[245] The note displays a frankness and friendliness that exist in few other Enmegahbowh letters. The Cutlerites and Enmegahbowh considered each other as equals, something very rare in Enmegahbowh's relationships with white people.

THE FIRST MOVE FROM GULL LAKE TO WHITE EARTH

Enmegahbowh recounted the first move of many Christian Indians from Gull Lake to White Earth in his letter of tribute to Chief Isaac Tuttle:

Six years ago, when he [Chief Tuttle] started for this unknown country, he came to see me and ask my advice on the subject. I told him, "arise and go and that was the best thing his people can do." The day was named when his Band and others should start and bid goodbye to their beloved land and country. Hole in the Day and a few of his warriors got ready to stop the movement, and made war dances before chief Tuttle, and threatened that the first man whoever moved one step toward the new country was a dead man. The day arrived when all should move. Tuttle had put on all his war costume, with feathers waving on his head, and led the moving caravan—four hundred in number. Hole in the Day with his warriors, had already posted on the road where Tuttle should pass. Tuttle, when he saw them, walked with firm steps before them, and passed unmolested. And when this was over, his people almost kissed him, and said, "Our Leader! Our Leader!" and his people loved him more and more."

I must hasten. I overtook them at their first encampment, and told Tuttle that it was uncertain whether I should follow them: previous to this I had made up my mind, that I would not take a step towards White Earth while Hole in the Day was a living man, for I know he was a man of blood and that he never would give a peace to Tuttle and his people until he carry out his wicked project against them. Tuttle grasped my hand, and that occasion I never shall forget.[246]

AN INTERIM IN CROW WING

Enmegahbowh continued his church work, holding services and doing parish work in Crow Wing and with the Mississippi Ojibwe. He had several offers of alternative work in the spring of 1865. Since Whipple was on leave at that time, Enmegahbowh wrote to Breck about his opportunities.[247] The Indian agent wanted him to be an interpreter and travel with him to Red Lake. In addition, he mulled the possibility of becoming a schoolteacher in a location where the agent would build him a house. He also had an offer from a large company in Otter Tail City. And, as previously noted, the Cutlerite Mormons offered him a position as high priest in their church in Clitherall. Enmegahbowh seemed not inclined to any of these opportunities, but perhaps he was suggesting hopes of being better compensated within the church.

MILLE LACS RESERVATION EVOLUTION

Mille Lacs was designated as a reservation in the 1855 treaty. During the Hole in the Day disturbance, the Mille Lacs Ojibwe remained peaceful, a stance much appreciated by the early white settlers. The successive treaties of 1863, 1864, and 1867 called for eventual removal to White Earth but did not mandate removal while the Ojibwe there remained peaceful.

A head chief had asked for instruction in Christianity, and many of his followers seemed similarly inclined. By 1865, Enmegahbowh had built himself a crude house in Mille Lacs and was instructing residents in Christianity.[248] He reported to Breck that four chiefs gave him a list of sixty-eight Ojibwe who were ready to "cut their hair," which was interpreted as being willing to adopt Christianity and live as white men. Enmegahbowh stated that the parents were his priority for baptism, and he felt uncomfortable baptizing children who were naked. The parents begged for clothing for the children.[249]

Enmegahbowh was a friend of Shabashkung, a Mille Lacs civil chief who consistently advocated friendship with the whites and nonremoval from Mille Lacs. He had strongly opposed the Hole in the Day disturbance. In 1867, he invited Enmegahbowh to go to Washington with him to ask that the agent release provisions and annuities to alleviate the effects of the harsh winter.[250] Enmegahbowh declined.

Shabashkung, Mille Lacs Chief

A removal from Mille Lacs was ordered in 1872. The Ojibwe refused to remove and were penalized by denial of annuities. When, in 1878, timber interests attempted to procure and harvest pine, Shabashkung along with other chiefs wrote President Rutherford B. Hayes informing him of the attempt to "rob us of our valuable lands."[251] No resolution resulted from the letter.

ENMEGAHBOWH'S CONTINUED WORK

The Indian agent continually called upon Enmegahbowh for purposes of communication and other tasks related to the Ojibwe. In June 1866, he testified in a trial at Winona of whiskey sellers who sold illegally to the Ojibwe.[252] They were acquitted by a white jury. It was the usual verdict for accused whiskey sellers. Enmegahbowh and three chiefs had been transported to Winona by boat. He intended to visit Whipple before returning home.

In July 1866, Bishop Whipple made his annual trip to Red Lake. The record of the trip is some doggerel about the adventure written by one of the four men, E. A. W.; it was sung to a popular tune at the time, "Believe Me, If All Those Endearing Young Charms."[253] Enmegahbowh was one of the voyageurs. The camping comradery, singalong, and tomfoolery seemed to be enjoyed by all involved.

Until August 1866, Edwin Clark had been the Indian agent and seemed well liked by many. Enmegahbowh commented that Clark did not work on Sundays and attended Christian services. His replacement was to be Charles Ruffee of Ruffee and Aspinwall traders. Being an agent and a former partner in a trading company was seen as a conflict of interest by Bonga and Enmegahbowh, and they protested to Whipple.[254] A month earlier, Whipple composed a letter to a senator (unnamed) and, on the previously mentioned grounds, stated his objection to Ruffee being confirmed as agent.[255] The letter on record appears to be a draft, and it is unknown whether it was sent.

Enmegahbowh was highly involved in the temporal as well as the spiritual well-being of the Ojibwe. He planned to attend the 1866 annuity distribution in Mille Lacs and Leech Lake as the "only man standing for the rights" of the Ojibwe.[256] Enmegahbowh's salary, presumably paid by the mission society, was $600 per year, of which $300 would go to rent in Crow Wing, but he chose to live in Mille Lacs where living was less expensive and he had more friends.

George Bonga accused Edwin Clark of being a tool of Ruffee and Aspinwall by preventing Bonga and any other traders from being licensed.[257] He denied selling liquor, which might have disqualified him. Hole in the Day and Henry Rice supported the concept of more traders.

BRECK STEPS DOWN AND ENMEGAHBOWH IS CONSECRATED AS A PRIEST

June 1867 was a turning point in the lives of several among the founders of the Episcopal Church in Minnesota. Breck resigned his position as head of the Seabury Divinity School and revealed his intention to go to California, where he would continue his missionary work. Enmegahbowh and Gear both attended the alumni dinner commemorating the event on June 17.[258] On June 20, Enmegahbowh was consecrated as an Episcopal priest in Faribault.[259] He had been examined for his fitness as a priest by the priests Knickerbacker, McMasters, and Welles. A dispensation was made in the requirement for Greek and Hebrew, and Bishop Whipple told of Enmegahbowh's courage in alerting whites to Hole in the Day's murderous intentions and of his service to the Ojibwe while "Standing before his People."

ENMEGAHBOWH VISITS CANADA

When he left Canada in 1834, Enmegahbowh had promised his parents that he would return to see them. His attempt to

Enmegahbowh in Priest's Robes

do so in 1844 had been thwarted by windstorms on Lake Superior. The long-delayed trip commenced in February 1868 with the company of the Mille Lacs chief Minogishick.[260] Enmegahbowh reported to Whipple from the Detroit home of Mr. Smith, a friend of Whipple's, that he was astonished to see such beautiful churches. Minogishick spoke in McCook Church, with Enmegahbowh probably interpreting. Enmegahbowh told of wanting to beg, which Whipple had proscribed in his diocese.

On April 2, Enmegahbowh was back to Faribault and filed a report on his trip to Canada.[261] Besides his birth area in Rice Lake, he visited eight settlements of "Chippewas," including Mohawk and Onondaga in Walpole Island, New Credit, Mud Lake, and Alnwick. In his native village, a brick Methodist church was being erected. He was asked to come back permanently and become a Methodist minister. Enmegahbowh declined this offer, as he had pledged his faithfulness to Bishop Whipple. He reported that the

Canadian Odawa were more advanced in civilization than the Minnesota Ojibwe. Indian women played piano, and a brass band was composed of Indians. Perhaps the population was on their best behavior, however, and an absence of drinking and gambling was reported. Churches, schoolhouses, fine houses, and large barns were reported in each settlement.

Enmegahbowh then lamented that his mission was not better supported.

THE ASSASSINATION OF HOLE IN THE DAY

Hole in the Day was a war chief who considered himself the leading chief of all the Mississippi Ojibwe. Other chiefs did not necessarily consider him as such, but the US government was happy to treat him as a prominent leader with whom they could deal. He was aggressive politically, having participated in several treaty negotiations, and employed an attorney, Judge David Cooper. Militarily, he had a group of several hundred warrior-followers who were willing to support him. Hole in the Day had accumulated considerable wealth through treaty clauses favoring him. His house was near the agency on the Crow Wing River, and he also had farmland south of the river, which he hired white farmers to farm. Hole in the Day had three Ojibwe wives, and on his last trip to Washington he married a fourth, a white woman named Helen Kater, who had worked in a hotel.[262]

Enmegahbowh had been associated with the family since 1839 when he camped at Little Elk River with Hole in the Day (the Elder). Enmegahbowh was accepted as a son by Hole in the Day (the Elder); his niece Charlotte was Enmegahbowh's wife. Hole in the Day (the Younger) was Enmegahbowh's neighbor at Gull Lake and participated in inviting Breck to bring his mission to Gull Lake. Enmegahbowh was alienated from the family by the 1862 disturbance and by Hole in the Day's drinking of alcohol. Their primary opposition to each other stemmed from the destruction of the St. Columba mission complex. At one point, in a letter to Whipple, Enmegahbowh suggested to "put a string around the neck" of Hole in the Day and four other leaders.[263]

Hole in the Day was assassinated on June 27, 1868, near the confluence of the Gull River with the Crow Wing River.[264] On that fateful day, he was on the beginning of a trip to Washington with his cousin, named Ojibwe, to try to renegotiate the Treaty of 1867 and prohibit those of mixed race from being traders at White Earth. Their buggy was intercepted by eleven Ojibwe from Leech Lake. Although he protested that he was unarmed, he was shot twice by two of the men. He was further given the coup de grace and left by the roadside. The Leech Lake Ojibwe then proceeded to Hole in the Day's large house and made off with horses, guns, and clothes. Helen Kater probably prevented further damage to the property since the raiders knew that molesting a white woman would result in their prosecution.

Two government investigations eventually revealed the names of the assassins, but it was deemed that the US government had no jurisdiction in the killing of an Indian by an Indian.[265] Neither investigation revealed a motive for the killing, although many—both whites and Ojibwe—frequently disagreed with Hole in the Day. Author Anton Treuer puts forth compelling evidence that a group of white and mixed-race traders from Crow Wing offered the killers $1,000 each to do the deed.[266] The plotters were identified as Charles Ruffee, Clement Beaulieu, George Beaulieu, George Fairbanks, George D. Morrison, Robert Fairbanks, William MacArthur, Peter Roy, and possibly others. Their motivation was thought to be Hole in the Day's trip to Washington, where he was expected to call for the exclusion of the traders in White Earth.[267]

Seven years later, a group confided to Mezhucegeshig, a leader at White Earth, that they had killed Hole in the Day.[268] They also stated that they were never paid the $1,000 promised by Clement Beaulieu. There was continued pressure for the Ojibwe of Mille Lacs to remove to White Earth, and while some did remove, most Mille Lacs Ojibwe made a point to remain peaceful and stay in their present habitat.

CHAPTER 14
Enmegahbowh Removes to White Earth

The White Earth Reservation, as defined by the Treaty of 1867, consisted of thirty-six townships located in northwest Minnesota. The reservation was eighty miles from the nearest civilization in St. Cloud, a three-day journey by horse and wagon. Sending freight to or from St. Cloud cost $4.50 per hundred pounds. As previously mentioned, one of the criteria for selection of the site was remoteness to prevent influence by whites and mixed-race people who were known to provide alcohol and were dishonest traders. The land was unoccupied, having been disputed Dakota and Ojibwe hunting ground. Most of the Dakota had been removed from the Mississippi River valley after the War of 1862. The divide between the Mississippi watershed and the Hudson Bay watershed runs approximately north and south through the middle of the White Earth Reservation. East of the divide are lakes and boreal forests.

The choice of the site for the purposes intended seemed very fortuitous. Pine timber was abundant in the eastern part of the reservation for building houses and other buildings. The central hilly, forested lands had lakes, abundant large and small game, and wild rice and fish in lakes that would support traditional Ojibwe lifestyles while they transitioned to agrarian pursuits. The western part of the reservation, the flat and fertile Red River valley land, was ideal for farming. The government intended the reservation to be home to the Mississippi Ojibwe plus any other Indians who were willing to move there. Some whites, including Whipple, envisioned that on this land, the Ojibwe would transition from their traditional lifestyle of hunting and gathering to an agrarian Christian lifestyle.

Major Joel Bassett was the Indian agent in charge of arranging the move of the Ojibwe to White Earth. He had attended the treaty negotiations with George Bonga, Hole in the Day, Peter Bottineau, and other Ojibwe.[269] The trader Paul Beaulieu, a son of Clement Beaulieu, explored the area and helped select a site for the agency, which became White Earth Village. A sawmill site was built at White Earth Lake. Paul also selected a site for his own home and was the first settler. He was employed by the Bureau of Indian Affairs as a surveyor and farmer. Some land was broken to facilitate farming. The administrative center of the reservation was established at White Earth Village.

By the middle of May 1868, the Ojibwe of Sandy Lake had been removed to White Earth. The first party of Ojibwe from Gull Lake under Chief Isaac Tuttle (Nay bon ash kung) and Chief Manitowab left for White Earth on June 6, 1868. Attacks by the Dakota were feared during their travels and after their arrival. The fears were not warranted since the Dakota had been removed to the Dakota Territory after the 1862 war. The two hundred Ojibwe in the Gull Lake party settled northeast of White Earth Lake in the hilly, deciduous forest.[270] The Ojibwe under Tuttle were generally favorable toward the Episcopal Church and to farming.

Having returned from his visit to Canada in April 1868, Enmegahbowh got involved in the politics of White Earth. He solicited Whipple's advice on removing in May 1868. Hole in the Day had vehemently opposed removal to White Earth, at least until promised houses were built and ground broken for planting. One reason may have been related to his property, which had been acquired as an inducement to sign treaties. Hole in the Day had a fine house near the agency plus farmland across the Crow Wing River. Removal would have meant losing this property without an equivalent replacement at White Earth. Upon Hole in the Day's death on June 27, 1868, Enmegahbowh decided to move quickly. Enmegahbowh's narrative of the trip follows.[271]

> In a few days I got ready to move my caravan, which consisted of three yoke of horned horses. I took a different route and came down to Swan River to strike the Long Prairie, once the home of the Winnebagos. My whole company consisted of fifteen persons, including myself and my wife. I took this route that no one might know that I had started for White Earth. I wanted to reach it secretly. I took my own time and camped when I thought best. I was my own master. On my route we met many whites, and they gave us all the flour and meat we wanted, though we needed nothing in the way of provisions.

Tents for the move had been supplied by the agent at Crow Wing Agency.

Upon arrival Enmegahbowh chose to join his friends from Gull Lake who had previously removed. He observed two impressions of the situation in White Earth: the promised provisions were in poor condition and poorly distributed, and the Ojibwe ranged from being enthusiastic to being resigned to the idea of adapting to Christianity and farming. Enmegahbowh erected temporary housing and wanted to immediately start building a church. Before the move, there was talk that the government would compensate the Ojibwe for the trip and that housing and sustenance for the winter would be waiting for them. None of this came to pass. Some money was paid to the Ojibwe to build their own houses. It was fortunate that the land had been unoccupied, and that game was abundant and wild rice plentiful. On January 29, 1869, Enmegahbowh had to buy staples for his family on credit, as he had already used the money Whipple had sent to buy clothing, soap, and candy for his family and others.[272]

Despite these struggles, Enmegahbowh felt at home on the White Earth Reservation because it resembled his childhood home—the land north of Rice Lake in Canada. The western part of the reservation sloped down through deciduous forested hills with lakes to the fertile Red River valley.

STRUGGLES AT WHITE EARTH

The first winter at the White Earth Reservation was very difficult. In March 1869, Enmegahbowh wrote of subsisting on hard bread, bacon, and coffee.[273] Sugar was scarce, and flour was either not available or "sour and bitter." Recently, he had purchased butter, tea, salt, medicine, thread, needles, and tobacco on credit and presented the bill to Bassett, the agent. Flour cost twenty dollars a barrel, and pork cost seventy dollars a barrel. When no other food was available, the family resorted to gathering acorns, which they boiled and ate.[274] Improving weather in the spring brought other problems. Two employees of the agency were accused of being drunkards, and the head farmer's son nearly stabbed Enmegahbowh.[275]

According to the Treaty of 1867, land was to be broken for cultivation, houses built, and sustenance provided over the next winter for the newly removed Ojibwe. None of these could be depended upon nor were needed supplies available. Houses would have to be built of logs, as hammers, saws, nails, windows, and foundation materials were not generally available on-site. The nearest settlement and post office was at Otter Tail Lake, forty or more miles away, and only limited supplies were available there.

Additional problems arose that spring. There were no teams of horses or oxen to till the soil, nor were there plows and other tools. Seed potatoes were scarce.[276] The Quakers had sent the settlement some seeds, which were divided among the inhabitants. Enmegahbowh wrote three letters to his friend Chauncy Whiting, the Cutlerite Mormon in Clitherall, inquiring about potatoes for seed.[277] (Availability of seed potatoes from the Mormons was not resolved in the historical record.)

Unrest and uncertainty led to further problems. Some feared that the Dakota would invade the settlement and retaliate. Flat Mouth, a Leech Lake chief, visited with a friendly Dakota couple who were nearby, and they ate and smoked together. Before leaving, Flat Mouth shot the Dakota and tomahawked his wife to death.[278] The government agency did nothing. Enmegahbowh advocated to Whipple that Flat Mouth be arrested and prosecuted as if he had killed a white man, but that did not happen.

The traders and those of mixed race soon abandoned Crow Wing and settled in what became White Earth Village.[279] Frank Campbell, Robert Fairbanks, Frank Roy, George Fairbanks, William MacArthur, and Clement Beaulieu came before 1874, and George Morrison came afterward. Game and pelts were plentiful, as the area had not been overhunted by the nonresident Ojibwe and Dakota. The mixed-race people were generally Catholic. Father Ignatius Tomazin came to White Earth in 1869 to minister to the Catholics.[280]

A PEACE MISSION TO THE DAKOTA

Enmegahbowh spoke with pride about the peace treaty he inspired between the Dakota and the Ojibwe the summer of 1869. Chiefs Waub-anaquort, or White Cloud; Nabnoshkung, or Isaac H. Tuttle; Meshakgeshig, or Horizon; and others risked their lives to secure this peace. Because the peace mission had to be accomplished in ten days, it is likely the Sisseton Reservation, located closest to White Earth, was where the negotiations took place. The Sisseton Reservation was led by Chief Gabriel Renville, or Tiwakan, meaning Sacred Lodge. He, his family, and the reservation members argued for peaceful means to settle grievances with the U.S. government. The Ojibwe could not have hoped for a better ally among the Dakota neighbors to advocate for peace.

ENMEGAHBOWH'S WORK CONTINUES

In White Earth Enmegahbowh had built a twenty-five-by-thirty-foot house and chapel that seated twenty.[281] A larger chapel was needed since people were standing outside during two services each Sunday. He felt proud that his work as a priest and missionary was successful. By August 1870, Enmegahbowh reported that he had baptized 123 Ojibwe.[282] Chief Tuttle was among those that Enmegahbowh baptized. Helping him in his proselytizing and teaching were his daughters Martha and Eliza, who had returned from school in New York sometime before August 1869.[283] The proud father said one of his daughters could play piano as well as a white woman. The daughter also played a keyboard instrument, probably a melodeon, to accompany the singing of hymns. One of Enmegahbowh's daughter (probably Martha) continued to teach and accompany singing at services.

That same August, Eliza became ill and was confined to bed; she was diagnosed with asthma, as was her mother.[284] Both were probably misdiagnosed, as Eliza was later found to have tuberculosis.

The lack of farm implements in the Gull Lake settlement was somewhat alleviated in the summer of 1871 by a donor whom the recipients gave the Ojibwe name Ne-gaun-ge-shig, meaning the Leading Day.[285] His gift included teams, wagons, plows, and other useful items. The chiefs signed their names to a thank-you note that Enmegahbowh composed; the names included G. D. Wright (White Fisher), A. T. Twing (Me-zhah-ze-zhick), J. H. Tuttle (Na-bura-shkong), E. A Washburn (Min-o-ge-shick), Isaac (Manitowab), and others.

Enmegahbowh himself was generally more charitable than his means allowed. Although Bishop Whipple and the Missionary Society frequently sent money and clothes to Enmegahbowh, there was never enough since he shared anything of worth with the less fortunate, which included just about everyone in the settlement. He also gave wherever he saw dire need and then asked Whipple to reimburse him.

On April 17, 1872, the white settler family of John and Diantha Cook were found murdered in the cellar of their burned home near Audubon, which was ten miles from White Earth.[286] Their murdered children were Freddie, 7; Mary, 6; and John W., 10 months. The response in nearby Lake Park was for families to put up barricades and occupy them for several days. A mixed Dakota-Ojibwe named Bob-O-Link was soon apprehended with some of the family's possessions; he was convicted of the murder, and he named two accomplices, one of whom was apprehended. Bob-O-Link died in jail before his execution. Since the only evidence of their complicity was his testimony, the prosecution of the supposed accomplices was halted. Enmegahbowh had known the Cooks well.

When the executive committee of the Indian Committee of the National Episcopal Church, along with Reverend David Knickerbacker as a representative of Bishop Whipple, visited White Earth on June 20, 1872, they found considerable apprehension among the whites about the Cook family murder. But when it came to the work that Enmegahbowh was doing, they were very cordial and approving. They estimated that half the Ojibwe residents on the reservation had an association with the St. Columba Church, the name of the new church in White Earth, and that two hundred were active members.

After crops had been planted and sprouted in June 1872, a plague of grasshoppers descended and ruined the prospect of a good crop. For winter food, the Ojibwe were then dependent on hunting, gathering, and government sustenance.

WHITE EARTH GROWS

The 1872 population of White Earth was 550 Ojibwe; three years later it had grown to eight hundred.[287] The Otter Tail Pillagers, who felt that they were being crowded out of their space, were planning to come to Pine Point on the White Earth Reservation.[288] Ojibwe from Mille Lacs relocated to Wild Rice River and Elbow Lake. The Pembina settled at a location that is the modern Mahnomen.

Apparently to gauge the suitability of White Earth as a future home, nine hundred Ojibwe from Turtle Mountain visited White Earth. Turtle Mountain is over two hundred miles from White Earth, making them a very isolated branch of the Ojibwe. In the end, the Turtle Mountain Ojibwe did not move to White Earth.

Each band on the reservation retained its traditional leadership and was isolated by several walking hours from the other settlements.

THE US INDIAN COMMISSION

The United States government, under the presidency of Ulysses S. Grant, initiated a program of oversight of Indian agencies by religious groups, which were organized under the name the US Indian Commission. It was part of the program to make Indians Christian agrarians. Each tribal group was assigned a religious organization as an overseer of that respective Indian agency. The Ojibwe were assigned to the Congregationalists. A meeting of the government and the US Indian Commission was held in Washington on January 11, 1872.[289] Representing the US Indian

Commission were the American Board of Commissioners for Foreign Missions (Congregational), the Presbyterian Board, the Methodist Board, Baptist Home Missions, American Mission Society (Congregational), Reformed Church, Orthodox Friends, Hicksite Friends, and the Protestant Episcopal Church. Some Creeks, Choctaws, and Chickasaws were also present. The government view was represented by an assistant secretary of the interior and the Bureau of Indian Affairs chief, General Walker. Those in the meeting came to the following conclusions:

- There is progress toward Christianizing and civilizing Indians.
- With exceptions, Indians were satisfied to accept government programs.
- Civilizing the Indians was no longer doubtful with the new policies of protected treaty rights and undisturbed reservation occupancy.

Fears were expressed that "corrupt men in and out of Congress" were conspiring "to procure lands of reservations for railroads and other interests." The Episcopal Church was mentioned for its exemplary efforts to support growth and prosperity among the Dakota and Ojibwe.

THE NEW ST. COLUMBA CHURCH

The consecration of St. Columba Church in White Earth in the summer of 1872 was a large, joyous event that seemed to signify that the policy of enabling Ojibwe to be Christian farmers would be successful. Enmegahbowh gave a speech at the consecration, and three hundred people gathered for a feast after the consecration. The celebration lasted for three days and all services were packed. An article in the *Spirit of Missions* describes Enmegahbowh's goals and accomplishments at White Earth.[290] White Earth was said to be capable of providing sustenance for all of the twelve thousand plus Ojibwe from Wisconsin, Minnesota, and North Dakota. After three years in White Earth, there were twenty-five tracts occupied, with a house, three to five acres of cultivated land, a well, and root houses. Under cultivation were 150 more acres of land. In addition to the church, a three-room, two thousand square foot schoolhouse had been built. The inhabitants of the reservation were described as well dressed, industrious, and sober. Church expansion, Enmegahbowh's debts, and funds for supporting teachers were paid for by the New York Indian Commission of the Protestant Episcopal Church, which E. C. K. Kemble headed.[291] Money for the church also came from anonymous sources, including a woman named Ellen Watkinson and her mother, as well as from the US government as compensation for the first St. Columba mission, which had been destroyed at Gull Lake.

Whipple wrote in *Spirit of Missions* of the consecration of the new St. Columba Church:

The service was one of those events which only come once in a lifetime. It is seldom that we who sow seed as I have with weeping, see here the ripe sheaves. If any had told me that I should live to see the day in the Indian country, I would have felt, in view of such a prospect, as though I could cry out when its realization came, "Lord, let thy servant depart in peace, for mine eyes have seen Thy salvation."

At an early hour, there might be seen, coming over prairie and from the woods, Indians, no longer clad as I used to see them in a blanket, paint and feathers of savage life, but Christian men and women, brought out of darkness, who could say: "We were glad when they said, We will go to the House of the Lord."

At half-past ten o'clock the church was packed, and many were standing outside who could not gain admission. Eleven Clergy besides the Bishop joined in the procession, reading alternately in Ojibway and English the twenty-fourth psalm. The Request to consecrate was signed by the chiefs, who, beside their old names, bore names such as Washburn, Tuttle, Twing and Wright. They and their fellows were clad neatly and showed in dress and person the benefits their households have reaped by learning to make soap.

Brother Enmegahbowh made a speech in behalf of his people, telling with tears the sad story of heathen darkness; of long dark nights when they felt that the sky was brass and the earth iron; of joy at the knowledge of

Jesus; of their feeling that they were only learners, and needed our prayers; of their desire to try and hold fast to Jesus' hand, Who is the good Shepherd; of their hope, although unworthy, to reach a better home.

There was never a more attentive congregation and I was deeply moved as I looked into the crowd of upturned faces who hung upon my words as if I were a messenger of life, bringing them pardon.

What touched me most was that, under God, this work is all due to the labors of Enmegahbowh.

Further in the letter, Whipple makes a plea to expand the mission to the Ojibwe. The Episcopal Church felt an urgent need for an additional missionary to the Ojibwe. Whipple saw Red Lake and Leech Lake as fertile grounds for missions. The Missionary Society agreed to pay Enmegahbowh a salary and authorized a salary for a full-time white missionary.[292] This financial support was very welcome. With no stipend, Enmegahbowh had been relying on hunting to get food for his family, which took time away from his religious and secular teachings. Whipple's only regret during the visit was when he was approached by a chief from the Turtle Mountain tribe in the Dakota Territory who asked him for the fourth time to send a missionary there. He was unable to honor that request.

As previously noted, Ellen Watkinson of Hartford, Connecticut, donated to the St. Columba Church. She had heard of Enmegahbowh's teaching and preaching, perhaps through a church publication, and invited him to visit in New Haven, Connecticut. He did so, staying in her house where they talked of his work as a priest and teacher.[293] Watkinson and her mother both anonymously donated money for the new St. Columba Church and an extension made necessary by expanding membership.[294] Watkinson also donated money to construct the Bishop Whipple Hospital at White Earth Village. Construction was completed in 1872. In 1900, Enmegahbowh recalled the donation, saying, "My heart was too full to give utterance."[295]

St. Columba Church

Chapter 14

Consecration of St. Columba

In a letter written from White Earth on April 13, 1900, to a Miss M. M. Johnson and the Ministering Children League of Ascension Church, Enmegahbowh recalled his visit with Watkinson, whom he viewed as a potential donor to the new mission at White Earth.[296]

While occupying my work received a letter from a young lady from Hartford Inviting me to visit her & in a few days got ready to go. Arrived in the city & on my arrival & on the second day came & found me in my hotel & invited (me?) longer & stay with her during my stay in the city.

She asked me many questions about my people and about the services. Whether I have church to hold my services? I said plenty of them. she ask who builded them. God made & created the trees & under their beautiful shade I hold my services.

Smiled & again whether my people have any Hospital? I said yes plenty of them, when any one taken sick, He or She is taken care of by his or her husband & again she asked what kind of a house that I was occupying. I said a log house. on next morning invited into the parlor. Mr Enmegahbowh I shall built your people a nice frame church & a Hospital and shall build you a nice

Bishop Whipple Hospital

frame house for yourself a present from me. The house shall be yours for your children after you.

I was struck dumb My heart was too full to give utterance.

She understood me full well that I was overwhelm with of thankfulness & gratitude for her great gift. & So the following year The frame Church & the Hospital and my house were built & completed with great joy of my people.

Here the beautiful buildings are now standing & in good condition.

In the following year the young lady died to the great sorrow of my people & on the (1st?) year our church began (to be) too small & need(ed) a larger church.

The two women also donated generously to the Seabury Divinity School in Faribault.[297]

Upon its opening, the hospital lacked a doctor. Sister Maria Selby, an experienced nurse, headed the hospital. Apparently, she ran a "taut ship" with little TLC, such that after a short period, the Ojibwe refused to be treated in the hospital, and it remained little used during her tenure. Joseph Gilfillan, an Episcopal priest who became Whipple's representative to the Ojibwe churchs in 1873, wrote to Whipple of the sister "blowing up" and of her "lack of charity, love and making allowances." The hospital had received $8,000 of clothes for distribution to the Ojibwe. Sister Maria dispensed the clothing with ill temper, causing ill will among the recipients.[298]

TUBERCULOSIS

Eliza Johnson, Enmegahbowh and Charlotte's daughter, died on May 23, 1874. She was twenty years old. Her death was likely from tuberculosis, which was endemic in the population and spread easily. Charlotte and many others in the family were also infected. The course of the disease is slow but relentless as the lungs are consumed (hence, the term consumption) by the disease. The diagnosis is not difficult; symptoms include a persistent cough along with phlegm from the chest and fatigue, not unlike a bad cold, except that the "cold" does not go away. The disease may be episodic with periods of quiescence, followed by "spreads." Although victims could, at the time, survive for years, the disease always resulted in death eventually. Death could come by simple decimation of the lungs or by hemorrhaging from the lungs. Eliza was buried in the St. Columba cemetery. Citing the deaths of his children, Enmegahbowh wrote to Cornelia Whipple in November 1875 that his family was thinking of leaving White Earth, ascribing illnesses to "bad water."[299]

CHAPTER 15

Joseph Gilfillan Comes to White Earth

Bishop Whipple was anxious to fill the position of missioner to the Minnesota population of Ojibwe beyond Enmegahbowh's congregation. He viewed Joseph Gilfillan, his priest in Brainerd, as a prime candidate for the position. One of Gilfillan's long-term ambitions was to be a missionary—to Africans.

Joseph Alexander Gilfillan was born in Londonderry, Ireland, on October 23, 1838. He studied medicine at the University of Edinburgh for two years, but then dropped out and came to Faribault, where he worked for his banker uncle for seven years.[300] In Faribault, Whipple and Breck awakened Gilfillan's religious interests and, through the generosity of his uncle, he attended General Theological Seminary in New York City. There, he excelled in languages. He graduated, then visited the Holy Land, again thanks to financing by his wealthy uncle. Upon Gilfillan's return, Whipple ordained him a deacon and then a priest. By 1872, Gilfillan had established himself as an Episcopal priest in Duluth, a rapidly growing city with a parish promising further growth. Sensing Gilfillan's interest in mission work, Whipple reassigned him to the frontier town of Brainerd. His assignment was to originate churches along the new rail line. In 1872, Brainerd was at the end of the Northern Pacific Railway line from Duluth; in 1873, the line was extended to Fargo.

The railroad eased access to land and brought more whites into the area as settlers and lumberjacks. This also led to more interactions between the whites and Ojibwe, as well as problems.

Brainerd was described as "an utterly Godless place: where all kinds of wickedness ran riot."³⁰¹ It had many saloons where men drank, gambled, fought, and worse. In the *Spirit of Missions,* an article signed by G (likely Gilfillan) deplored the Ojibwe participation in drinking, which produced moral degradation, starvation, and deadly fights. The article advocated that Indians be confined to reservations.³⁰² The same article described two Ojibwe couples who bought corn to eat from a farmer, then camped near another farm. In the morning, they picked corn for breakfast and were confronted by the owner's brothers, who shot and killed the two Ojibwe men. No action was taken against the brothers.

THE MURDER OF HELEN MACARTHUR

On April 28, 1872, a young woman named Helen MacArthur and her sister left their farm to walk toward Crow Wing, two miles away, to visit a friend. ³⁰³At a halfway point, the sister turned back toward home while Helen, age twenty-two, continued on alone toward the friend's house. Helen, who was described as having one leg shorter than the other, was never seen again. A search was conducted, but no trace of her could be found. In mid-July of that year, the wife of an Ojibwe man named Tebekeckickwabe, upset at her husband, told authorities that her husband and his brother, Begoonce, had "followed Helen McArthur into the woods, seized her, ravished her, killed her, cut her body into small pieces and trampled the pieces into the mud."³⁰⁴ The two Ojibwe brothers, ages twenty-two and twenty-four, were arrested at White Earth and jailed in Brainerd for the murder.³⁰⁵ The brothers and the wife each told conflicting stories of the killing. Joseph Gilfillan, now a priest in Brainerd, visited the men and determined that the older one had been baptized by Enmegahbowh.³⁰⁶ Public indignation arose, and a mob raided the jail. The two Ojibwe were removed from their cell and taken to a pine tree on Front Street in front of the Last Turn Saloon. It was later reported that the local sheriff was powerless to stop the mob of about fifty men. Gilfillan appeared at the scene and asked for permission to pray with the captives. The mob agreed, and many knelt while Gilfillan prayed. The lynching then took place but with complications. The first man was hanged, but the second was able to climb to a tree limb with the noose around his neck. Shots were fired from the crowd, and he fell to dangle from the rope.³⁰⁷

Front Street, Brainerd, Minnesota

After the lynching, many Ojibwe were seen gathering in Brainerd. Fearing an uprising in retaliation for the lynching, authorities called out the National Guard. The guardsmen responded, but before engagement it was determined that the Ojibwe had been congregating to sell blueberries. The aborted engagement was dubbed "the Blueberry War."[308]

Gilfillan

GILFILLAN AND ENMEGAHBOWH

Gilfillan was assigned to White Earth. After he settled in, his first task was to learn the Ojibwe language. This was done by immersion in the home of Enmegahbowh with whom he lodged.[309] Also, he talked the language with an old Ojibwe every morning and heard "myths, legends, gossip, everything" with gestures, for which he paid a half dollar per session. In a letter written two months after his arrival, he described being able to recite the Lord's Prayer and the Apostles' Creed in Ojibwe.[310] He described the language as consisting largely of conjugated verbs with inflections that gave shades of meaning.

In 1873, Gilfillan reported assisting Enmegahbowh in services, hospital visitations, preparing a mission service book in the Ojibwe dialect, farming, and putting the finances of the mission in order. Soon after his arrival, Gilfillan also started a program that aimed to educate Ojibwe men to be missionaries. Nine or more were thus educated by Gilfillan.[311] He began the training by carefully selecting men for the program. The first who became deacons were Fred Smith and Samuel Madison in July 1876. George Johnson, son of Enmegahbowh and Charlotte, was ordained a deacon in July 1877, as was Charles Wright. George Smith and John Coleman, brothers of Fred Smith, together with George Morgan, were ordained deacons in July 1878. Charles Wright, Fred Smith, George Johnson, and Samuel Madison all had previously been educated for two years, including learning English, at Faribault under James Lloyd Breck. The diaconate was conferred on Mark Hart in July 1879. Joseph Wakazoo, after becoming a lay reader, was ordained a deacon in 1887. Gilfillan had considered educating Gaius Johnson, son of Enmegahbowh, for the deaconate but found his orientation unsuitable. Gaius was primarily a hunter, but also farmed.

GILFILLAN'S MISSION WORK

During Gilfillan's tenure, twelve churches, including St. Columba, were consecrated on Ojibwe reservations.[312] In 1871, Epiphany Church was built in Wild Rice River on the White Earth Reservation to serve the Otter Tail Pillagers and was successively led by deacons Samuel Madison, Charles Wright, George Morgan, and Mark Hart. Church of the Holy Spirit at Mahnomen, built in 1870, served the Pembina settlement. It was first staffed in 1876 by Samuel Madison followed by George Johnson, George Morgan, Charles Wright, Gilfillan, and Mark Hart; it was closed in 1900. The fourth White Earth Reservation church, at Pine Point, later Ponsford, and named Breck Memorial Church, was built start-

Ojibwe Deacons

ing in 1886. In 1891, Joseph Wakazoo presided in the church, followed by George Smith in 1896. The fifth church on the White Earth Reservation was at the original Gull Lake settlement; named after Shay-Day-Ence, it was built in 1892. Clergy duties were provided by the staff of St. Columba.

Two of the outlying churches from the White Earth Reservation were at Red Lake and were named St. John's at Redby and St. Antipas at the Old Chief's Village. St. John's was built in 1876 and was first served by Samuel Madison, followed by Fred Smith, Mark Hart, Edwin Benedict, and Francis Willis. Services began at St. Antipas in 1878 with Deacons John Coleman and George Smith.

On Leech Lake at Onigum, the Church of the Good Shepherd was consecrated in 1879. Edwin Benedict was the first rector, and in 1885 he was followed by Charles Wright. Another church, St. John's, also existed at an unknown location from 1881 through 1884 and was staffed by clergy of the Church of the Good Shepherd. St. Philip the Deacon Church was located on Lake Winnibigoshish from 1881 through 1893. George Smith was succeeded by Joseph Wakazoo as resident clergy in 1885. The first Cross Lake church was the Church of the Holy Spirit built in 1878. The Church of the Holy Spirit was apparently succeeded by the Prince of Peace Church in 1879 with John Coleman presiding, followed by George Morgan.

As part of his administrative and ministerial duties, Gilfillan toured the churches under his direction every two months. He counseled with his deacons, held communion services, and generally fostered the development of Christian communities. The circuit to visit the churches was a three hundred mile trip, which he made even in the cold of winter and during the mosquito season. Trips to Red Lake required sleeping outside and traveling by railroad, buggy, canoe, and walking. Winter and summer, he traveled by foot, canoe, and snowshoes, despite mosquitos and very cold weather.[313] His report of travels in 1895 indicated more, but easier traveling. He went 6,312 miles by rail, 5,009 miles by wagon team, 951 miles on horseback, 438 miles by birchbark canoe, 12 miles by steamboat, and 272 miles on foot.[314] On his travels he ministered in logging camps, settlements, and in homes.

Gilfillan in Traveling Furs

Gilfillan's travels to remote missions taught him about life in a wigwam: all wigwams were entered without announcement.[315] Hospitality of food and a place to sleep could be assumed. While a wigwam in winter was cold and drafty by white standards, it was a welcoming shelter after a long walk through the wilderness. A fire burned in a fire circle in the center. Storage was around the edges. Sleeping and sitting space on the ground was covered with reed mats. The owner's place was opposite the entrance, which was covered with a blanket. The wife's place for sleeping was near her husband and children, and visitors found places with feet toward the fire. The fire died during the night, and the temperature approached that of the outside. A white man kept on his winter clothes and was very uncomfortable. The Ojibwe, seemingly used to the cold, wrapped themselves in a blanket and never complained. Unless food was unavailable, or sickness was present, the occupants of a wigwam were talkative and jovial.[316]

Even after settling in cabins, Gilfillan observed that the Ojibwe roamed in a pattern during the seasons of the year, and this made education and mission work difficult. The beginning of a year was the arrival of the first crow, which portended the thawing of the snow.[317] Maple sugaring by the women and hunting and trapping by the men followed and lasted about a month until the maples sprouted. Sugaring was done from remote camps in maple groves, and the small children accompanied their mothers. Summer brought a time for planting potatoes and corn, and picking strawberries, raspberries, and blueberries. Then rushes were picked and woven into mats. Cranberries and wild rice were harvested in the fall by the women, while the men again hunted. During the winter, which was the "starving time," the families were together in their village.

Gilfillan built and paid for his own house, perhaps from funds provided by his Faribault banker uncle. In 1877, Gilfillan and Harriet Woodbridge were married in Ripon, Wisconsin. Woodbridge had been working at the government school in White Earth when they met. The couple had two sons and three daughters. Early in the marriage, the Gilfillans hosted multitudes in their house for meals and lodging. Everyone was welcome. However, Harriet's constitution was not robust, and she and the children spent more time in St. Paul when they became of school age. When she was absent from home, Gilfillan resided in the Bishop Whipple Hospital, where meals were provided.

In 1873, Gilfillan estimated that there were seventeen hundred Ojibwe at White Earth, many of whom were of mixed race.

Many of the residents stayed to cohesive groups, as from Otter Tail, Pembina, and Leech Lake and they were not open to the agrarian-Episcopalian ideas. The presence of many mixed-race people tended to incline the new residents to Catholicism. Although President Grant had appointed the Congregationalists as advisors/overseers of the affairs of the Ojibwe, they ceded their role to the Episcopalians in 1874.[318] Edward Smith had been named agent at White Earth in 1873 and was subsequently promoted to the Bureau of Indian Affairs in Washington. In 1874, the Catholic Church appointed Ignatius Tomazin to be missionary on the White Earth Reservation.

AGENT LOUIS STOWE

Under the influence of Bishop Whipple, an Episcopalian, Louis Stowe became agent at White Earth in 1874. The Catholics, now in the majority at White Earth, soon protested that they were being discriminated against. They accused Stowe of fraud, of selling Ojibwe pine trees, and of profiting personally.[319] Ignatius Tomazin, in a November 25, 1874 letter to prospective donors for an orphanage in White Earth, described the extravagance that the Episcopalians had expended, with a result "half a dozen Indians, who believe in that religion."[320] In contrast, he cited Father Pierz who converted one thousand Indians to Catholicism, eight hundred of whom lived at White Earth. Tomazin[321] wrote, "The Indians after they have been well instructed, follow their religion very strictly and always listen with pleasure to the advices and instructions of their priest."

Stowe wrote to Whipple that Tomazin, Henry Beaulieu, John Morrison, John St. Luke, and Joseph Perault were the leaders who had petitioned Washington three times to give oversight of the reservation to the Catholics. Stowe accused Beaulieu of bringing whiskey to the reservation and St. Luke of raiding the agency warehouse. Edward Smith, the former agent at White Earth, wrote to Whipple citing the good crops and prosperity, and he argued that Episcopal efforts should assure continued Episcopal oversight of White Earth. In a long letter to Whipple, Gilfillan denied most of the allegations made against Stowe and declared that he fully supported him. Gilfillan also called the conflict over Stowe's performance a fabrication of Tomazin. He then reported to Whipple an incident that is best expressed in his own words:

The priests here had a violent argument; the one I speak of, Father Tomazin cast out the other out of the house, because, as the one who was cast out told me he had been seen and talked with Father Tomazin's paramour down below. The one who was cast out appealed to the agent to get him his clothes and personal property, which Father T. would not give him, keeping them locked up in the house, the agent forced his door (on his refusal to open it) and gave the cast-out priest his goods. Then the priest, Father T. rang his fire alarm like a madman, summoned people of the reservation, vowed that in revenge he would have the agent in Stillwater making shoes,[322] and since then has been inviting the Indians to councils, writing letters all over the country, and moving heaven and earth to put the agent out.[323]

Tomazin was reassigned away from White Earth well before 1878 when the Benedictines formed a mission on the reservation.[324]

THE BENEDICTINES COME TO WHITE EARTH

On November 5, 1878, the Catholic Benedictines Father Aloysius Hernanutz, Sister Philomia Ketten, and Sister Lioba Braun arrived in White Earth Village from the St. John's monastery and St. Benedict's school near St. Cloud. They judged the reservation to be a place of poverty. The building they first occupied had a room for Father Hernanutz, a living room, a very small chapel, and a garret bedroom for the sisters. Within a month, they had established a school, which was attended by seventeen boys and twenty-three girls.[325] The cornerstone for a forty-by-eighty-foot church was laid in June 11, 1882, and was soon dedicated along with the confirmation of 250 Ojibwe. By 1885, the school, now named St. Benedict's Orphan School, housed twenty-seven children. A government subsidy of $108 per quarter, per student, funded the housing and care of the children.

In 1891, a new building was opened, which housed 150 children and seven staff. It was financed by the Drexel family. Katharine Drexel had formed the Sisters of the Blessed Sacrament for black and Native American people and became the head of the order that staffed the new building. The building continued to be used as an orphanage and school until 1945. Teaching was primarily done in English.

An 1892 census of the Duluth Diocese of the Catholic Church recorded 7,416 Ojibwe, of whom 3,755 were listed as Catholics, 315 as Protestant, and 3,346 as pagans.[326] The numbers probably reflected the judgments of the census takers.

AGENCY OF STOWE IS INVESTIGATED

Henry Rice and William Lyon were called upon by the commissioner of Indian affairs, L. L. Smith, to investigate Stowe's agency at White Earth.[327] On August 10, 1877, they reported the following to the commissioner: $300,000 had been expended on removal of the Ojibwe to White Earth and on improvements; 1,400 acres had been prepared for tillage by the Ojibwe. Not all the broken land was tilled, primarily due to the recent plague of grasshoppers. One hundred log houses had been completed, but their quality was poor. The report characterized some of the houses as mud-covered hovels, unfit for habitation. The school and public buildings were reported to be well built and adequate. Two lumber mills had been built, but neither was operational. The first had burned to the ground, and the second at Wild Rice River was inoperable because the dam providing waterpower had been swept away twice. A third attempt to dam the river was underway, but soil conditions made its permanence doubtful. These efforts had cost $50,000. Rice and Lyon judged that only "a half dozen" Ojibwe families operated farms that gave them an independent income. Of the four hundred Pembina Ojibwe who had removed to White Earth, three-fourths had returned to their previous homes near the Canadian border. The hiring of relatives rather than the Ojibwe was considered an ethical breach. The religious feud between Catholics and Protestants was discussed and deplored as being preventable.

The report concluded that progress on White Earth toward being a model reservation accommodating all the Ojibwe as Christian agrarians was not sufficient. Although Stowe was exonerated of wrongdoing, the powers that be—including Whipple—advocated assigning a new agent to end the conflict. Stowe resigned in 1878 and was replaced by Charles Ruffee, a former trader.

One of the most ardent Ojibwe supporters of the Christian-agrarian program was Shay-Day-Ence (the Little Pelican). As a Midewiwin medicine man, he had opposed the efforts of Breck on farming and religion at Gull Lake, but when Breck returned to Faribault, he took Shay-Day-Ence's son with him to be schooled for two years.[328] The son was baptized with the name Samuel Madison, and he later became an Episcopalian deacon. After Shay-Day-Ence moved to White Earth, there was a period during in which he drank to excess. By 1875 he was abstinent and led a group of up to thirty singers who visited Ojibwe homes where they sang and preached.[329] He was also a frequent correspondent to Whipple, with Gilfillan as his scripter. In his letters, he expressed his joy in Christianity and his progress in becoming a farmer. Shay-Day-Ence worked eleven years for the church before he died in about 1883.

Among the Ojibwe women, Suzanna Roy was a leader who worked to spread Christianity and advocated a role of housekeeping and domestic skills for women.

DANCING

The former enemies of the Ojibwe, the Dakota, began visiting White Earth in 1878. Gilfillan complained that the Ojibwe and Dakota visitors were "dancing themselves wild, day and night."[330] The practice of exchanging gifts was impoverishing the Ojibwe, as an ox a day was being killed to provide feasting. The visiting became common and involved Ojibwe from the Leech Lake Reservation who invited the White Earth Christians to join them. About 100 Ojibwe from White Earth journeyed in ten ox wagons to Leech Lake to dance.[331] The trip took place at a time when Gilfillan had expected the Ojibwe to be tending their gardens and fields. Eight hundred Leech Lake and White Earth Ojibwe participated in the dance in a hall. The Leech Lake Ojibwe had made the trip to White Earth the previous winter for dancing. Gilfillan felt that the present agent was encouraging the gathering and that some of those of mixed race were profiting from it by the sale of whiskey.

A TRIP TO WASHINGTON

Enmegahbowh went to Washington in 1881 to discuss payments overdue to the Ojibwe under treaties.[332] Although he was very cordially received by the secretary of the interior, he was told that the payment depended on an appropriation by Congress. He talked to Senator William Windom of Minnesota, Representative Benton McMillan of Tennessee, and Representative William Washburn of Minnesota. Of the experience, he said, "I never knew I was such a big Injun." He used the term "Injun" when he was treated with deference but ignored. Congress was set to adjourn, and no payments resulted from Enmegahbowh's visit.

A STONE CHURCH

Enmegahbowh expressed his desire for a substantial church to honor Bishop Whipple in early 1880. Whipple must have approved the idea, as he recruited Rev. Tomas Yarnell to lead a drive for funds through the *Spirit of Missions*.[333] Enmegahbowh had suggested that Philadelphia was "the very best hunting ground" for funds. By September 1880, nearly $5,000 had been donated for the church, primarily from the East. One of the appeals was that the Catholics were building an impressive brick church in White Earth Village and that the Episcopalians must not be overshadowed. By June 1881, an additional $4,222 had been raised for the cause.[334] Enmegahbowh favored a stone church, arguing that the building material was all around them. The cornerstone of the new church was laid on July 6, 1881, next to the old St. Columba Church, which remained in place. Stonework was completed in the fall of 1881, but the building was not roofed and finished until 1883.[335] The slow progress on the church was reportedly due to the contractor, who was said to be a drinking man whose frequent sprees kept him from his work. The church was completed and dedicated in 1883.

St. Columba Stone Church

MILLE LACS BECOMES A PERMANENT RESERVATION

In March 1880, Chief Mooseomona from Mille Lacs appealed to a group in Little Falls, which included Nathan Richardson. Richardson was the mayor of Little Falls and a lawyer who was friendly to the Mille Lacs Ojibwe. Mooseomona complained that 350 claims had been filed for timbered land in the reservation. Richardson commented, "It does really appear that the Pine grabbers and ringsters will not be content as long as there is pine tree in the state they do not own."[336] A petition was circulated and sent to Carl Schurz, the secretary of the interior, for relief from the timber cutting. The petition was successful. Richardson effectively continued to act as attorney for the Ojibwe. In 1884, Richardson successfully restored the annuities of the Mille Lacs Ojibwe the year after they had been suspended by agent Luse, who alleged the Ojibwe were prospering when they were in poverty.[337]

By 1883 the reservation at Mille Lacs had been reduced to sixty-one thousand acres as a result of railroad claims, state claims, and claims by individuals. As a member of the northwest commission, Whipple advocated that Shabashkung remove to White Earth, but he remained firm in his refusal. Shabashkung died in 1890.[338]

The Nelson Act of 1889 allowed allotments to individuals in either White Earth or Mille Lacs. Richardson again acted as attorney for the Mille Lacs Ojibwe and after explaining the law urged them to take their allotments at Mille Lacs and not sell them. Enmegahbowh wrote to Richardson in thanks for his involvement: "I never thought that such a bighearted paleface man would come out from such a place as Little Falls. I hope I shall grasp his hand at some future day."[339]

MISSISSIPPI RIVER HEADWATERS DAMS

The US Army Corps of Engineers built dams to control the headwaters of the Mississippi at the outlets of Leech Lake, Lake Winnibigoshish, and other river sources.[340] The Leech Lake dam was completed in 1884, and the depth of the lake was increased by 2.5 feet. The Winnibigoshish dam was also completed in 1884, and it raised the water level by 14 feet. The primary beneficiaries of the dams were the lumbermen, who wanted better navigation during the summer low levels of the river. Also, evening out the flow of water through the year was intended to prevent the rapid erosion of St. Anthony Falls.

Gilfillan wrote of the dams in a letter to Whipple on July 13, 1885.[341] One of his first comments is that the dams are "contrary to the law," according to the commissioner of Indian affairs. Leech Lake had been the "great storehouse" of fish on which the Ojibwe subsisted when the ice was out. The rising of the waters changed habitat such that fish could no longer be caught in abundance. The wild rice fields had been flooded, and no fall harvest for winter survival could be expected. At Lake Winnibigoshish, the water covered hay meadows, graves, fields, and habitations. Some forests were flooded, and dead trees were standing in the water. The Ojibwe were forced to evacuate to higher land.

Gilfillan journeyed to Red Lake and witnessed Ojibwe setting fires to the forest in retaliation for the flooding. He called for quick settlement of the dispute lest the destruction continue. The US government offered the Ojibwe $15,000 for the damage to the lakes. Since the lives of two thousand Ojibwe were hugely affected by the flooding, Gilfillan considered the offer grossly inadequate.

ST. COLUMBA CHURCH BURNS

Other troubles plagued the White Earth Ojibwe in 1889. Gilfillan informed Whipple that the roof was burned off the stone church in December.[342] A door had been left open on a furnace after Sunday service, and wind had blown fire to the woodwork. Gilfillan pointed out that the old church still existed beside the burned church and was quite adequate to fill the needs of the congregation since the membership had not grown as expected to fill the new church. The church had been built anticipating that more Ojibwe would be removed to White Earth. Gilfillan estimated that 250 to 300 men, women, and children were members of the church.

CHAPTER 16

Strike!

Another crisis was brewing at the Episcopal mission among the Ojibwe in the fall of 1877, this one involving Enmegahbowh's son George Johnson. A precipitating event cannot be better told than in Gilfillan's letter to Whipple, which follows:[343]

A painful occurrence has taken place here which however you must know.

You know that Rev. George Johnson went to Canada to find a wife. When he returned unsuccessful about two weeks ago, his father the Rev. Mr. Johnson [Enmegahbowh] came over to my house, and he, my wife and I held a consultation about procuring a proper wife for George. We unanimously settled on a grand-daughter of Major Harriman's; my wife immediately went over and proposed it to her; she was agreeable; Rev Mr. Johnson proposed it to George; he was agreeable; we invited them to a party at our house, and all was settled for last Thursday the 27th. On that evening when on my way to church to perform the service and when the people had already assembled, the sister of Rev. George Johnson's deceased wife, who died a year ago last spring, met me, stopped me and asked to speak with me. She told me that the Rev. George Johnson had begun cohabiting with her since last sugar-making, and had done so regularly for about three months; that he had told her to keep it quiet as were it known, he would be broken, deprived of his office; that he had spent the night at her house pretty regularly—I think every night; and that she did not think it right for him now to marry another person and cast her off. In answer to my question she told me she was not with child. I was as you may imagine thunder-struck and ran immediately to Rev. George Johnson to know if it were true. He admitted it was. I told him I thought the right thing under the circumstances for him to do was to marry that girl, (more particularly as she is a very nice-looking Indian girl, and I had never heard anything against her reputation). I started to find her and bring her to the church immediately, to have her married to him instead of the other, while he was willing, being satisfied that that was his duty; found her and brought her to the church, met her mother who corroborated her story entirely. George then positively refused to marry her. As soon as I heard of the story, I told his father, Rev. John Johnson, and he and I were agreed as to the only thing that could be done. The second day I called to talk again with Rev. Mr. Johnson about it; and mentioned a plan I had heard L. Bodle speak of by which George might not be entirely cut off from future usefulness, of course if you approve of it, namely that George should go to Red Lake to assist Rev. Fred Smith by visiting and catechizing only, not preaching nor officiating until you saw fit to restore him; if even which would afford Rev. Fred Smith all needed help, and let Rev. Charles Wright take Wild Rice River; that in this way his salary would still be continued to him, and if he were really repentant he could show it and do as much for his Master as by preaching; even more if he had the right spirit in him, Rev. Mr. Johnson was pleased with this and said he would propose it to George.

Since then his mother-in-law, the girl herself, and others have come to me at my house and told me, that the first two nights after this discovery George spent at their house abusing them violently, so much so that the mother hid her daughter from him lest he should injure her, as his mother-in-law says he struck her on the neck with a stick, hurting her a good deal, and the third night being last Saturday (this is Monday morning) George came back quietly, asked for the girl, and resumed his usual marital relations with her, spending the night as usual at the home. She also informs me that the same evening on which George came back from Canada, he went to the house and passed the night with her daughter and as I understand her to say he had been regularly in the habit of doing right along since the first commencement. I give you all the facts, however painful to me, that you might be in possession of them for your action. George's going back to live with her since the exposure does not seem to show that he is repenting, or that he would do good to the church visiting among people at Red Lake or anywhere else. I have not seen him since the evening of the intended marriage, judging from the temper of mind he was in then, that to urge him at present to what was right, would only make him more obstinate. He was then disposed to be angry and throw the blame on others.

I feel deeply sorry for his father at this sad occurrence. It is a great pity too to lose a laborer at this time when we need one so much at Red Lake or Wild Rice River.

George Johnson

What in the Ojibwe culture was the couple's personal business was a serious breach of the Christian moral code. Gilfillan and Whipple, while deploring George's indiscretion and pondering their investment in George's education and their need for missionary workers, looked for facts. They determined that George lived with "that girl" from April to October while he courted Miss Harriman. After the wedding had been called off, George continued to correspond with Miss Harriman while still living with "that girl."[344] George's stipend was suspended, and he returned to being a blacksmith.[345] The money that George Johnson was denied is suggested by a yearly stipend schedule recommendation that Gilfillan made in 1878 as follows:[346]

Rev. Fred Smith, wife, 3 children $425
Rev. Charles Wright, no children $350
Rev. John Coleman, no children $335
Rev. Mark Hart, unmarried $300
Rev. George Smith, unmarried $300
Rev. George B. Morgan, unmarried $300
Rev. John Johnson $500
Rev. J. A. Gilfillan $500

A year later, Gilfillan, on instructions from Whipple, talked to Enmegahbowh and George Johnson and reported the results to Whipple.[347] George was still living with the girl and supporting her and their newborn child. George said he would marry her if his salary was restored. In his response, Whipple insisted that George marry her, then he would see about the salary being restored. Gilfillan doubted George's grace and noted that he was drinking and gambling. Gilfillan claimed a state of "Perfect love and harmony" with Enmegahbowh and the Ojibwe deacons. But the Ojibwe deacons and Enmegahbowh carried considerable animosity about the public rebuke to George Johnson, the expectation that the Ojibwe would become independent farmers sooner, and the way Gilfillan meted out funds to the Ojibwe.

By 1880, Gilfillan informed Whipple that George had been penitent and recommended him for a position as deacon in several venues, including Mille Lacs, Winnibigoshish, Leech Lake, White Earth, and the Pembina settlement.

Another indiscretion of an Episcopal deacon occurred when John Coleman became a father without marrying.[348] His salary was suspended.[349] Similarly at Leech Lake, Edwin Benedict, an Episcopal missionary, fathered a child out of wedlock, but his salary was not suspended nor was he officially chastised. This became known and was much resented by the Ojibwe as unequal treatment.

In the fall of 1878, Gilfillan wrote in a letter to Whipple that Enmegahbowh had made (unspecified) charges against him, had "evil feelings" toward him, and was jealous of him.[350] He also wrote that Enmegahbowh had told others that Gilfillan prevented him from getting clothes. Gilfillan denied this but stated that, after ten years, he no longer advocated donating clothes to the Ojibwe. He reflected that Enmegahbowh had not lost his Ojibwe viewpoint. This letter reflects a smoldering cultural split between the Episcopal hierarchy and the Ojibwe people.

ENMEGAHBOWH'S FAMILY ILLNESS

In September 1878, Enmegahbowh wrote to Whipple regarding the health of his family. Charlotte and the children were reported to be dying of worms caused by stagnant drinking water, according to Dr. Flagg of St. Paul. Not only was his family dying, but many other Ojibwe had the same affliction.[351] Charlotte expressed a wish to go back to the old county of Crow Wing. Enmegahbowh had just conducted the funeral of "our daughter's oldest boy" (a child of Martha). Enmegahbowh was severely depressed and complained of getting old.

Two years later, in December 1880, the dreaded word—tuberculosis—was again spoken to Enmegahbowh's family by the sympathetic Catholic priest Father Hernanutz. Charlotte, with Enmegahbowh's approval, sought help from the Catholic Church, which was perceived to have more effective prayers. Whipple severely chastised Enmegahbowh for this belief. Tuberculosis is, of course, a highly infectious disease, spread by the product of the cough. There were no preventative measures for tuberculosis in the nineteenth century. All of Enmegahbowh's children died of tuberbulosis.[352]

Both Charlotte and Enmegahbowh appreciated the sympathetic treatment by Father Hernanutz and responded somewhat positively to his appeal for them to become Catholics. When Whipple heard this, he was flabbergasted. Whipple admonished him by letter, and Enmegahbowh responded, "I read your rash letter to me. It stun me, I felt it all over my frail body."[353] Enmegahbowh ended his letter with these words: "Dear Bishop, forgive me all my fault and sin which I have committed against man and God. Should I remain here any length of time, I hope I shall never again cause you to be upset over my fault and me."[354]

GROWING TENSIONS

In a December 10, 1880, letter to Whipple, Enmegahbowh apologized profoundly for writing begging letters to people in the East. Despite his profound apology, in a

February 1882 letter, Gilfillan told Whipple that Enmegahbowh had continued writing begging letters, which stretched the truth, to contacts in the East.[355]

In early 1882, Enmegahbowh told of an honest agency clerk who accused his boss, the agent of embezzlement. Gilfillan denied Enmegahbowh's accusation to Whipple, and Gilfillan was apparently was believed. Enmegahbowh then wrote to Whipple that Gilfillan "Strike my words before you, and because he is a white man and I am an Indian, make no difference what I say."[356]

Another example of unequal treatment became evident when Edwin Benedict, a white teacher at Leech Lake fathered a child with an Ojibwe woman out of wedlock. Unlike George Johnson, he remained a teacher at full salary.

A DEACON'S STRIKE

The crux of the discord between Gilfillan backed by Whipple and Enmegahbowh and the Deacons was different understanding of cultural values. The Ojibwe wanted respect for their efforts to adapt to American standards while Gilfillan and Whipple disparaged their efforts as inadequate. The Ojibwe did not feel they were being treated as equals.

Whipple and Gilfillan became estranged from Enmegahbowh and the deacons. Perhaps, this resulted in a meeting of the Ojibwe clergy to plan an action deemed a deacons' strike.[357] In November 1882, Charles Wright at Leech Lake and George Smith withdrew their services, and Fred Smith joined the strike in January 1883. Wright let it be known that he wanted the Leech Lake agent, Henry King, to be removed, teacher Sela Wright to be removed, and Edwin Benedict to be exposed for fathering a child out of wedlock. Benedict was a white missionary who remained unrebuked and salaried. The strike action was generally supported by the Ojibwe leadership, Enmegahbowh, and the other deacons. The general complaint was unequal treatment of the Ojibwe compared to whites.

Without apparent concessions on either side, the strike was over by June 1883. The needs of both sides—the church for support by the deacons, and the Ojibwe for support by Whipple—were apparently more important than the issues between the disputants. Yet bad feelings remained on both sides. The salaries of the Ojibwe clergy remained essentially unchanged. Whipple's idea of Ojibwe swiftly becoming Christian farmers, which started with enthusiasm on both sides, was not progressing and possibly regressing. Meanwhile, Whipple had been politicking for consolidating all Ojibwe to White Earth. He wrote to Representative Washburn of Minnesota on the subject, and Washburn thanked him for the idea.³⁵⁸

DISCORD ON THE RESERVATION

In the fall of 1883, potatoes that Gilfillan intended to be used for seed potatoes for the Ojibwe the next spring were stored in White Earth. During the winter, the potatoes were dispensed by Clement Beaulieu to the Ojibwe either for money, furs, or to needy Ojibwe as charity. These events led to a long-standing disagreement between the two men that soured relations between them and spread among their supporters for several years.³⁵⁹

In the spring of 1884, Gilfillan, upon finding the potatoes dispensed and consumed, claimed Beaulieu owed him $200 for their full value and reported the incident to Whipple and Timothy Sheehan, the agent at White Earth. Sides were taken to support Beaulieu or Gilfillan, and the feud became more intense when the White Earth paper, published by Gus Beaulieu, a son of Clement, backed the position of Beaulieu.

In 1885, upon the urging of Gilfillan, an order was issued by Sheehan to expel Beaulieu from the White Earth Reservation.³⁶⁰ The order by Sheehan was preceded by a directive from the secretary of the interior.³⁶¹ The Ojibwe chief Waubanakwad protested the order. Beaulieu rallied his supporters, and the issue was brought before the US Senate, which considered the matter.

In July 1886, Gilfillan wrote to Whipple that Enmegahbowh made "a passionate call upon the congregation to throw overboard all white people connected with the mission including myself, though no names were given and for the Chippewas to take all into their own hands and carry everything forward to glorious success!! Of course, old Clem is behind it all and Satan behind him."³⁶²

Enmegahbowh wrote a letter to the Senate, dated February 8, 1887, in which he expressed his support for Beaulieu:³⁶³

To say one or two words for my friend, Mr. Beaulieu. I have been personally acquainted with Clement H. Beaulieu Sr. a half-blood Indian of the Mississippi Chippewas for over forty-six years and have known him to be always upright and honorable, and zealous in the civilization and advancement of his tribe. His loyalty to the great father is too well known to be questioned. And, therefore, under these circumstances any interference by any party or parties with his right as a member of the tribe without having an opportunity for self-defense, in my opinion is unwarrantable and savors much of malicious persecution.

Reverend E. Steele Peake and Edwin Benedict, two Episcopal priests with congregations near White Earth, counseled Whipple that in Gilfillan's zeal, he unnecessarily disparaged his associated clergy and the Ojibwe.[364]

In the end, the Senate concluded that Beaulieu should not be banned from White Earth. With less-sharp tones on both sides, the controversy abated. Following these events, church leadership on the reservation began to improve, and leadership styles became more respectful and collaborative.

AN ASSOCIATE BISHOP FOR NORTHERN MINNESOTA

By 1886, Whipple was heavily loaded with church work, tending to general Indian affairs, representing the Indians to the government, and directing charity to the Ojibwe. To lessen his load, an associate bishop position was created for northern Minnesota. Reverend Mahlon N. Gilbert was elected to the position, which was to be headquartered in Duluth. Yet even with this help, Whipple's intense interest in and involvement with the Ojibwe continued.

CHAPTER 17

Red Lake Timberland Ceded, 1889, the Dawes and Nelson Acts

The political power of Indians in the United States changed drastically in 1888 when Congress passed the Indian Appropriations Act and President Grover Cleveland signed it into law.[365] With this law, no additional treaties would be made with what had been considered "nation tribes," but existing treaties would remain in place. Instead of viewing Indians as independent nations, they were now to be considered wards of the US government. The law, which increased federal power over the Indians, was a response to the desire of settlers and the government to gain easier access to lands occupied by Indians. Indians retained little power under the new law, yet they still had their tenacity and love of their land. One of the few white advocates for Indians was Bishop Henry Whipple. He held power indirectly—through government connections, his moral speaking ability, and writing power that he used to communicate his ideas, which were advanced for the time.

NORTHWEST INDIAN COMMISSION TRIP

To facilitate the white settlement of northern Minnesota and make the pine forests and lands in the possession of the Ojibwe available to the lumber industry and for settlement, Congress, in an Indian Appropriation Act dated May 15, 1886, called for the establishment of a Northwest Indian Commission. The commission members named were John V. Wright, chair; Charles F. Larrabee, secretary; and Henry Whipple. This commission was tasked with securing agreement for removal to White Earth of most of the Ojibwe, especially the bands from Winnibigoshish, Leech Lake, White Oak Point, Cass Lake, and Mille

Lacs. The commission met on August 3, 1886, in St. Paul and organized their work. They proceeded to White Earth and related how land on the reservation would be apportioned to removed Ojibwe. Interestingly, they stated that any land left after allotment would be held in common. White Earth was praised for its advancement toward civilization.[366]

From White Earth, the commission members journeyed eighty miles to Red Lake (perhaps by horse and wagon) and conferred until August 23. According to the agreement reached, two-thirds of Red Lake land would be ceded, an area of two million acres. Timbered land would be sold at auction, and agricultural land would be sold to settlers, with funds accumulating for the Red Lake Ojibwe. The land retained by the Red Lake Ojibwe was not to be allocated to individual Ojibwe immediately, though it would be later. Schools were to be provided shortly. The main negotiator for the Red Lake Ojibwe was He Who Is Spoken To, or Madweganonind. He was insistent that if the land of Red Lake was taken from the Ojibwe, the proceeds should be used for the education and welfare of the band. He Who Is Spoken To drew a perimeter around the lakes, and he and the commission agreed that a permanent reservation would be retained within this perimeter.

The commission returned to White Earth before traveling sixty-five miles to Leech Lake.[367] Leech Lake Ojibwe were divided on the commission's proposals for removal, the young being somewhat willing while the older men resisting. After spending two weeks at Leech Lake, the commissioners were discouraged.

The commissioners did form an agreement with the Cass Lake and Winnibigoshish Ojibwe—which numbered around four hundred—that met their objectives. The nearby White Oak Point Ojibwe were a scattered group, who were considered to be depraved by alcohol and prostitution. Some of the scattered band agreed to the commission's proposals, and this was deemed approved by that group.

Wright and Larrabee continued on to Mille Lacs on October 9 without Whipple, who had other business. The first session was unproductive, as the Mille Lacs Ojibwe refused to consider removal. After consultation, the commission resumed their negotiations on November 3; this time they were joined by Whipple. Only twelve Ojibwe from Mille Lacs agreed to the commission's proposal for removal.

The commission found that the Sandy Lake Ojibwe dispersed to avoid having discussions.

On November 16, the commission met with Fond du Lac Ojibwe. The members of the commission found that these band members were living in comfortable homes, were well dressed, and were prospering by working in mills and lumber camps. No removal was deemed necessary for this band.[368]

The commission intended to visit the Bois Forte and Grand Portage bands, but winter weather prevented further travel. Their report, generally referred to as the Northwest Indian Commission Report,[369] to J. C. Atkins, commissioner of Indian affairs, was submitted on December 1, 1886. Along with their report, they submitted the agreements they had made with various bands, most important among them the agreement with the Red Lake band.

The report and agreements were approved by the head of the Department of the Interior and forwarded to Knute Nelson, Minnesota representative in Congress. Nelson added his complication to the bill for "The Relief and Civilization of the Minnesota Chippewa" by setting up a fund to benefit *all* the Ojibwe of Minnesota, which was to be approved by all Ojibwe in the state. The fund would receive the proceeds of the sale of Red Lake lands. The bill as modified drew a comment from Larrabee that the preface should read, "Whereas Indians have pine lands and the white man wants them, be it enacted."[370] The last change to the bill allowed removal to either Red Lake or to White Earth. The unpopular allotment was never enforced at Red Lake.[371] Whatever agreements were made by the commission were used by Congress as a basis for the Dawes Act. However, Congress acted largely without regard for many of the provisions in the agreements.

DAWES ACT AND THE NELSON ACT

A huge factor to consider in the evolution of the Ojibwe reservations in northern Minnesota is the value of land resources that were in Ojibwe hands in 1890. Much of the land on reservations was not very useful for agriculture. There were no exceptional stands of pine timber nor large tracts of fertile land on the Leech Lake, Cass Lake, Lac du Flambeau, Grand Portage, or Bois Forte reservations. White Earth was an exception. The western third of White Earth was prime agricultural land on the Red River floodplain, requiring no great expenditure to raise grain and other crops. The eastern third of White Earth was prime pine forest that had been untouched, while such forests were being rapidly depleted outside of reservations. The relative wealth of White Earth assets made them the focus of politics, greed, and fraud; much of White Earth land was ultimately transferred from the Ojibwe into the hands of white landowners and timber companies.

In 1887, the Dawes Act was passed by Congress and signed into law. Under this law, individual Indians had the right to be allotted up to 160 acres of land on reservations; accepting such allotments also made the recipients US citizens.[372] The stated purpose of the act, as expressed in its first paragraph, was "to provide for the allotment of lands in severalty to Indians on the various reservations and extend the protection of laws of the United States and Territories over the Indians, and for other purposes." The "other purposes" included fostering assimilation among the Indians by encouraging farming. The allotted land was to be held in trust for twenty years, during which time it could not be sold and would not be taxed. After all Indians received an allotment, the remaining land was to be sold, with the proceeds being put into funds for the benefit of Indians. The Dawes Act applied to all Indians in the United States.

The Nelson Act of 1889 tailored the Dawes Act to the situation in Minnesota related to the value of the pine forests. Four townships on the eastern border of White Earth were heavily timbered with pine forest, which were at the time threatened—the Ojibwe were allowed to harvest and sell "dead and down" timber,[373] and they could increase their supply by burning the crowns of trees. The first action of the Nelson bill was to remove the White Earth Reservation ownership of the four eastern townships. Money from the sale of the four townships' land was to go to the "Chippewa in Minnesota Fund" to benefit all Minnesota Ojibwe rather than White Earth residents. However, it was found that over $150,000 was spent fraudulently from this fund on surveys and resurveys, and the land had not been sold.[374] The four timbered townships were sold at auction in 1900 in Crookston. An investigation later deemed that the auction had been fixed and that the winners had bought the land at $1.60 per thousand board feet rather than the targeted $3.00 per thousand board feet.

The Nelson Act allowed the Ojibwe of Minnesota to take allocations of 160 acres of land in either their home reservation or in White Earth. The land was not to be taxed nor could it be sold for twenty-five years. The provision was intended to allow the Ojibwe a period in which they could adjust to market farming. By 1900, 1,198 Ojibwe had moved to White Earth.[375] The Ojibwe tended to settle in the central lakes and forest area of the reservation. Most sought to live in a way that was similar to the hunting and gathering culture from which they came. The government's efforts to get the Ojibwe to transition to a farming lifestyle had little success. The acreage under cultivation by the Ojibwe in White Earth grew from 5,703 acres in 1887 to 6,075 acres in 1904—less than 6 percent.[376] Ojibwe did participate in the market economy by selling products they gathered, which included snakeroot, maple syrup, berries, ginseng, fish, and hides.[377]

A commission was created to apply the provisions of the law and administer the Chippewa in Minnesota Fund. Its members did not include any Ojibwe, nor was there any way they could represent their thoughts to the commission.

Nathan Richardson, the mayor of Little Falls, acted as attorney for the Ojibwe of Mille Lacs in their negotiations for land before a special Indian commission chaired by Henry Rice.[378] Richardson advocated for the repulsion of white squatters and the rejection of fraudulent land transactions.[379] He recommended that the agreement with the United States relating to the allotment under the Nelson Act be signed, as it allowed allotment to the Mille Lacs land as an alternative to land on White Earth. In exchange for rights of citizenship and continuing rights to some of their land, the Ojibwe reluctantly ceded land that had been illegally entered by Amherst Wilder and Senator Dwight Sabin.

Allotments in White Earth were encouraged, and by 1900, 4,446 allotments had been made on the reservation land, though many Ojibwe did not occupy their allotment.[380] The allotment plan encouraged some to remove from Mille Lacs, Leech Lake, and Gull Lake to White Earth. The Ojibwe at White Earth continued to be forest and lake oriented. Traditional hunting and gathering continued to be a large factor in the economy, and most preferred the forested eastern area for their homes.

Most of the Ojibwe exercised their allotments in the forested eastern parts of the White Earth Reservation, which fulfilled their cultural needs. The Ojibwe experienced little pressure to remove from other reservations and take allotments at White Earth. There was little competition in the bidding for pine lands, with possible collusion, and the result was that the lumber companies bought pine near their mills. The money from sales went to the Chippewa in Minnesota Fund. Money was paid from the fund to effect removals and provide support until the removed people were settled.

Edward Neal, US court commissioner, wrote to Whipple in 1893 about an investigation into "pine land stealing of this state."[381] T. B. Walker and others were accused of securing power of attorney from hundreds of Native Americans and soldiers through Indian agents and others in consortium with the government with apparently no compensation to the Native Americans. Some legal papers were alleged to have been signed by dead people. It was alleged that the 1863 treaty with the Red Lake Ojibwe was not actually confirmed, which would invalidate many transactions involving scrip and power of attorney.

Chapter 17

THE BATTLE OF SUGAR POINT

In 1898, people charged with bootlegging liquor were being prosecuted in Duluth. Ojibwe suspects and witnesses who were called to court were not provided transportation to their homes.

This resulted in the last engagement between US troops and Native Americans, which occurred on the Leech Lake Reservation. Bugonaygeshig, an Ojibwe from Leech Lake also known as Old Bug, had been taken into custody on a whiskey bootlegging charge. He was subsequently moved to Duluth in April 1898 for a trial but was acquitted for lack of evidence. He then had to walk a hundred miles home to Leech Lake.[382] Such trials happened frequently in either Duluth or St. Paul. On September 15, at an annuity payment in Onigum, Old Bug and another Ojibwe were seized as witnesses for another bootlegging trial in Duluth. A melee ensued, and a number of Ojibwe helped the two men escape. Military assistance was requested, and a force of twenty soldiers under Chauncey Humphreys responded. They were unable to find Bugonaygeshig or catch the other twenty Ojibwe from Onigum who had been accomplice in his escape. A larger force was summoned and seventy soldiers under Melville Wilkinson were dispatched to Walker; there they boarded two steamboats on October 5 and reached Sugar Point, where Old Bug had a cabin in the middle of a two-acre clearing.[383] Two accomplices were arrested, and the force searched the surrounding woods and began setting up battle stations. The soldiers stacked their rifles in preparation for the noon meal. Meanwhile, the Ojibwe occupied much of the brush and undergrowth around the cabin. Firing began at about 11:30 a.m., probably started by an accidental discharge of a rifle by a troop. Gunfire was exchanged for the next half hour. Six soldiers, including Wilkinson, were killed.[384] Ten additional troops were wounded. The fighting continued until the boats were boarded and steamed back to Walker. One Ojibwe police officer was also killed. All the Ojibwe fighters at Sugar Point retreated into the woods and were never identified or apprehended. Several Ojibwe who surrendered spent two to six months in jail in Duluth.[385] The incident highlighted the forcing of witnesses to be transported to faraway trials. Secretary of the Interior Cornelius Bliss wrote of the Ojibwe, "They may now go back to their homes and live peaceably if the whites will treat them fairly."[386]

Old Bug (with Other Ojibwe)

CHAPTER 18

Turtle Mountain Becomes a Reservation, 1888, and the Ten Cent Treaty, 1892

By 1880, the Ojibwe had extended their territory from Pembina across North Dakota and into Montana. This far west branch of the Ojibwe had adapted their lifestyle—from being lake and forest Indians to being hunters of buffalo—and lived in tepees rather the wigwams. Horses were used for hunting buffalo. The Sweet Corn Treaty of 1858 between the United States, the Ojibwe of North Dakota and Montana, and the Dakota defined the border between the Ojibwe and the Sioux.[387] The described Ojibwe territory contained about eleven million acres. By 1882, settlers were occupying some of this land while the Ojibwe were on the hunt.[388] Under pressure to expand the land available for settlers, President Chester A. Arthur proclaimed that the Ojibwe holdings in North Dakota would be reduced to twenty-two townships in the Turtle Mountains, a lakes and hills area in north central North Dakota.[389] In 1884, again by presidential proclamation, the Turtle Mountain Reservation was reduced to two townships, an area of seventy-two square miles. Removals to the reservation proceeded slowly. It was proposed that the North Dakota Ojibwe be removed to the White Earth Reservation, and some did indeed move there. But by 1892, the situation was very confusing. The Dawes Act required that the land of the Turtle Mountain Reservation be allotted to individuals. The problem was that the small reservation would not accommodate all the North Dakota Ojibwe with a 160-acre allotment. The Ojibwe, under the leadership of Chief Little Shell, contended that the land defined in the 1858 Sweet Corn Treaty had never been ceded and therefore belonged to the Ojibwe.

P. J. McCumber was appointed by the US government to resolve the situation.[390] Although Little Shell was a recognized chief of the Turtle Mountain Ojibwe and a relatively strong negotiator, McCumber chose to form a committee of thirty-two Ojibwe with which to meet and negotiate "the cessation and relinquishment of the lands claimed by them, and to determine the number to be listed on the rolls." Further, a listing of the Ojibwe at Turtle Mountain excluded Little Shell and his contingent from the roll of tribal members. The resulting agreement between McCumber and the committee ceded the eleven million acres and awarded the enrolled tribal members a million dollars. The agreement has come to be known as the "Ten Cent Treaty." Congress ratified the agreement. Little Shell and five hundred others from the tribe were excluded from the benefits of the treaty. Little Shell and his followers wanted no part in the agreement, and they moved to Montana, which remained Indian territory.

CHAPTER 19
Whipple, Gilfillan, and Enmegahbowh, 1889 to 1903

The lives of Whipple, Gilfillan, and Enmegahbowh changed greatly as they aged. Wives died, and remarriages happened. Retirements and disabilities came to pass. The withdrawal from active participation in religious and political affairs by these men, and ultimately their deaths, ended an era in which the Ojibwe came to reside largely on reservations.

WHIPPLE

Whipple continued to be very politically active and wrote letters, even when he was in Florida, to the Bureau of Indian Affairs noting his opposition to the Red Lake cession legislation. Whipple's opinions had little effect, as revealed in letters from the bureau by Larrabee[391] and Vilas.[392] Larrabee agreed that the Red Lake legislation was unfair, and Vilas agreed that Sheehan would be a good choice for the next agent, but both said it would make no difference. The agency went to Ruffee, which Gilfillan told Whipple was a poor choice.

In 1889, Whipple and his wife, Cornelia, attended the General Convention of the Episcopal Church in New York, where he preached the opening sermon.[393] After the convention, they were traveling to Florida on a train when it crashed near Albany, Georgia. The bishop was bruised, but Cornelia suffered a broken rib, a concussion, spinal injuries, and an injured kidney, which was not diagnosed until later. Although they continued to Maitland, Florida, Cornelia had problems with memory, balance, and speech. She was mostly bedridden. The Whipples returned to Faribault in April, but her condition worsened, and she died on July 16, 1890.

Cornelia Whipple

To soothe his sorrows, Whipple made a visit to England, met Queen Victoria, and then went to Egypt and steamed up the Nile River.[394]

WHIPPLE REMARRIES

Rose Cleveland, daughter of President Cleveland, spent the winter of 1895 in Maitland, Florida, with the company of Evangeline Marrs Simpson, the widow of a wealthy manufacturer.[395] When Whipple and Simpson met at a Christmas dinner, a romance ensued. They were married on October 22, 1896, in St. Bartholomew's Church by Bishop Potter. Whipple was seventy-six years old and Simpson was thirty-eight.

Whipple with Evangeline Whipple

Bishop Henry Whipple had not visited the White Earth Reservation for several years before the year 1899, which marked his forty-year anniversary of being a friend, benefactor, and spiritual leader to the Ojibwe in the area.[396] The Ojibwe were no

SYBIL CARTER AND LACE MAKING

Sybil Carter was associated with the Domestic and Foreign Missionary Society in New York. She had apparently met Whipple and recognized a need to usefully employ Indian women. Her idea was to teach Indian women lace making. With great industry, she gathered materials and tools, brought them to the Dakota at Birch Coulee and to the Ojibwe, and remained in Minnesota starting in July 1890.[430] She personally financed the operation and then marketed the lace products in the East.

Sybil Carter

Carter employed lace-making instructors at White Earth, Red Lake, and Leech Lake. Mrs. Wiswell presided at White Earth, and she taught Pauline Colby the trade. Colby was then reassigned to Leech Lake. She wrote of her experiences in a 115-page typescript, addressed to "Fidus Achates" (Faithful Friend).[431] On the wagon trip to Leech Lake from White Earth, the driver got lost. Their attempt to get accommodations for the night resulted in being chased away by an angry man, and they spent the night in the forest. In the morning, they found that their resting place was near Leech Lake. Carter's cabin at Leech Lake was primitive, until the agency built her a new home. Carter's lace-making operation lasted about ten years.

longer in his bishopric, or district, since Duluth was now the missionary base for northern Minnesota. Yet, over the years, Whipple had developed an unbreakable bond with the Ojibwe through his work, political advocacy, and charity. He was invited and came to White Earth for three days in 1899. The first day, a Saturday, was spent meeting with Ojibwe who came from as far as a hundred miles to see and greet the bishop. On Sunday, a church service was held, at which all the Ojibwe clergy described how the bishop had influenced their life work. On Monday, a great feast was prepared for an outdoor picnic. Game, produce, fruits, vegetables, and desserts had been prepared in abundance. Enmegahbowh and Minogishick sat at the head table along with Bishop Whipple. After the feast, the principals circulated among the crowd and told and listened to stories of the work that had been accomplished over the past forty years. The bishop's benediction ended the celebration.

Whipple's vision for the Ojibwe had been for them to reside at White Earth Reservation, where they would be far away from whiskey traders and other bad influences, and where they would become Christian (hopefully Episcopalian) farmers. Many factors prevented this vision from being realized: First, the vision was utopian; second, it did not consider the culture of the Ojibwe; third, the lust for land and resources by whites continually decreased Ojibwe land holdings; and fourth, acts of Congress removed Ojibwe from desirable land. The result was an impoverished White Earth Ojibwe population of about five thousand. The land allotments also had the effect of breaking up tribal loyalties.

WHIPPLE DIES

Bishop Henry Benjamin Whipple died on September 19, 1901.[397] Enmegahbowh wrote the following tribute to him:[398]

I write in the language of my sorrowful heart. I cannot say much at this time; my heart is too heavy. When I heard that our Bishop had died, I said, "No, this cannot be." I did not think our Bishop could die. But in another hour a second messenger entered my house to assure me that the beloved Bishop had died truly. I and my wife wept aloud in our lonely room, and then for hours spoke not to one another.

The Indians began to come from all directions and asked with startled faces what it meant. I said, "My friends, the best friend our people ever had in the world, the great warrior, the great bishop, the great loving man has fallen." The grief was terrible to see. They could not believe it. Some went away with bitter weeping; other stole to their homes stunned silent.

I went to Faribault for the last time with my sorrowing people. I said to them, "This time we go to Faribault with feelings unlike any that we ever had. Before we had gone with bounding step and happy hearts. We have known that we were to look on the face of our loving Bishop, the friend of our lives. It was our joy to see the face of the man who loved and sympathized with my people. Before we have been going to get inspiration, courage, counsel. We have gone away full of hope and courage, blessing our Bishop and with our hearts ready to go on as he had bidden us.

Our Bishop was all LOVE. He preached always from the beginning, LOVE, LOVE! "My children love the Great Spirit—Love one another. Love other tribes." His one great aim has been to unite us by close connection in Christian fellowship.

He is no more here to give us these lessons. His loving face is hidden from us. His voice is silenced—SILENCED did I say? Yes and no. His voice shall sound, and be forever ringing in our ears—yes, and it shall be ringing as long as his Red Children live, throughout the Indian country.

More than forty years ago when I went to him through the forests, he carried his blanket, his robe case and many other things, and many times the Indians said, "We cannot let him do this. He will kill himself. He cannot work this way and live." But he would smile—"O, THIS is nothing! This does not tire me!" and his voice filled us with hope and courage.

Our beloved Bishop has stood for over forty years and defended the defenseless. He has spoken for the rights of his red children, and THAT when no man gave much thought to the forlorn outcast of the world. He alone, the first Bishop who entered into the Chippewa heathen land. Today throughout the Chippewa Country tears are blinding *the eyes, hearts heavy loaded with sorrow and are looking upward crying, "My Father, My Father" like Elisha of old when his friend was taken away from him. In a loud voice he cried "My Father, My Father." The double portion of Elijah's spirit was given him. May the double portion of our departed Bishop's love be given us! His was a long battle for us. His Indian work has been blessed in the conversion of many. He has built churches and has ordained many Indian Deacons who are doing their work faithfully. How truly can he say in the language of St. Paul; "I have fought the good fight, I have kept the faith."*

But WE, what are WE to do? What courage can we take away? We are lost children. Our hearts are lead. I bid you farewell.

J. J. Enmegahbowh

Enmegahbowh in Old Age

PETER MARKSMAN

After serving as a Methodist missionary in Minnesota, Peter Marksman, or Kawgodahewag, was transferred to the Michigan conference. He served at Sault Ste. Marie from 1839 to 1841, at which point he was again transferred to the Big Iron River, Michigan, ten miles west of Ontonagon. In 1842, he was assigned to Lakeville in Michigan's Lower Peninsula, and the same year he became a deacon in the Methodist Church.[399] Marksman was married to Hannah Morien, who was of mixed race, in 1844.[400] Their wedding took place in La Pointe, where Hannah had lived and absorbed American culture, such that she moved confidently among Americans. The couple had no children of their own but adopted a boy and raised him to adulthood.

From 1848 to 1852, Marksman served as a missionary at Tahquamenon Bay, Michigan, under several Methodist missionaries. At some locations he became the preacher in charge. In 1862, Marksman was ordained as an elder in the Methodist Church.[401] He served an Ojibwe congregation at Point Iroquois near Sault Ste. Marie from 1861 to 1870[402] and received a salary of $300 per year.

Marksman's assignments from 1872 to 1880 included Kewawenon, Indian Point, Cedar River, and Hannahville as preacher in charge. He died on May 28, 1892.

Peter Marksman

GILFILLAN'S ARCHDEACONATE

Gilfillan operated under several titles during his twenty-five years in White Earth.[403] His first title was simply missionary. Later he was addressed as superintendent of missions to the Ojibwe. In November 1890, he was first referred to as archdeacon.

The archdeaconate of Gilfillan included five churches on the White Earth Reservation, two on Red Lake, and outlying churches at Leech Lake, Cass Lake, and Lake Winnibigoshish.[404] While St. Columba at White Earth Village was Enmegahbowh's base, where he presided from 1868 to 1889 and continued to provide ministry until 1893, he was occasionally incapacitated by arthritis. At these times, Gilfillan became the rector at St. Columba.

Nine deacons were consecrated between 1874 and 1879, after which no more were consecrated. No deacons were advanced to priesthood.

In 1898, Gilfillan's separation from his family, the rigors of work over a large area, and perhaps disappointment with the Ojibwe not becoming Episcopalian farmers in the numbers he had hoped caused him to retire from his archdeaconate. He was granted a leave by Bishop Morrison of northern Minnesota, and he moved to Washington, DC. There he became politically active for the Ojibwe cause and served as minister in Esther Memorial Chapel. In 1904, he published a novel, *The Ojibway*. He died on November 19, 1913, shortly after moving to New York.

ENMEGAHBOWH

Enmegahbowh became infirm in 1887, and Whipple ordered Gilfillan and a deacon to take over services in St. Columba. Enmegahbowh was to continue doing whatever he could for the welfare of the Ojibwe, and he would receive his full salary. His daughter Martha lived to the age of forty-six, dying in 1888. His son Gaius, the hunter, died at age forty that same year. Enmegahbowh's dear wife and companion, Charlotte, died of tuberculosis on April 30, 1895.[405] The last remaining offspring of Enmegahbowh and Charlotte, Sarah Jamison, died on October 27, 1897, at age thirty-two.

The remaining survivor in the family was a grandson whose father was probably William Augustus (Gus).[406] In a letter to Whipple, Enmegahbowh identified the grandson as "the son of her [Charlotte's] youngest son." It must be assumed that Enmegahbowh meant his youngest son who survived to maturity. The grandson was born six months before his father died. Since Gus died on September 7, 1883, that would make the boy referred to as Johnny thirteen years old in 1896. Enmegahbowh and Charlotte raised their grandson after both of his parents died. Johnny had accompanied Enmegahbowh on trips to Washington and Canada. Johnny died of tuberculosis before the time of the August 11, 1896 letter.[407] The deaths of Charlotte in 1895 and Johnny left Enmegahbowh alone and grieving.

Later in the letter, Enmegahbowh self-consciously asked Whipple for permission to remarry. Gilfillan had encouraged him to do so. While Enmegahbowh referred to his stipend, he considered himself poorer than he had ever been in his life as a missionary.[408] He reported that he had preached at Wild Rice River and that Chief Twing had attended to hear Enmegahbowh, whose appearance at that church was apparently infrequent.

John Johnson Enmegahbowh married Nogahnigijigoque (Mary) on October 4, 1896.[409] The marriage took place in Enmegahbowh's home and was performed by Gilfillan. Witnesses were Wassesau, Nindoling, Apishkin, and Miss Mark.

In an 1899 letter, Enmegahbowh reminisced fondly of his camping trips with Whipple to Red Lake. He described one incident when Whipple reached Red Lake, had unpacked in a wigwam, and was preparing to go to the morning service: "Your things were scattered [and] you asked the old chief whether your things would be safe. The old chief throw very strong insinuation said, 'Yes, all will be safe because there were no white men within a hundred miles.'"⁴¹⁰

Enmegahbowh also wrote of another camping site near White Oak Point:

> After retiring, here all at once the wild whippoorwills began singing of their captivating songs very near us & almost you can distinguish the words of the birds, thus, "Whip him well, whip him well, whip him well."
>
> Someone spoke out in your tent, I believe it was you or Dr. Washburn and said, "Here, dear friends, some of us have done wrong & deserve punishment & punishment has been delayed & now someone is calling for punishment, forthwith." And bye and bye comes another bolder song from the water (from a bullfrog), "Mod-er-ation, Mod-er-ation."⁴¹¹

In 1902, Nathan Richardson, a former mayor of Little Falls, urged Enmegahbowh to write of his life. Enmegahbowh obliged in several long letters, which Richardson collected. In 1904, a year after Enmegahbowh's death, arrangements were made for the material to be published as "En-me-gah-bowh's Story" by the Women's Auxiliary of St. Barnabas Hospital in Minneapolis. The book of fifty-six pages covers notable events from Enmegahbowh's life written from memory.

Enmegahbowh died in 1903. His death was unheralded. He had served his church until his death, despite rheumatism and old age. He was buried in the St. Columba Cemetery. No dignitaries attended the funeral: he had outlived his supporter, Bishop Whipple, and Joseph Gilfillan lived in Washington and New York and was out of touch with the affairs of the Episcopal Church in Minnesota.

Theodore Holcombe wrote of Enmegahbowh just before his death:⁴¹²

> Enmegahbowh was the herald of all our Indian work; the man who cried in the wilderness, "Come over and help us", the man who first opened the door for all that has since followed of God's work for the Indians, even to the Pacific Coast. Let honor be given where honor is due and may a sense of appreciation warm his heart before the sun sets upon his earthly pathway.

ENMEGAHBOWH'S LEGACY

Enmegahbowh spent his entire life working for the betterment of the Ojibwe: as a cleric, in the political realm, as an educator, and as a community member. His clerical functions resulted in several hundred conversions to Christianity, and his moral teachings affected many more. He was honorably involved in local and national politics. During his lifetime, he had truly "stood before his people."

CHAPTER 20

The Ojibwe at the Beginning of the Twentieth Century

The beginning of the new century coincided with the ability of the Ojibwe to sell land they had been allotted. Nationally, Indian allotments, which were inherited, could be sold after 1902. Five thousand acres of mostly Red River valley allotted land was sold by 1905 for $57,760.[413]

STEENERSON ACT WITH CLAPP RIDER OF 1904

The allocation of land under the Dawes and Nelson Acts had taken place fairly equitably on White Earth. Full-blooded Ojibwe tended to select land in eastern White Earth forests.

The railroad was extended along the western fringe of the White Earth Reservation in 1902, and the ready availability of transportation increased the value of Red River valley farmlands on the reservation.

The 1904 Steenerson Act provided an additional allotment of eighty acres or a pro rata share of unallocated forestland in the White Earth Reservation.[414] There was less land to allocate than expected, since eighty-six thousand acres of swampland and lakes had been previously claimed by the State of Minnesota.[415] On the allocation day in May 1905, mixed-race people were largely more aware of the value of the timberland and lined up ahead of time so they would be the first to receive an allotment. Eighty-acre allocations were made and the pro rata requirement of the law was ignored; several hundred Ojibwe in line received no allocation.[416]

The Clapp Rider of 1904 allowed the timber on allotted land to be sold. Under the act, contracts for cutting had to be approved, and the process prevented most sales.[417]

The allotment results were protested but with political pressure, Commissioner Francis Leupp of Indian affairs determined that the allotment was valid. Charles Wright later went to Washington in 1905 with a petition signed by 376 Ojibwe to protest the allocation. His petition was rejected. A 1911 commission investigated the allocation and found there had been fraudulent collusion with the lumber companies. However, the timber had already been cut and marketed, and no action resulted from the investigation.

THE CLAPP RIDER TO THE BURKE ACT OF 1906

The land that had been allocated to the Ojibwe could not be immediately sold, as the allocation agreement stipulated that the land was not outright owned by the Ojibwe but had been placed in a twenty-five-year trust held by the US government. This arrangement was based on the premise that the Ojibwe were not sophisticated property owners. The 1906 Clapp Rider assumed that mixed-race Ojibwe were more sophisticated, and so they were allowed to sell their property.[418] The result was a huge controversy over who was eligible to sell their property, as "mixed blood" was a criteria that could not objectively be determined. The Clapp Rider of 1906 created a controversy that lingers on, with many titles to land in White Earth clouded.

Many mixed-race Indians, including Gus Beaulieu, facilitated such sales through a mortgage scheme.[419] The owner of an allotment was induced to mortgage the allotment to obtain immediate cash. Within three weeks of the Clapp Rider becoming effective, 250 mortgages had been issued.[420] Provisions in the mortgage made immediate payments necessary and, when not paid, the mortgages were foreclosed. By such means, land was procured for $4 per acre, although it was worth $25 to $400 per acre.

Through legislation, administration, corruption, and aggressiveness on the part of whites, less than 10 percent of land in the thirty-two townships of White Earth was owned by Ojibwe by 1915. Moving more people onto less land tended to impoverish the Ojibwe at White Earth. Much of the clan structure of the bands was broken up, but the lifestyle of most Ojibwe remained one of hunting and gathering.

Acquisition of land on other Ojibwe reservations by whites depended on the quality of the land for farming; whites did not actively seek the less valuable land. Red Lake was not allocated nor sought after by whites by some quirk in the administration of the laws.

In Minnesota, the approximately eighty-five hundred Ojibwe were concentrated on reservations at Red Lake, White Earth, Mille Lacs, Leech Lake, Grand Portage, Fond du Lac, and Bois Forte.[421] In Wisconsin, the Ojibwe were concentrated at Lac Courte Oreilles, Lac du Flambeau, Bad River, and Red Cliff. Ojibwe reservations were also located at L'Anse, Michigan, and Turtle Mountain, North Dakota. The approximate total Ojibwe population in 1910 was eleven thousand. With all of the changes imposed on the Ojibwe by the US government, the traditional leadership of chiefs became less important. The dominant political force in the reservations was the agent—he was the law and the person who dispensed any annuities or benefits derived from the sale of timber.

After Whipple became less active in Ojibwe affairs after 1895, the Christian-agrarian initiative died. The general policy of the Bureau of Indian Affairs was acculturation, and the main vehicle for acculturation was the schools. There were on-site schools and boarding schools. On-site schools were not greatly funded, and most of the pupils tended to be of mixed race. Those who were full blood were less punctual attendees and might have received corporal punishment for their truancy. Traditional hunting and gathering continued on a much-diminished land base. Typical employment of the Ojibwe involved intermittent work in the forests and mills. After 1900, most of the Ojibwe lived in a restricted area, were ruled by an agent, and made a marginal living from hunting-gathering, intermittent labor, and government handouts.

In the period after Enmegahbowh's death, the Ojibwe were largely confined to reservations. Each reservation fared differently depending on its location, resources, the skills of its leadership, and happenstance.

White Earth, which had high-value agricultural land and timber resources, had fared poorly through allocation and subsequent, somewhat fraudulent, land transactions. Of thirty-six original townships, four were separated and sold to timber interests under a Nelson Act provision for approximately half their value. Although the money from the sale was put into the Chippewa in Minnesota Fund, the fund was not managed for the benefit of the Ojibwe. A poor definition of what it meant to be of mixed race allowed for sales of some lands, which resulted in clouded titles of White Earth lands. As of 1983, 7 percent of White Earth land was owned by the Ojibwe or Ojibwe interests.[422]

Leech Lake was similarly subjected to checkered landownership, with only 4 percent remaining in Ojibwe hands by

2003.[423] Red Lake, through its remoteness and the persistence of its leadership, avoided allocation; today, most Red Lake land is communally owned.[424] Remoteness and lower resource value left the Bois Forte Ojibwe with just 34 percent of their original land[425] and Grand Portage reservation with 78 percent of its original land.[426] Mille Lacs, with persistence and the help of Nathan Richardson, retained its reservation. Timber-interest encroachment reduced Ojibwe ownership to 4 percent of the original reservation land.[427] . The Fond du Lac Ojibwe retained 23 percent of the land within its reservation boundaries.[428]

In North Dakota, the Turtle Mountain Reservation of two townships was hardly adequate to sustain the Plains Ojibwe who had previously ranged over a huge territory while hunting buffalo. Little Shell of the Turtle Mountain band became disgusted with land allocation in the 1890s and led part of his band to unorganized Montana.

Wisconsin reservations were subject to allocation but survived somewhat intact.

Michigan's lone L'Anse Reservation was remote and had a fate similar to that of Bois Forte. The Ojibwe in Upper Michigan, being sparsely populated, were able to survive in the wilderness near Ontonagon and Watersmeet.

Each reservation was ruled by an agent of the Bureau of Indian Affairs until about 1930, when some democratic credence was given to reservations.

The religious legacy of Enmegahbowh, Whipple, and Gilfillan produced enduring Episcopal communities at White Earth, Leech Lake, and Red Lake. Many Ojibwe became Catholic through association with mixed-race people and through the work of missions and schools. The orphans housed and educated in the orphanage established by the Drexels were effectively set on a path to Catholicism.

By 1910, poverty among the Ojibwe was as great as at any time in their transition away from being hunter-gatherers. They lived on a tiny fraction of their original land on which they foraged for food and trapped for income.

ENDNOTES

1. Smith, Donald, *Miississauga Portraits* (Toronto, University of Toronto Press, 2013), 171. The passage refers to Enmegahbowh being in his "mid-twenties" in 1834. While Enmegahbowh is identified as being Ottwa, his cousin, George Copway was identified as being Ojibwa. Perhaps the difference is inconsequential.
2. Doane, *Enmegahbowh of the Chippewas* (National Council of the Protestant Episcopal Church, 1962).
3. Ibid., 168.
4. Vance, Bruce, *Reverend Doctor John Strachman, Reverend Samuel Armour, and the Old Blue School* (Toronto: Toronto Board of Education, 1995), 94.
5. Whipple, Henry, *Lights and Shadows of a Long Episcopate* (New York: MacMillan, 1912), 407.
6. Pitezel, John H., *The Life of Reverend Peter Marksman* (Cincinnati, OH: Western Methodist Book Concern, 1893), 26.
7. Whipple, 500.
8. Smith, 169.
9. Jones, Peter, *The Sermons and Speeches of the Reverend Peter Jones* (Leeds, England: H. Spine, 1831), 12.
10. Smith, 170.
11. Ibid., 171.
12. Ibid., 171.
13. Doane, 3.
14. Whipple, 498.
15. Ibid., 499.
16. Smith, 171.
17. Pitezel, 62.
18. Smith, 26.
19. Jackson, Leroy, *Enmegahbowh, Chippewa Missionary* in Collections of the State Historical Society of North Dakota, vol. II, 475.
20. Ibid., 475.
21. Ibid., 475. Keoche-we-kwa-doong is probably now Keewatin, Michigan.
22. Pitezel, 20. Pitezel is ambiguous about Marksman's origin. Page 20 states he appeared "on an island in the St. Croix River" while page 3 states "his parents lived near the St. Louis River above Fond Du Lac."
23. Smith, 21.
24. Ibid., 172.
25. Copway, George, *The Life, History and Travels of Kah-ge-ga-gah-bowh (George Copway)* (New York: B. W. Benedict, 1847), 117.
26. Ibid., 120.
27. Doane, 5.
28. Brunson, Alfred, *A Western Pioneer*, vol. 2 (Cincinnati, Hitchcock and Walden, 1879), 65.
29. Brunson, Alfred to Lewis Cass, August 31,

1835, State Historical Society of Wisconsin, Brunson Papers.

30 Brunson, 81.

31 Smith, 176.

32 Danziger, Edmund, *The Chippewas of Lake Superior* (Norman: University of Oklahoma Press, 1979), 7.

33 Danziger, 10.

34 Blegen, Theodore, *Minnesota, a History of the State* (Minneapolis: University of Minnesota Press, 1964), 21.

35 Risjord, Norman, *A Popular History of Minnesota* (St. Paul: Minnesota Historical Society, 2005), 4.

36 Wingert, Mary Lethert, *North Country: The Making of Minnesota* (Minneapolis: University of Minnesota Press, 2010), 83.

37 Northwest Ordinance.

38 Folwell, William, *A History of Minnesota*, Vol. 1 (St. Paul: Minnesota Historical Society, 1956), 90–100.

39 Ibid., 93.

40 Ibid., 132.

41 Ibid., 133.

42 Blegen, 99.

43 Wingert, Mary, *The Making od Minnesota*, (Minneapolis, The University of Minnesota Press, 2010), 83.

44 Treaty of Prairie du Chien of 1825, Wisconsin Historical Society

45 Blegen, 127.

46 Shortridge, Wilson Porter, *The Transition of a Typical Frontier, with Illustration from the Life of Henry Hastings Sibley* (Menasha, Collegiate Press, George Banta Publishing Co., 1922), 13.

47 Ibid., 19.

48 Gale, George, *Upper Mississippi Historical Sketches* (Chicago: Clark and Company, 1867), 143.

49 Whipple, 252.

50 Brunson, 85.

51 Ibid., 83

52 Shortridge, 24.

53 Zapffi, Carl H., *Minnesota's Chippewa Treaty of 1837* (Brainerd, MN: Historic Heartland Association, 1994), 3.

54 Hansen, Marcus, *Old Fort Snelling* (Iowa City: State Historical Society of Iowa, 1918), 173.

55 Zapffi, 33.

56 Wingert, 133.

57 Zapffe, 5.

58 Hole in the Day the Elder to Taliaferro and Maj. Plimpton, June 3, 1839, Library of Congress, M234, roll 378.

59 Enmegahbowh to Whipple, December 11, 1898, Minnesota Historical Society, Whipple Papers.

60 Shortridge, 7.

61 Carroll, Jane Lamn, "Who Was Jane Lamont?" *Who Was Jane Lamont*, Anglo-Dakota Daughters in Early Minnesota, Minnesota History Magazine, Spring 2005, 192

62 Ibid., 7.

63 Brunson, 88.

64 Pitezel, 68.

65 Copway, 122.

66 Hobart, Chauncy, *The History of Methodism in Minnesota*, (Red Wing, Red Wing Printing Co. 1897), 24.

67 Copway, *The Life, History and Travels of Kah-Ge-G-Gah-Bowh*, 122.

68 Gale, 144.

69 Collections of the Minnesota Historical Society, vol. 6, 1876, 141.

70 Hobart, 144.

71 Diedrich, Mark, *The Chiefs Hole in the Day of the Minnesota Chippewa* (Minneapolis: Coyote Books, 1986), 2.

72 Ibid., 15.

73 Smith, 177–78.

74 Ibid., 183.

75 Ibid., 186.

76 Ibid., 208.

77 Gale, 145.

78 Hobart, 26.

79 Whipple, 502.

80 van Herk, Aritha, "Travels with Charlotte," Canadian Geographic Magazine, July–August 2007.

81 Peyer, Bernd C., ed., *American Indian Non-fiction: An Anthology of Non-Fiction, 1760-1930s* (Norman: University of Oklahoma Press, 2007), 9.

82 Extract from report of John Johnson of Sandy Lake Station, August 1, 1842, Index of Executive Documents, Twenty-Third Congress, Third Session.

83 St. Columba Church Register.

84 Peyer, 9.

85 Tanner, George Clinton, *Fifty Years of Church Work in the Diocese of Minnesota, 1857–1907* (St. Paul: Published by the committee and sold by W. C. Pope, 1909), 54.

86 Tanner, 52.

87 Doane, *Enmegahbowh of the Chippewas*, 8.

88 Whipple, 501.

89 Enmegahbowh to James P. Hayes, Subagent, Indian Department, June 8, 1846, in *Collections of the State Historical Society of North Dakota*, vol. 2, 473.

90 Peyer, 231.

91 St. Columba Church Register.

92 Danziger, 78.

93 Ronald Satz, *Chippewa Treaty Rights of Wisconsin Chippewa Indians* (Madison: University of Wisconsin Press, 1996), 40.

94 Ibid., 44.

95 Ibid., 44.

96 Folwell, 310.

97 Ibid., 321.

98 Copway, George, *Organization of a New Indian Territory East of the Missouri River* (New York: S. W. Benedict, 1850).

99 Satz, Ronald, "Chippewa Treaty Rights," *Transactions of the Wisconsin Academy of Sciences, Arts and Letters* 79, no. 1 (1991), 51.

100 Ibid., 55.

101 Treaty to Commission of Indian Affairs, April 13, 1850, Minnesota Historical Society.

102 The Reverend Sherman Hall to unknown, December 30, 1850, The Newman Library.

103 Satz, 58.

104 Ibid., 56.

105 The number 4,000 is taken from a commemorative sign on the Sandy Lake Tragedy site.

106 Whipple, 252.

107 December 3 is the date for clearing of the encampment on the commemorative plaque at Sandy Lake.

108 Enmegahbowh to Whipple, December 11, 1898, Minnesota Historical Society, Whipple Papers.

109 Satz, 58.

110 Flat Mouth to Ramsey, December 3, 1850, delivered at Sandy Lake to the Chip-a Agent, J. S. Watrous, December 3, 1850, and as it was interpreted by (name obscured), J. G. Minnesota Historical Society, Alexander Ramsey papers, Roll 5. Transcribed by Verne Pickering, January 8, 2019.

111 Tanner, 52.

112 Ibid., 52.

113 Dawden to secretary of war, September 23, 1851, National Archives, M234, Rolls 148 and 149.

114 Enmegahbowh to Lee, August 4, 1851, National Archives, Chippewa Agency, M234, Roll 149.

115 Satz, 56.

116 Ibid.

117 Ibid., 76

118 Family Research website, "Chippewa Indian Agency (Minnesota)" with further references to Edward Hill and the National Archives.

119 Ojibwe Treaty of 1854.

120 Satz, 69.

121 Stone, Anthony, Mnopedia.

122 Ojibwe Treaty of 1855.

123 Enmegahbowh to Whiting, September 15, 1855, National Archives Microfilm, M324, Roll 151, 1855-09-15-ENM.

124 Ibid.

125 Breck, Charles, *The Life of Reverend James Lloyd Breck* (New York: E. & J. B. Young and Co., 1883), 133.

126 Ibid., 178.

127 Ibid., 166.

128 Ibid., 175.

129 Tanner, 58.

130 Ibid., 25

131 Breck, 179.

132 Ibid., 184.

133 Ibid., 182.

134 Holcombe, Theodore, *An Apostle of the Wilderness: James Lloyd Breck, D. D., His Missions and Schools* (New York: Thomas Whittaker, 1903), 95.

135 Ibid., 69.

136 Ibid., 79.

137 Ibid., 82.

138 Diedrich, Mark, *Ojibway Chiefs* (Rochester, MN: Coyote Books, 1999), 102.

139 Tanner, 65.

140 Ibid., 72.

141 Ibid., 200–37.

142 Holcombe, 91.

143 St. Columba Church records.

144 Tanner, 70.

145 Ibid., 70.

146 Weber, Eric W., MNopedia.

147 Enmegahbowh to Whipple, December 11, 1898, Minnesota Historical Society, Whipple Papers.

148 Tanner, 70.

149 Ibid., 95.

150 Holcombe, 98.

151 Ibid., 98.

152 Tanner, 76.

153 Breck, 288

154 Tanner, 19.

155 James Breck, *Chippewa Pictures, 1857* (Church Missions Publishing, 1929), 16.

156 Tanner, 80.

157 *Brainerd Daily Dispatch*, September 18, 1911. A record collected by Mr. E. Leon Lum of reminiscences of Mrs. E. Steele Peake, prepared to be filed with the Minnesota Historical Society.

158 Ibid.

159 Holcombe, 119.

160 Plan for the buildings at Leech Lake. In Enmegahbowh Archive as 1856-05-00-BUI, source unknown.

235 Enmegahbowh to Whipple, April 28, 1864, Minnesota Historical Society, Whipple Papers.

236 Minnesota Indian Affairs Council, tribal nations, website, Bois Forte.

237 Bassett to Whipple, January 23, 1867, Minnesota Historical Society, Whipple Papers.

238 Enmegahbowh to Whipple, January 1, 1867, Minnesota Historical Society, Whipple Papers.

239 Batterson to Whipple, March 29, 1867, Minnesota Historical Society, Whipple Papers.

240 Whipple, Henry, "Bishop Whipple's Report on the Moral and Temporal Condition of the Indian Tribes on Our Western Border," a typescript of nineteen pages coded as 1866-00-00-WHI in Enmegahbowh Archive.

241 Bilione Whiting Young, *Obscure Believers: The Mormon Schism of Alpheus Cutler* (Apple Valley, MN: Pogo Press, 2002), 65.

242 Ibid., 44.

243 Enmegahbowh to Breck, May 16, 1865, Minnesota Historical Society, Whipple Papers.

244 Enmegahbowh to Whiting, April 30, 1867.

245 Whiting to Enmegahbowh, 1869, National Episcopal Archives, Austin, Texas.

246 Enmegahbowh, January 13, 1894, from White Earth Reservation, Published in the Spirit of Mission periodical of the National Episcopal Church 1894, 223–25. Archives of the Episcopal Church USA.

247 Enmegahbowh to Breck, May 16, 1865, Minnesota Historical Society, Whipple Papers.

248 Enmegahbowh to Whipple, December 4, 1865, Minnesota Historical Society, Whipple Papers.

249 Enmegahbowh to Breck, January 27, 1866, Minnesota Historical Society Whipple Papers.

250 Diedrich, *Ojibwe Chiefs*, 96.

251 Ibid., 100

252 Enmegahbowh to Whipple, June 7, 1866, Minnesota Historical Society, Whipple Papers.

253 E. A. W. record dated July 19, 1866. Minnesota Historical Society, Whipple Papers.

254 Bonga to Whipple, November 23, 1866 and November 21, 1866, Minnesota Historical Society, Whipple Papers; Enmegahbowh to Whipple, October 19, 1866, Minnesota Historical Society, Whipple Papers.

255 Whipple to unnamed senator, September 20, 1866, Minnesota Historical Society, Whipple Papers.

256 Enmegahbowh to Whipple, October 19, 1866, Minnesota Historical Society, Whipple Papers.

257 Bonga to Whipple, October 21, 1866, Minnesota Historical Society, Whipple Papers.

258 Tanner, 351.

259 Whipple, 178.

260 Enmegahbowh to Whipple, February 16, 1868, Minnesota Historical Society, Whipple Papers.

261 Enmegahbowh to Whipple, April 2, 1868, Minnesota Historical Society, Whipple Papers.

262 Melissa Meyer, *The White Earth Tragedy: Ethnicity and Dispossession at a Minnesota Anishinaabe Reservation, 1889–1920* (Lincoln: University of Nebraska Press, 1999), 45.

263 Enmegahbowh to Whipple, August 25, 1662.

264 Anton Treuer, *The Assassination of Hole in the Day* (St. Paul: Minnesota Historical Society Press, 2011), 3.

265 Ibid., 6.

266 Ibid., 173–75.

267 Ibid., 176.

268 Meyer, 46.

269 Viznor, Gerald, *Escorts to White Earth,* (Minneapolis, Four Winds, 2968), 133.

270 Michael McNally, *Ojibwe Singers* (New York: Oxford University Press, 2000), 82.

271 Enmegahbowh, *Enmegahbowh's Story*, 40.

272 Enmegahbowh to Whipple, January 29, 1869, Minnesota Historical Society, Whipple Papers.

273 Enmegahbowh to Whipple, March 9, 1869, Minnesota Historical Society.

274 Enmegahbowh in "Missions," volume 34, 1869 1869-00-00-ENM.

275 Enmegahbowh to Whipple, March 9, 1869, Minnesota Historical Society.

276 Enmegahbowh to Whipple, May 18, 1869, Minnesota Historical Society.

277 Enmegahbowh to Whiting, April 4, April 6 and May 23, 1869.

278 Ibid.

279 Meyer, 89.

280 The Minnesota Chippewa Tribe, *White Earth, a History* (Cass Lake, Minnesota Chippewa Tribe, 1989).

281 Enmegahbowh to Whipple, August 18, 1869, Minnesota Historical Society, Whipple Papers.

282 Enmegahbowh to Hollingsworth, August 23, 1870.

283 Enmegahbowh to Whipple, August 18, 1869, Minnesota Historical Society, Whipple Papers.

284 Enmegahbowh to Hollingsworth, August 23, 1870.

285 *Spirit of Missions*, September 18, 1871.

286 Trennery, Walter, *Murder in Minnesota* (St. Paul: Minnesota Historical Society, 1985), 62.

287 Hollingsworth to Enmegahbowh, March 3, 1871.

288 McNally, *Ojibwe Singers,* 83.

289 David Knickerbacker, *Spirit of Missions*, 1873, volume 37.

290 Whipple, October 1872, *Spirit of Missions*.

291 Kemble to Whipple, July 7, 1872, Minnesota Historical Society, Whipple Papers.

292 Whipple, *Spirit of Missions*, October 1872, 579.

293 Enmegahbowh to M. Johnson, April 13, 1899, Newberry Library, Box 3042.

294 Ellen Watkinson to Whipple, October 29, 1872, Minnesota Historical Society, Whipple Papers.

295 Enmegahbowh to M. Johnson, April 13, 1900, Newberry Library, Box 3042.

296 Enmegahbowh to M. Johnson, April 13, 1900.

297 Watkinson to Whipple, October 29, 1872, Minnesota Historical Society, Whipple Papers.

298 Gilfillan, Joseph to Whipple, February 22, 1875, Minnesota Historical Society, Whipple Papers

299 Enmegahbowh to Cornelia Whipple, November 23, 1875, Minnesota Historical Society, Whipple Papers.

300 Marston, Eliot, *The Apostle to the Ojibway, Joseph Alexander Gilfillan, Archdeacon* (Nashotah House Library, 1938), 1 (a typescript).

301 Ibid., 4

302 Whipple, *Spirit of Missions*, September 1872, 579.

303 Trenery, Walter W., *Murder in Minnesota* (St. Paul: Minnesota Historical Society, 1985), 76.

304 Ibid., 77

305 *Weekly Record*, Detroit Lakes, MN, December 1872.

306 *Brainerd Tribune*, July 27, 1872.

307 Trenerry, 81.

308 Ibid., 81.

309 Gilfillan, Mrs. *A Hero of Minnesota, Joseph Alexander Gilfillan, Archdeacon* (Hartford: Church Mission Publishing Company, 1920), 8. (A pamphlet number 18 in the Soldier and Servant Series)

310 Gilfillan to Office of the Indian Commission, Prot. Episcopal Church, November 1873.

311 Joseph Gilfillan, "History of the Indian Missions in Minnesota," *Church Review*, October 1885, 539–53.

312 Tanner, *Fifty Years of Church Work*, 512–15.

313 Marston, *Apostle to the Ojibway*, 14.

314 Ibid., 19.

315 Joseph Gilfillan, "The Ojibwe in Minnesota," vol. 9, Collections of the Minnesota Historical Society, 68.

316 Ibid., 65.

317 Ibid., 70.

318 Rebecca Kugel, *To Be the Main Leaders of Our People: A History of Minnesota Ojibwe Politics, 1825–1898* (East Lansing: Michigan State University Press, 1998), 121.

319 Ibid., 121.

320 Tomazin to Catholic Clergy, November 25, 1874, Minnesota Historical Society.

321 Ibid.

322 A discussion between Pickering and Brent Peterson, executive director of the Washington Country Historical Society, revealed that shoes were not made in the Stillwater Prison until the 1890s. Perhaps it was a common job in other prisons.

323 Gilfillan to Whipple, March 1877, Minnesota Historical Society, Whipple Papers.

324 Carol J. Berg, "Agents of Change. The Benedictines at White Earth, Minnesota History Magazine, Winter 1982, 162.

325 Ibid, 165.

326 Ibid., 168.

327 Henry Rice to L. L. Smith, August 10, 1877, Minnesota Historical Society.

328 McNally, 96.

329 Ibid., 105.

330 Gilfillan to Whipple, October 10, 1878, Minnesota Historical Society, Whipple Papers.

331 Gilfillan to Whipple, July 15, 1891, Minnesota Historical Society, Whipple Papers.

332 Enmegahbowh to Whipple, December 6, 1881, Minnesota Historical Society, Whipple Papers.

333 *Spirit of Missions*, June 1880, 189–93.

334 Enmegahbowh to Whipple, September 19, 1881, Minnesota Historical Society, Whipple Papers.

335 Enmegahbowh to Knickerbacker, September 28, 1871. Minnesota Historical Society, Whipple Papers.

336 Warner, Mary E. *A Big-Hearted Paleface Man* (Little Falls: Morrison County Historical Society, 2006), 102.

337 Ibid., 105.

338 Ibid., 100.

339 Ibid., 105.

340 Army Corps of Engineers, Leech Lake website.

341 Gilfillan to Whipple, July 13, 1885, Minnesota Historical Society, Whipple.

342 Gilfillan to Whipple, December 14, 1889, Minnesota Historical Society, Whipple Papers.

343 Gilfillan to Whipple, October 1, 1877,

344 Gilfillan to Whipple, November 5, 1877, Minnesota Historical Society, Whipple Papers.

345 Gilfillan to Whipple, December 29, 1877, Minnesota Historical Society, Whipple Papers.

346 Gilfillan to Whipple, 1878, Minnesota Historical Society, Whipple Papers. The proposed funds were to be paid from the legacy of Miss Josie Smith.

347 Gilfillan to Whipple, November 11, 1878, Minnesota Historical Society, Whipple Papers.

348 McNally, 100.

349 Kugel, 149.

350 Gilfillan to Whipple, November 10, 1878, Minnesota Historical Society, Whipple Papers.

351 Enmegahbowh to Whipple, September 23, 1878, Minnesota Historical Society, Whipple Papers.

352 Jackson, 496

353 Enmegahbowh to Whipple, December 10, 1880, Minnesota Historical Society, Whipple Papers.

354 Ibid.

355 Gilfillan to Whipple, February 8, 1882, Minnesota Historical Society, Whipple Papers

356 Enmegabowh to Whipple, 1882, Minnesota Historical Society, Whipple Papers.

357 Kugel, 148.

358 Washburn to Whipple, February 27, 1882, Minnesota Historical Society, Whipple Papers [1882-02-27-WAS].

359 This incident is not well documented, but the story was repeated and became White Earth lore.

360 Kugel, 151.

361 White Cloud to Whipple, August 17, 1885, Minnesota Historical Society, Whipple Papers.

362 Gilfillan to Whipple, July 19, 1886, Minnesota Historical Society, Whipple Papers.

363 Vizenor, 203.

364 Kugel, 158.

365 Appropriation Bill for Indian Affairs, Ch. 14, 9 Stat. 547, passed on February 27, 1886.

366 Northwest Indian Commission Report, December 1, 1886, 14.

367 Ibid., 15.

368 Ibid., 19.

369 Senate Executive Document 2449, number 115, 49 Congress, 2 session (1887), 10,53 Communication from the secretary of the interior, with papers relating to Chippewa Indians in Minnesota.

370 Oberly, commissioner of Indian Affairs, to Whipple, February 21, 1889. Minnesota Historical Society.

371 Anton Treuer, *Warrior Nation* (St. Paul: Minnesota Historical Society Press), 72–91.

372 Meyer, 51.

373 Ibid., 138–140.

374 Ibid., 139–140.

375 Bureau of Indian Affairs Census, 1900, Microfilm Roll 653, National Archives.

376 Meyer, 75.

377 Ibid., 80.

378 Warner, *Big-Hearted Paleface Man*, 104.

379 *Little Falls Transcript* (newspaper), October 11 and 13, 1889.

380 Meyer, *White Earth Tragedy*, 65.

381 Neal, US Court commissioner, to Whipple,

381 March 5, 1893, Minnesota Historical Society, Whipple Papers.

382 William Matsen, "The Battle of Sugar Point," *Minnesota History Magazine,* Fall 1987, 270.

383 Ibid., 272.

384 Ibid., 273.

385 Ibid., 274.

386 Ibid., 275.

387 Patricia Poitra, *The History and Culture of the Turtle Mountain Band of Chippewa* (Bismarck: North Dakota Department of Public Instruction, 1997), 12.

388 Ibid., 16.

389 Ibid., 17.

390 Ibid., 15.

391 Larrabee to Whipple, January 29, 1889, Minnesota Historical Society, Whipple Papers [1889-01-29-LAR]; Larrabee to Whipple, February 4, 1899 [1889-02-04-LAR]; and Larrabee to Whipple, February 11, 1899 [1889-02-11-LAR].

392 Vilas to Whipple, February 11, 1899, Minnesota Historical Society, Whipple Papers [1889-02-11-VIL].

393 Allen, 226, 227.

394 Ibid., 229, 231.

395 Allen, Anne Beiser, *And the Wilderness Shall Blossom,* 242.

396 The description of the celebration is contained in a typed script, collected by Mr. Schaitberger, unsigned and undated. The script readily identifies itself to be a description of the event.

397 Allen, Anne Beiser, *And the Wilderness Shall Blossom,* 252.

398 *The Church Record,* official paper of the Diocese of Minnesota and District of Duluth, 1902.

399 Pitezel, 88.

400 Ibid., 93

401 Ibid., 164.

402 Ibid, 216.

403 Marston.

404 This information is derived from a massive chart prepared by George Schulenberg.

405 St. Columba Register.

406 Enmegahbowh to Whipple, August 11, 1896, Minnesota Historical Society, Whipple Papers.

407 Ibid.

408 Enmegahbowh to Whipple, 1898, Minnesota Historical Society, Whipple Papers.

409 St. Columba Register.

410 Enmegahbowh to Whipple, February 13, 1899, Minnesota Historical Society, Whipple Papers.

411 Ibid.

412 Holcombe, 96.

413 Ibid., 141.

414 Ibid., 142–48.

415 Ibid., 143.

416 Ibid., 147.

417 Ibid., 151.

418 Ibid.

419 Ibid., 155.

420 Peterson, Ken, *Ransom Powel and the Tragedy of White Earth,* Minnesota History Magazine, Fall 2012, 93.

421 Meyer, 55. The approximate number 8,500 is derived from information in the *White Earth Tragedy,* which numbers the Ojibwe population of Minnesota in 1890 as 8,304. The population of Ojibwe moved much after 1890, particularly to White Earth to receive allotments. The movements took place mostly in Minnesota, and it is assumed that the total number of Ojibwe in Minnesota did

not change much in twenty years.

422 Ebbott, Elizabeth, *Indians of Minnesota* (Minneapolis: University of Minnesota Press, 2006), 31.

423 Ibid.

424 Ibid.

425 Ibid.

426 Ibid.

427 Ibid.

428 Ibid.

429 Ibid., 78, 79.

430 Carter, Sybil to Whipple, November 11, 1892, Minnesota Historical Society, Whipple Papers.

431 Colby, Pauline, *Fidus Achates* (a typescript of 115 pages with few errors and an upbeat attitude to the rigors of life on the frontier).

BIBLIOGRAPHY

Allen, Anne Beiser. *And the Wilderness Shall Blossom: Henry Benjamin Whipple, Churchman, Educator, Advocate for the Indians.* Afton, MN: Afton Historical Society Press, 2008.

Blegen, Theodore. *Minnesota, A History of the State.* Minneapolis: University of Minnesota Press, 1963.

Breck, Charles. *The Life of Reverend James Lloyd Breck.* New York: E. & J. B. Young and Co., 1833.

Breck, James Lloyd. *Chippewa Pictures in Early Days in Minnesota.* Hartford Church Missions Publishing, 1857.

Brunson, Alfred. *A Western Pioneer,* Cincinnati, OH: Hitchcock and Walden, 1879.

Colby, Pauline. *An Account of the Work of Pauline Colby* (a typescript).

Coleman, Sister Bernard. *Old Crow Wing.* Brainerd, MN: Evergreen Press, 2000.

Copway, George (Kahgegagahbowh). *Life, Letters and Speeches.* Lincoln: University of Nebraska Press, 1850.

Copway, George. *The Life, History and Travels of Ka-gi-ge-gah-bowh.* Philadelphia: James Harmstead, 1847.

Copway, George. *Organization of a New Indian Territory East of the Missouri River.* New York: S. W. Benedict, 1850.

Danziger, Edmond Jefferson, Jr. *The Chippewas of Minnesota.* Norman: University of Oklahoma Press, 1938.

Diedrich, Mark. "Chief Hole in the Day and the 1862 Chippewa Disturbance, a Reappraisal." *Minnesota History*, Spring 1987.

Diedrich, Mark. *Ojibway Chiefs.* Rochester, MN: Coyote Books, 1999.

Doane, Gilbert. *Enmegahbowh of the Chippewas.* National Council of the Protestant Episcopal Church, 1962.

Enmegahbowh. John Johnson, *Enmegahbowh's Story.* Women's Auxiliary Saint Barnabas Hospital, Minneapolis, Minn. 1904.

Enmegahbowh. John Johnson, *Enmegahbowh's Story.* St. Paul's Episcopal Church Brainerd, MN and the Committee on Indian Work of the Diocese of Minnesota Reprint June 1985, June 1994 and September 2013. Compiled and Edited by Rev. Canon Stephen Schaitberger, Printed by Bang Printing 2013.

Folwell, William Watts. *A History of Minnesota,* revised ed.. St. Paul: Minnesota Historical Society Press, 1956.

Gale, George. *Upper Mississippi Historical Sketches.* New York: Clarke and Company, 1867.

Gilfillan, Joseph. *The Ojibwe in Minnesota.* Minnesota Historical Society Collection.

Hadden, Jeanette. Ebenezer. Published by the Morgan County Historical Society, Printed by TRE, LTD Jacksonville, Illinois, 1998.

Hanson, Marcus. *Old Fort Snelling.* Iowa City: State Historical Society of Iowa, 1918.

Hobart, Chauncey. *History of Methodism in Minnesota.* Red Wing, MN: Red Wing Printing Company, 1847.

Holcombe, Theodore. *An Apostle of the Wilderness: James Lloyd Breck, D. D., His Missions and Schools.* New York: Thomas Wittaker, 1903.

Jackson, Leroy. *Enmegahbowh, Chippewa Missionary.* Collection of the State Historical Society of North Dakota, Volume 2. Bismark, North Dakota, 1908.

Johnson, John. *Enmegahbowh's Story.*

Jones, Peter. The Sermons and Speeches of Reverend Peter Jones, Leeds: H. Spink, 1831.

Jones, Peter. History of the Ojibway Indians. Published by A.W. Bennett, 5 Bishopsgate Street Without. Houlston and Wright, Paternoster Row, London. Published Posthumously, 1861.

Kugel, Rebecca. *To Be the Main Leaders of Our People: A History of Minnesota Ojibwe Politics, 1825–1898.* East Lansing: Michigan State University Press, 1998.

Marston, Eliot. *The Apostle to the Ojibwe, Joseph Alexander Gilfillan, Archdeacon* (a typescript). Nashotah House Library, 1938.

Matson, Donald, Waltz, Louis. *Old Fort Snelling,* St. Paul: Minnesota Historical Society Press.

McNally, Michael D. *Ojibwe Singers.* New York: Oxford University Press, 2000.

Meyer, Melissa. *The White Earth Tragedy: Ethnicity and Dispossession at a Minnesota Anishinaabe Reservation, 1889–1920.* Lincoln: University of Nebraska Press, 1999.

Nichols, David A., *Lincoln and the Indians.* St. Paul: Minnesota Historical Society Press, 2012.

Payer, Bernd C. *American Indian Nonfiction: An Anthology of Writings, 1760s–1930s.* Norman, University of Oklahoma Press, 2007.

Pitezel, John H. *The Life of Peter Marksman,* Cincinnati, OH: Western Methodist Book Concern, 1901.

Risjord, Norman. *A Popular History of Minnesota.* St. Paul: Minnesota Historical Society, 2005.

Satz, Ronald. *Chippewa Treaty Rights.* Madison: University of Wisconsin Press, 1996.

Shortridge, William Porter. *The Transition of a Typical Frontier, with Illustrations from the Life of Henry Hastings Sibley, Fur Trader, First Delegate in Congress from Minnesota Territory and First Governor of the State of Minnesota,* Menasha, WI: The Collegiate Press, 1923 or before.

Smith, Donald B. *Mississauga Portraits.* Toronto: University of Toronto Press, 2013.

Tanner, George E. *Fifty Years of Church Work in the Diocese of Minnesota, 1857-1907.* St. Paul: Published by the committee and sold by W. C. Pope, 1909.

Trenerry, Walter. *Murder in Minnesota: A Collection of True Cases.* St. Paul: Minnesota Historical Society Press, 1985

Treuer, Anton. *The Assassination of Hole in the Day.* St. Paul: Minnesota Historical Society Press, 2011.

Treuer, Anton. *Indian Wars.* National Geographic Society, Washington, undated.

Treuer, Anton. *Ojibwe in Minnesota.* St. Paul: Minnesota Historical Society Press, 2010.

Treuer, Anton. *Warrior Nation.* St. Paul: Minnesota Historical Society Press, 2015.

Warner, Mary E. *A Big-Hearted Paleface Man.* Little Falls, MN: Morrison County Historical Society, 2006.

Wingert, Mary Lethert. *North Country: The Making of Minnesota*. Minneapolis: University of Minnesota Press, 2010.

Vance, Bruce. *Reverend Doctor John Strachan, Reverend Samuel Armour and the Old Blue School, 1812-1825*. Toronto: Toronto Board of Education.

Vizenor, Gerald, and Jill Doerfler. *The White Earth Nation*. Lincoln: University of Nebraska Press, 2012.

Whipple, Henry. *Lights and Shadows of a Long Episcopate, 1899*. New York: Macmillan, 1912.

Young, Bilione Whiting. *Obscure Believers: The Mormon Schism of Alpheus Cutler*. Apple Valley, MN: Pogo Press, 2002.

Zapffe, Carl A. *Minnesota's Chippewa Treaty of 1837*. Brainerd, MN: Historic Heartland Association, n.d.

INDEX

Aitkin, William, 28, 89
Akers, Peter, 14, *33*, *33*
alcohol. *See* whiskey, availability of
Aldrich, Cyrus, 93
American Fur Company, 21, 22
Anishinaabe
    medicine men, 10
    migration of, 17
    westward movement of, 7
annuities
    Beaulieu investigations into payments, 94–95
    Dole payment changes, 102, 103
    Enmegahbowh and, 52–53, 63–64, 114
    Hole in the Day (the Younger) and, 95
    non-recipients (1843-1844), 45
    payment irregularities, 63–64
    payments (1843-1849), 51, 52
    payments to La Pointe Ojibwe resumed, 59
    payments to mixed-race Indians, 28, 29
    recipients (1843-1844), 42–44
    reduced, 58
    Treaty of 1837 and, 28, 29, 30
    Treaty of 1842 and, 47, 48
    Treaty of 1854 and, 61–62
    Treaty of 1855 and, 62–63
    Treaty of 1863 and, 102, 103, 104
    Treaty of 1867 and, 105, 106
    voucher system for, 94

Armour, Samuel, 8–9
Arthur, Chester A., 161
Ashwinn, 71
Astor, John Jacob, 21
Ayer, Fredrick, 97

Bad Boy, 69
    Breck and Christianizing of Ojibwe, 68
    characteristics, 68
    Treaty of 1855 and, 62, 63
    Treaty of 1863 and, 101
Bad River Reservation, 61
Baraga, Fredric, 91
Bassett, Joel, 105, 120
Battle of Sugar Point, 158
Beaulieu, Clement, 95
    assassination of Hole in the Day (the Younger), 117
    in Crow Wing, 77
    Gilfillan and, 151–152
    investigations into annuity payments, 94–95
    Treaty of 1863 and, 101
Beaulieu, George, 117
Beaulieu, Gus, 151
Beaulieu, Paul, 77, 120
Benedict, Edwin, 135, 148, 150
Benedictines, 138–139
Bishop Whipple Hospital, 127, *129*, 129–130

"Bishop Whipple's Report on the Moral and Temporal Condition of the Indian Tribes on Our Western Border" (Whipple), 106–108
Bliss, Cornelius, 158
Blueberry War, 133
Bob-O-Link, 123–124
Bois Forte Treaty of 1866, 105
Bonga, George, 71
    background, 71
    Breck and, 72
    Edwin Clark and, 114
    Ruffee and, 114
    Treaty of 1863 and, 101
    Treaty of 1864 and, 104
Bonga, Jean, 71
Bonga, Pierre, 71
Bonga, Stephen, 71
Brainerd, 131–132, *133*
Braun, Lioba, 138
Breck, James Lloyd, *66*, *67*, 70
    background of, 4, 65
    characteristics, 70
    Enmegahbowh's return to missionary work and, 4
    Faribault Seminary and, 78
    Flat Mouth and, 71
    Gull Lake Mission, 4
    Holcombe on, 70
    Hole in the Day (the Younger) and, 67, 68
    Leech Lake Mission and, 74, 75
    marriage, 73
    Otter Tail Lake Mission, 72
    plans for Ojibwe, 67
    resignation from Seabury, 114
    St. Columba Mission, 69
    St. Paul and Minnesota mission, 65–66
    Whipple and, 82
Breck, Jane Marie, 90
Brown, William and Martha, 30
Brunson, Alfred
    education of Enmegahbowh, Copway, and Marksman, 14, 33
    land payments in 1837 and 1842 treaties, 48
    mission to Dakota, 15
    replaced, 34
    on Treaty of 1837, 25
Buffalo, Chief, 59
    removal order rescinded through efforts of, 59
    Treaty of 1855 and, 62, 63
    Treaty of 1854 negotiations, 61–62
Bugonaygeshig (Old Bug), 158, *159*
Buh, Joseph, 92
Bureau of Indian Affairs, 93–94
Burien, Peter, 33

Cahbeach, John, 13, 14
Carter, Sybil, 165, *165*
Cartwright, Peter, 14
Cass Lake Ojibwe, 154
Catholic Diocese of St. Paul, 91–92
Chippewa in Minnesota Fund, 157, 175
Chippewa Indian Agency, established, 59
Clapp Rider to the Steenerson Act of 1904, 174
Clapp Rider to the Burke Act of 1906, 174
Clark, Edwin, 114
Clark, John, 11, 23, 33
Cleveland, Grover, 153
Colby, Pauline, 165
Coleman, John, 133–134, 135, 148
Cook family, murder of, 123–124
Cooper, David, 97, 116
Copway, George, *11*

baptized, 11
Christian education of, 33–34
creation of one large reservation for all Indians between the Missouri and James Rivers in Dakota Territory, 51
Dakota and, 15
further Christian education of, 14–15
initial missionary work, 3–4
marriage, 35
at missions, 11, 13–14
names of, 11
overview of life of, 35
Treaty of 1837 and, 25

Craig (Captain, colleague of Breck), 68
Cretin (Catholic Bishop), 91
Crossing Sky (Rabbit Lake Chief), 95–96, 101
Crow Wing, 78
Enmegahbowh at, 99, 112
growth of, 77–78
logging at, 64
whiskey at, 64, 77, 100
Crow Wing Indian Agency, 59
Cullen, Superintendent Major, 94
Cutler, Alpheus, 109
Cutlerites, 109–111

Dakota
Brunson mission to, 15
capture of Enmegahbowh, Copway, and Marksman, 15
fur trading posts, 22
Ojibwe and, 18–19, 22, 35, 161
peace treaty with, 122
Treaty of 1826, 21
White Earth Reservation land and, 119
Dakota Uprising, 98

Dawden, R. P., 58
Dawes Act (1887), 155–158, 161
Day, E. H., 93–94
Denna, Lewis, 110
Dodge, Henry, 17, 28
Dole, William P., 93, 94, 95, *97*, 97–98, 102–103
Doolittle, James, 93
Dousman, Hercules, 27, 28
Drexel, Katharine, 138

Ebenezer Manual Labor Training School, 14, 33–34
Enmegahbowh, *70, 168*
accepted as son by Hole in the Day (the Younger), 116
alcohol and, 11
annuities and, 52–53, 63–64, 114
baptized, 11
begging letters, 149–150
biography, 171
George Bonga and, 71–72
Catholicism and, 149
children of, 38, 42, 70, 83, 149
Christian education of, 14–15, 33–34
conditions at White Earth Reservation and, 121, 122
consecrated as Episcopal priest, 114, *115*
at Crow Wing, 99, 112
Cutlerites and, 110–111
Dakota and, 15
death, 171
deaths of family members, 170
Deena and, 110
education of Alfred, 67
escape to Fort Ripley with family, 96
Gear and, 4, 57, 58, 66

generosity of, 123
Gilfillan and, 133–134, 149–150
health, 169
Holcombe on, 70
Hole in the Day (the Younger) at White Earth and, 112
Hole in the Day (the Younger) attacks and, 96, 98–99
journey to White Earth Reservation, 120–121
Kavenaugh and, 35–36
legacy, 172
at Little Elk, 34
marriage to Charlotte, 36–37, 42
marriage to Nogahnigijigoque, 170
Mille Lacs Ojibwe and, 112–113
mission trip, 11–12
at missions, 13–14
names of, 3, 8, 11
ordained as deacon, 37–38, 78
overview of life of, 3–4, 5
peace treaty with Dakota, 122
Pillager warrior attacks on whites and, 95–96
planned attack on frontier forts and, 4
as priest and missionary at White Earth, 123, 125, 126–127
with Rabbit River tribe, 38–39, 42
recruitment of Ojibwe into Union Army and, 88–89
return journey to Rice Lake, 39–42
return to missionary work and Breck, 4
Rice Lake missionary school and, 11
Richardson and, 142
Ruffee and, 114
St. Columba Churches and, 82–83, 125, 126–127, 128, 141
at St. Columba Mission, 69, 76–77, 169

support for Clement Beaulieu in dispute with Gilfillan, 151–152
as teacher, 38
Treaty of 1837 and, 25
Treaty of 1863 and, 101–102
Treaty of 1864 and, 104–105
Treaty of 1867 and, 105
trips to Washington, DC, 56–58, 140
Turner and, 38
visit to Canada, 114–115
visit to Ojibwe at Red Lake, 89–90
visit to Watkinson in Connecticut, 127, 128–129
Henry Whipple and, 4, 82–83, 149–150, 166–168, 170–171
at Whitefish Lake, 35
Sylvester Whiting and, 110
as youth, 8–9
Episcopal Church
first in Minnesota, 65
Ojibwe deacons' strike, 150–151
salaries for Ojibwe deacons, 148, 150
split with Ojibwe people, 149
Evans, James, 11, 12
Ewing, Thomas, 52

Fairbanks, George, 117
Fairbanks, John, 77
Fairbanks, Robert, 117
Faribault, Alexander, 83
Faribault Seminary, 78–79, 83, 114
Flat Mouth, 54–56, 56, 71, 122
Fond du Lac Ojibwe, 61, 154–155, 176
Fort Crawford, 21
Fort Gaines, 50, *50*
Fort Ridgley, planned attack on, 4
Fort Ripley, *50*

Enmegahbowh and family escape to, 96
established, 50
planned attack on, 4
as refuge during Hole in the Day (the Younger) attacks, 98
Fort Snelling, 21–22, 25, *26*
fur trade
1816 law and, 21
American Fur Company, 21, 22
decrease in, by 1831, 27
goods traded for furs, 22–23
Hudson's Bay Company, 19
Ojibwe and, 19, 22
St. Paul and, 65
value of (1835), 23
See also traders

Galbraith, Thomas, 94
Gear, Ezekiel, 67
Breck and, 4, 65
Enmegahbowh and, 4, 57, 58, 66
Gilbert, Henry, 61
Gilbert, Mahlon N., 152
Gilfillan, Joseph Alexander, *133*, *135*
as archdeacon at White Earth, 169
background, 131
Clement Beaulieu and, 151–152
death, 170
Enmegahbowh and, 133–134, 149–150
on intended marriage, sex scandal, and abuse by George Johnson, 145–148
mission work, 134–137
on Mississippi River dams, 142–143
murder of Helen MacArthur and, 132
on Sister Mary Selby, 129–130
on Stowe, 137–138

in Washington, DC, 169–170
Gorman, Willis A, 73
Grace, J. L., 102
Grand Medicine (Midewiwin) tradition, 8–9
Grand Portage Reservation, established, 61
Grant, Ulysses S., 124
Great Spirit (Gitchi Manidoo) origin story, 9
Gull Lake Mission
approved by Ojibwe chiefs, 67–68
atmosphere at, 72–73
building of, 68–69
Enmegahbowh and Breck at, 4
overview of, 73–74
See also St. Columba Mission

Hall, Sherman, 14, 75
Halstead (colleague of Breck), 68
Harriman, David, 59, 62
Hart, Mark, 134, 135
Hatch, E. A., 97
Hayward, Stephen, 67
He Who Is Spoken To, 154
Hernanutz, Aloysius, 138, 149
Herriman, David, 73
Hill, James, 104
Ho-Chunk (Winnebago), 48, 49–50
Holcombe, Theodore, 68, 70, 171
Hole in the Day (the Elder)
background, 34–35
death, 50
goods promised and, 28–29
Huddleston and, 34–35
planned attack on frontier forts, 4
Warren and, 28
Hole in the Day (the Younger), *68*
annuity payments and, 95

assassinated, 116–117
attacks on whites and, 95–98, 99, 102
as band leader, 50
birth, 35
Breck and Christianizing of Ojibwe, 67, 68
Enmegahbowh as son of, 116
house on Crow Wing River, 78
named Boy, 35
Treaty of 1855 and, 62, 63
Treaty of 1864 and, 104
Treaty of 1867 and, 105, 106
as war chief, 116
White Earth Reservation and, 112, 120
Homestead Act (1862), 91
Horizon (Meshakgeshig), 111–112
Howell, Elizabeth, 35
Huddleston (Reverend), 34–35
Hudson's Bay Company, 19, 20, 22
Humphreys, Chauncey, 158

Indian Appropriations Act, 153–155
Indian Removal Act (1830), 47

Jackson, Andrew, 47
Jacksonville, Illinois, 33–34
John Jacob Astor, 39–42
Johnson, Alfred
   baptized into Episcopal Church, 70
   birth, 38
   Breck and, 67
   death, 98
   education of, 88
   escape to Fort Ripley, 96
   trip to Rice Lake and, 39
Johnson, Charlotte, *38*
   attacks on whites and, 96
   children of, 38, 42, 70, 83, 149
   death, 170
   as "effective helpmeet," 70
   health, 99, 130, 149
   Holcombe on, 70
   Hole in the Day (the Younger) and, 95
   journey to Rice Lake, 39–40
   marriage, 36–37, 42
Johnson, Eliza, 70, 123, 130
Johnson, Gaius
   baptized into Episcopal Church, 70
   birth, 42
   death, 170
   education of, 87–88, 134
Johnson, George, *148*
   baptized into Episcopal Church, 70
   birth, 42
   Cutlerites and, 111
   as deacon, 133–134
   at Faribault Seminary, 79
   intended marriage, sex scandal, and abuse by, 145–148
Johnson, Gus, 170
Johnson, Henry Whipple, 83, 96, 98
Johnson, Jane Maria, 70
Johnson, John. *See* Enmegahbowh
Johnson, Johnny, 170
Johnson, Martha
   baptized into Episcopal Church, 70
   birth, 38
   death, 170
   trip to Rice Lake and, 39
   at White Earth, 123
Johnson, Sarah Jamison, 83, 170
Johnson, William Augustus (Gus), 70
"Jonah experience," 39–42

Jones, Augustus, 10
Jones, Peter
    arrival at Rice Lake, 10
    baptized and ordained, 13

Kadawabide, Fred Smith, 79
Kah-ge-ga-gah-bowh (Standing Firm). *See*
    Copway, George
Kater, Helen, 116, 117
Kavenaugh, B. T., 34, 35–36
Kemble, E. C. K., 125
Kemper, Jackson
    Breck and, 66
    consecration of St. Columba Church, 69
    Gull Lake Mission, 4
    ordination of Enmegahbowh by, 78
    Whipple and, 82
Ketten, Philomia, 138
King, Henry, 150
Kittson, Norman, 104
Knickerbacker, David, 124

La Pointe Mission, 14
La Pointe Ojibwe
    annuity payments to, 28, 59
    as stronghold, 17, 19
Lac Courte Oreilles, 14
Lac Courte Oreilles Reservation,
    established, 61
Lac du Flambeau Reservation
    established, 61
lace making, 165
Lamanites, 110–111
land
    amount set aside for reservations, 62
    ceded (shown by date), 31
    ceded in Bois Forte Treaty, 105
    ceded in Treaty of 1837, 25, 28
    ceded in Treaty of 1842, 47, 48
    ceded in Treaty of 1847, 48–49
    ceded in Treaty of 1854, 61
    ceded in Treaty of 1855, 62
    ceded in Treaty of 1863, 102, 104
    ceded in Treaty of 1867, 105
    Dawes Act allotments, 156
    gold on, 105
    held in common on White Earth
        Reservation, 154
    Indian Appropriations Act and, 153
    Indian relocation to west of Mississippi
        River, 47
    Lake Superior band request for
        "permanent home," 51–52
    Manifest Destiny and, 90–91
    Nelson Act and, 156
    Northwest Ordinance and, 20–21
    Ojibwe attitude toward, 19–20
    Ojibwe fear of out-of-state removal, 99
    Ojibwe removal from some North Dakota
        areas, 161
    Pike and, 21
    reasons Ojibwe traded, 27
    Red Lake, 154
    Red Lake cessation, 163
    of Red Lake Ojibwe, 106, 154, 163, 176
    removal from White Earth Reservation, 156
    removal of Lake Superior Ojibwe to
        Minnesota, 52
    reservation, owned by Ojibwe (1983-2003),
        175–176
    value of Ojibwe, in northern Minnesota, 155
    white Americans on Ojibwe land (1830), 23

White Earth allotments, 157
See also timber
L'Anse Mission, 13
Larrabee, Charles F., 153–155
Lautischar, Lawrence, 91–92
Leech Lake Mission, 74, 75, 76
Leech Lake Ojibwe, 154, 175–176
Leupp, Francis, 174
Lincoln, Abraham, 102
Lind, Jenny, 57
Little Crow, 4, 98
Little Shell, 161–162, 176
Lynde, Joseph, 59
Lyon, William, 139

MacArthur, Helen, 132
MacArthur, William, 117
Madeline Island, 14
Madison, Samuel, 79, 133, 134
Manifest Destiny, 90–91
Manitowab, Isaac, 78, 89–90, 120
Manney, Solon, 68, 71, 72
Manypenny, George, 62
Marksman, Peter, *169*
   background, 14
   Christian education of, 14–15, 33–34
   Dakota and, 15
   initial missionary work, 3–4
   at Little Elk, 34
   at missions, 14
   overview of life of, 168–169
   Treaty of 1837 and, 25
McCumber, P. J., 162
medicine men (mide), 10
Mendenhall, Cyrus, 58–59
Menomonie, 49

Methodist Episcopal Church
   alcohol and, 11
   failure to convert Indians, 38–39
   missions in Minnesota terminated, 38
   Rice Lake missionary school, 10–11
   See also specific missions
Midewiwin tradition, 8–9
Mille Lacs Ojibwe, 62, 112–113, 142, 154, 176
Mills, Jane Maria, 60, 73
Minneapolis (1860), 83
Minnesota
   frontier justice, 76–77
   land transportation in (1850s), 75
   Sioux war in, 98
   statehood, 78
   Territory organized, 51
Minogishick, 115
Mississauga area, 7
Mississippi Ojibwe, 104–105, 119
Mississippi River dams, 142–143
Mix, Charles, 93, 94
"mixed bloods." *See* mixed race *under* Ojibwe
Mooseomona, 142
Morgan, George, 135
Morien, Hannah, 168
Mormons, 109–111
Morrill, Ashley, 97
Morrison, Allen, 37, 75, 77, 94
Morrison, George D., 117
Morrison, William, 77

Nanabozho, 9
Nashotah, Charles Wright, 79
Neal, Edward, 157
Nelson Act (1889), 142, 155, 156
Nogahnigijigoque (Mary), 170

Northwest Indian Commission, 153–155
Northwest Ordinance (1787), 20–21

Odawa, 7, 17, 116
The *Ojibway* (Gilfillan), 170
Ojibwe
    accommodation of Winnebago and Menomonie, 49
    band not participating in Hole in the Day's (the Younger) attacks on whites, 99
    bands in Minnesota, 19
    bands recognized by US government (1844), 46
    conditions of (1860), 83
    Dakota and, 18–19, 22, 35, 161
    Episcopal deacons' strike, 150–151
    Episcopal stipends for deacons, 148, 150
    excluded from Treaty of 1854, 62
    excluded from Treaty of 1855, 62
    fear of out-of-state removal, 99
    frontier justice and, 76–77
    fur trade and, 19, 22
    Hunter's Island band, 42
    land occupied by (1800), 17
    land set aside for reservations, 62
    leaders, 18
    migration of, 17
    in Minnesota, Michigan, and Wisconsin ruled one nation, 47
    Mississippi River dams and, 142–143
    mixed-race, 19, 28, 29, 42, 136, 173, 174, 175
    murder of Helen MacArthur, 132–133
    non-annuity recipients (1843-1844), 45
    Pillager attacks on whites, 95–98
    population (1843), 42
    population (1910), 175
    removal order rescinded, 58–59
    request for land for "permanent home," 51–52
    split with Episcopal hierarchy, 149
    at St. Columba Mission, 82
    Union Army and, 88–89
    See also specific bands and tribes
Ojibwe way of life
    beliefs of whites as confusing to, 74
    Bible translation and, 14
    Christianizing, 15, 27, 67, 68, 106, 124–125, 139, 154–155, 156, 175
    clans, 18, 174
    Grand Medicine (Midewiwin) tradition, 9–10
    hunting, fishing, and gathering, 17–18, 29, 136, 175
    lace making on reservations, 165
    marriage, 18
    names and naming, 7–8, 37
    sexual relations, 148
    tepees and buffalo hunting, 161
    values of, 11, 18, 19–20
    wigwams, 17–18, 136
    work differentiated by sex, 18
Old Crossing Treaty (1863)
    with Mississippi, Pillager, and Winnibigoshish Ojibwe, 101–103
    with Pembina and Red Lake Ojibwe, 104, 106, 157
Otter Tail Lake Mission, 72

Parker, John, 75
Peake, E. Steele
    with family, 75
    journey to Leech Lake, 74
    move to Crow Wing, 77
    in Union Army, 100
    visit to Ojibwe at Red Lake, 89–90

Pembina Ojibwe, 104, 106
Pierce, Franklin, 61
Pierz, Francis, 77, 91–92
Pike, Zebulon, 21
Pillager Ojibwe, 95–98, 101–103, 124
pine, 27, 62
Potawatomi, 7, 17, 34
Prairie du Chien, 21
Puk-O-Nay-Keshig. *See* Hole in the Day (the Elder)

railroad, 131, 173
Ramsey, Alexander, 51, 52–56, 97, 104
Red Blanket Woman, 30
Red Cliff Reservation
    established, 61
Red Lake Ojibwe
    communal ownership of land, 176
    Enmegahbowh and, 38, 89–90, 170
    timber lands of, 106, 143, 154, 155, 163
    Treaty of 1863 and, 101, 104, 157
    Treaty of 1867 and, 106
Reese, Tom, 75
Renville, Gabriel (Tiwakan), 111–112
reservations, 61, 62, 173–175
    See also specific reservations
Rice, Henry
    accused of fraud, 94
    Chippewa in Minnesota Fund, 157
    Leech Lake Mission and, 74
    money for St. Columba Mission, 73
    Pillager warrior attacks on whites and, 97
    Stowe and, 139
    Treaty of 1855 and, 62, 63
    Treaty of 1863 and, 101–103
    Treaty of 1864 and, 105
    Winnebago and, 49

Rice Lake, 7, 8, 10–11
Richardson, Nathan, 142, 157, 171, 176
Robinson, Peter, 8
Rolette, Joseph, Sr., 22
Roy, Peter, 117
Roy, Suzanna, 140
Ruffee, Charles, 114, 117, 139

Sabin, Dwight, 157
Sakaogan Ojibwe, 62
Sandy Lake Mission, 35–38
Sault Ste. Marie Mission, 13
Schaitberger, Stephen, 4, 89
Seabury University, 78–79, 83, 114
Selby, Maria, 129–130
Shabashkung, 113, *113*
Shawundais, 11
Shay-Day-Ence (the Little Pelican), 139–140
Sheehan, Timothy, 151
Shubway (French-Canadian trader at Red Lake), 90
Sibley, Helen Hastings, 30
Sibley, Henry Hastings
    elected governor, 78
    personal life, 30
    Treaty of 1837 and, 30
    Winnebago removal and, 49
Simpson, Evangeline Marrs, 164, *164*
Sioux war in Minnesota, 98
Small, Charlotte, 37
Smith, Edward, 137
Smith, Fred, 133, 134, 135, 150
Smith, George, 133–134, 135, 150
Snelling, Josiah, 22
Spates, Samuel, 34, 35
Spirit of Missions (Whipple), 125, 126–127
St. Benedict's Orphan School, 138–139

St. Columba Church
    Gilfillan at, 169
    new, 124, 125–127, *127*, *128*

    original, 69, *69*, 70, 82–83
St. Columba Mission, 69
    attacks on, 96, 116
    described (1862), 83–87
    destroyed, 98
    Enmegahbowh at, 69, 76–77, 169
    financing of, 73
    growth of, 72
    Ojibwe at, 82
    school and staff, 69–70
St. Columba Stone Church, 141, *141*, 143
St. Croix Ojibwe and Treaty of 1854, 62
St. Paul
    in 1860, 83
    Catholic Diocese of, 91–92
    in 1850s, 65, 74
St. Paul Mission, 65, 66
Stands Before His People. *See* Enmegahbowh
Steenerson Act (1904), 173
Stowe, Louis, 137–138, *139*
Stuart, Robert, 47–48
Sugar Point, Battle of, 158
Sunday, John, 11, 13
Superior, William, 89–90
Sweet, George, 97
Sweet Corn Treaty (1858), 161

Taliaferro, Lawrence, 22, 28, 29
Tanner, George C., 71
Taunchey, John, 13
Taylor, Zachary, 52
"Ten Cent Treaty" (1892), 162

Thompson, C. W., 93, 94
Thompson, Clark, 98
Thompson, David, 37
timber
    cutting on Mille Lacs land, 142
    illegal cutting on Indian land, 94
    Manifest Destiny and, 90
    "pine land stealing," 157
    of Red Lake Ojibwe, 106, 143, 154, 155, 163
    Treaty of 1837, 27, 30
    Treaty of 1855 and, 62
    Treaty of 1867 and, 105, 106
    White Earth allotments, 173–174
    on White Earth Reservation, 119, 155
Todd (Captain with Breck), 71
Tomazin, Ignatius, 92, 122, 137, 138
traders
    move from Crow Wing to White Earth, 122
    payments to, from Indians' annuities, 63–64
Treaty of 1837 and, 28, 29
Treaty of 1855 and, 62
Treaty of 1863 and, 102
Treaty of 1826, 21
Treaty of 1837
    delivery of goods promised to Ojibwe, 28
    impetus for, 27
    land ceded, 25, 28
    negotiations, 25–27, 28
    Ojibwe bands represented at, 28
    payment to traders of Ojibwe debts, 28, 29
    payments to Ojibwe and mixed-race Indians, 28, 29, 48
    signers, 29
    timber and, 27, 29
Treaty of 1842, 47–48
Treaty of 1847, 48–49

Treaty of 1854, 61–62
Treaty of 1855, 62–64, 112
Treaty of 1858 (Sweet Corn Treaty), 161
Treaty of 1863
   with Mississippi, Pillager, and Winnibigoshish Ojibwe, 101–103
   with Pembina and Red Lake Ojibwe, 101, 104, 106, 157
Treaty of 1864, 104–105
Treaty of 1867, 105–106, 121
Treaty of 1892 ("Ten Cent Treaty"), 162
Treaty of Bois Forte (1866), 105
Treaty of 1864 with Leech Lake and Mississippi Ojibwe, 104–105
Treuer, Anton, 117
Turner, James, 38
Turtle Mountain Reservation, 161–162, 176
Tuttle, Isaac (Nabnoshkung), 111–112, 120, 122, 123, 124

US Indian Commission, 124–125

Wahkiyee ("Bird"), 30
Wakazoo, Joseph, 134, 135
Walker, Lucius
   appointment as Crow Wing agent, 93
   Hole in the Day (the Younger) and suicide, 96–97, 98
   investigation of and illegal actions by, 94, 95, 99
Walker, T. B., 157
War of 1812, 21
Warren, Lyman W., 28
Watkinson, Ellen, 126, 127, 128–129
Watrous, John, 52–56, 59
Waubanakwad, 151
Wautaub, *70*
Wells, Eliza, 69
Whipple, Cornelia, 81, 163–164, *164*
Whipple, Henry Benjamin, *82, 164*
   as annuity payments overseer, 102, 103
   background, 81
   on Bureau of Indian Affairs, 94
   death, 166
   on effects of treaties on Ojibwe, 106–108
   elected bishop for Minnesota, 82
   Enmegahbowh and, 4, 82–83, 149–150, 166–168, 170–171
   Gilfillan and, 131
   marriage to Simpson, 164
   new St. Columba church and, 125, 126–127
   Northwest Indian Commission, 153–155
   Red Lake legislation and, 163
   on Treaty of 1863 with Pembina and Red Lake Ojibwe, 104
   visit to Faribault Seminary, 83
   visit to Ojibwe at Red Lake, 89–90
   visit to St. Columba, 82–83
   visit to White Earth (1899), 165–166
Whipple, Sarah, 81
whiskey, availability of
   Battle of Sugar Point, 158
   in Brainerd, 132
   at Crow Wing, 64, 77, 100
   Enmegahbowh and, 76–77
   at Leech Lake, 76
   prohibited on reservations, 61
   remoteness of White Earth and, 106
   trials of sellers, 113
white Americans in Minnesota
   1837, 30
   1849, 51

1850, 65
1860, 83
1882, 161
acquisition of Ojibwe reservation land, 174–175
Hole in the Day (the Younger) attacks, 96–98, 102
on land Ojibwe allowed Menomonie and Winnebago to settle, 50
murder of Cook family, 123–124
Pillager attacks on, 95–98
White Cloud (Waub-anaquort), 122
White Eagle, 68
White Earth Reservation
Benedictine mission, 138–139
churches built, 134–135
conditions at, 119, 121–122, 125, 139, 166, 174, 175
created, 5, 35, 101, 105, 119
dancing at, 140
land allotments, 157, 173–174
land owned by Ojibwe (1983), 175
move of Christian Indians to, 111–112
North Dakota Ojibwe at, 161
population, 124, 136–137
purpose of, 106
religious oversight of, 137–138
removal of bands to, 120, 153–154
removal of land from, 156
value of land, 155
Whipple 1899 visit to, 165–166
White Oak Point Ojibwe, 154
Whiting, Chauncy, 109, 110, 111
Whiting, Francis, 110
Whiting, Sylvester, 110
Wilcoxson, Timothy, 65
Wilder, Amherst, 157
Wilkinson, James, 21

Wilkinson, Melville, 158
Williamson, Thomas, 102
Willis, Francis, 135
Wilson, W. D., 81
Winnebago, 48, 49–50
Winnibigoshish Ojibwe, 101–103, 154
Woodbridge, Harriet, 136
Wright, Charles, 133, 134, 135, 150, 174
Wright, John V., 153–155
Wright, Sela, 150

Zuzek, John, 92